What Is Crime?

Controversies over the Nature of Crime and What to Do about It

Edited by
Stuart Henry
and
Mark M. Lanier

ROWMAN & LITTLEFIELD PUBLISHERS, INC.
Lanham • Boulder • New York • Oxford

To all victims of power.—S.H.

To my father, Col. Lawrence H. Lanier (USAF), who saw everything in black and white, which helped me to see all the gray, and to Katie who provided a much-needed epiphany of color.—M.M.L.

ROWMAN & LITTLEFIELD PUBLISHERS, INC.

Published in the United States of America
by Rowman & Littlefield Publishers, Inc.
4720 Boston Way, Lanham, Maryland 20706
www.rowmanlittlefield.com

12 Hid's Copse Road, Cumnor Hill, Oxford OX2 9JJ, England

British Library Cataloguing in Publication Information Available

Library of Congress Cataloging-in-Publication Data

What is crime? : controversies over the nature of crime and what to do about it / edited by Stuart Henry and Mark M. Lanier.
      p.   cm.
   Includes bibliographical references and index.
   ISBN 0-8476-9806-8 (alk. paper)—ISBN 0-8476-9807-6 (pbk. : alk. paper)
   1. Crime.   I. Henry, Stuart.   II. Lanier, Mark M.
   HV6025.W44   2001
   364—dc21   00-062694

Printed in the United States of America

♾ ™ The paper used in this publication meets the minimum requirements of American National Standard for Information Sciences—Permanence of Paper for Printed Library Materials, ANSI/NISO Z39.48-1992.

Contents

Acknowledgments

In any collaborative enterprise such as this, many people need to be thanked. Our first thanks go to those who encouraged the initial project. Martha Myers and Vic Kappeler are owed our sincere appreciation for encouraging us to do what we did not have time to do, important though it is. Others who deserve our thanks are our colleagues, mentors, and friends who have always stimulated our debate about the varied dimensions of crime; these include Gregg Barak, John Sloan, Joe Rankin, Tilden Bybee, John Smykla, Karol Lucken, Trung Le, and Robert "Bob" Bohm. Our editor, Dean Birkenkamp, has been the shadow editor in several of our projects, and we thank him for that support. Jill Rothenberg, our acquisitions editor, has contracted us to write two books for two different publishers. We owe you many thanks for having confidence in another of our projects and look forward to working with you again in the future.

Introduction

Mark M. Lanier and Stuart Henry

It is surprising to us that the defining feature of criminology and criminal jus-tice—crime—is itself often left undefined; or, at best, it is inadequately defined. It is typically a taken-for-granted concept that many scholars, students, and prac-titioners presume to understand, yet they may not understand it completely or may even misunderstand it. To date, the defining concept of our discipline has not been comprehensively presented in a manner that allows serious contempla-tion, comparison, and debate. The contemporary practice among criminologists is to briefly consider competing positions on crime and then rapidly proceed to adopt a narrow legal definition such as "acts or omissions in violation of the criminal law." In fact, the majority of criminologists and many criminology text-books begin with a discussion about the competing views on crime with "most of them settling for the legalistic definition" (Gibbons 1994: 45). At best, a smaller number of criminologists identify a social, cultural, or contextual definition and leave the reader dangling with the differences. A problem with this abandon-ment of criminological responsibility is that, while allowing some comparison and selection (based on one's particular ideological/theoretical view), such a dis-cussion does nothing to incorporate the different and competing views. Thus, *crime*, the core concept of the discipline, remains a taken-for-granted concept, one that either relies on state legal definitions, which leave out the multiple components of the crime phenomenon, or presents us with multiple contradic-tory approaches that lead more to confusion than comprehension. Indeed, so undefined is the field that we may not even be talking about the same thing when we talk about crime. The deficiency we note above led us to commission and compile this collection of articles.

In this context, the genesis of this book is interesting and worthy of comment. While conducting research for our textbook *Essential Criminology* (Lanier and Henry 1998), it became apparent that while most textbooks include a review of the different approaches to defining crime, the only serious treatment of the subject has been via journal articles, dictionaries, and encyclopedias. Moreover, most of the criminological writing simply reviews different positions on what *should* count as crime; very few attempts have been made to integrate these into a single comprehensive approach. Indeed, even those who claim to have developed an integrated approach ultimately come up short of delivering the goods. For example, Barak's (1998) recent pioneering definitive statement on integrating criminological knowledge relies on a review of the various definitional components, but Barak does not integrate them.

As a result of these deficiencies, we developed what we call the "crime prism." Several reviewers of our textbook commented on our own introductory definitional chapter that outlined the concept of the prism of crime, and some suggested that we write a journal article that expounded on our concept of the crime prism. We thought the arguments warranted at least a spirited attempt to trigger the debate. We submitted the resultant article at first to *Criminology*, whose reviewers were less than enthusiastic. Without revision, we submitted the same article to *Justice Quarterly* (*JQ*), whose reviewers were much more favorably disposed; indeed, revising the article to meet their constructive comments resulted in the article's publication (Henry and Lanier 1998). Then editor of *JQ*, Victor Kappeler, suggested that the concept and further discussion be not only worthy of an article but also of a book-length analysis. In short, independent of us, several criminological scholars noted the need for a book devoted to exploring the issue of defining crime. These comments and suggestions inspired us to put this book together.

In *Essential Criminology* (Lanier and Henry 1998), and subsequently in our crime prism article for *JQ* (Henry and Lanier 1998), we argued the case that criminology should move beyond competing definitions to a definition that would take into account the multiple dimensions of crime within one framework. We saw these competing definitions as mutually constitutive of crime's content. We argued that each of the different dimensions that make up the concept of "crime," like the different wavelengths of light that make up the visible spectrum, are important in our comprehension of the subject. For example, critics of the legal definition of crime argue that *who* makes the law is as important as whose behavior is defined as crime. These critics argue for an expanded definition of crime based on harm and social injury (Sutherland 1945; Schwendinger and Schwendinger 1970; Michalowski 1985; Tifft 1995). Does taking their arguments into account mean that state definition of crime should be abandoned in favor of a broader sociological definition, or does it mean that definition should be a part of the reality of defining crime? We argue that many definitions, including those identified as "state" or governmentally constituted, contribute important dimensions and should be included in any assessment of criminological attempts to determine crime's content. We argue that to focus on one or other of these positions excludes some of what is essential to an understanding of not only how we see crime but also what it is and the reality of what it becomes. Thus, we argue that comprehension of the criminological process and theories explaining crime is contingent on the kind of definition that we assume. We believe that any serious discussion of criminology, criminological theory, and criminal justice policy is ultimately dependent on our assumed definition of crime, whether or not this is made explicit. Thus, we believe that an extended treatment of this topic is long overdue.

In *What Is Crime?* we present leading advocates for the different perspectives taken when defining crime. The book includes both reprints of classic articles on the subject, revisions of well-known statements by the original authors, and several new pieces written specifically for this book. Reflecting this, the book is divided into three main parts: (1) classic statements, (2) new directions, and (3) integrating approaches. We begin with our own cursory overview of varied crime definitions and theoretical arguments in chapter 1, which we call "Crime in Context: The Scope of the Problem." This is followed in chapter 2 by the first of four articles in the "classic statements" part, "The Nature of Crime" by Jerome Michael and Mortimer Adler (1933). The chapter is edited from their seminal book *Crime, Law and Social Science* in which the authors argue that "social interests" may shape crime. Ultimately, however, they see these interests expressed in law. Indeed, echoing Durkheim ([1893] 1984), they argue:

> The question of what behavior shall be made criminal, will be answered in terms of our likes and dislikes. If our dislike for any conduct is sufficiently strong, we will make it criminal, and the seriousness or magnitude of the resulting crime can be measured only by the intensity of dislike for that type of conduct . . . the question of what behavior shall be made criminal, seems to resolve itself into the question of what behavior arouses our indignation. (Michael and Adler 1933: 23)

Of course, this begs the question of who are the "we" whose indignation is aroused, and how is that articulated? Tappan's (1947) classic statement on the legal definition, which he titled "Who Is the Criminal?" was first published in 1947 and is included as chapter 3. Tappan had no hesitation in asserting that the "we" is perfectly expressed by law and the legislative process and that no other Tom, Dick, or criminologist should be in the business of claiming to know what was crime. He was writing in response to a provocative statement by Edward Sutherland (1940, 1945) a few years earlier who had questioned the strict "legal" definition for failing to acknowledge that the law could be blind to social injury or harm. Such social harm, argued Sutherland, was just as qualitatively criminal, even if it had not been seen as such by the legislators, not least because they were influenced by the harm creators, particularly corporate interests and their lobbyists. Many scholars agree that Tappan, albeit outraged by Sutherland, provides one extreme in any academic discussion of crime.

Chapter 4, "Defining Patterns of Crime and Types of Offenders," follows Tappan's article and was prepared for this text by Don Gibbons and Kathryn Ann

Farr. It is an update and revision of Gibbons's classic statement in the "legal" tradition of defining crime (Gibbons 1975, 1992, 1994). He states, "My own position is a legalistic one—crime is defined by the criminal law. 'Criminals' are persons who violate criminal laws, whether or not they become detected and identified as law breakers" (Gibbons 1994: 45). Here Gibbons and Farr explore the consequence of the legal definition: the attempts that have been made to establish both a taxonomy of crimes and a taxonomy of offenders.

Finally, chapter 5 is a reprint of the classic counterstatement to the legal definition, entitled "Defenders of Order or Guardians of Human Rights?" by Herman Schwendinger and Julia Schwendinger (1970). It includes a new introduction placing their original statement in the historical context of its time. In the article the Schwendingers summarize the then thirty-year debate and go on to develop a modern version of Sutherland's radical criminological stance on social harm as crime.

In part II we explore the new directions in defining crime that have spun off the classic debates. Each of these chapters has been specifically commissioned for this book. They represent a variety of different positions within social science. Indeed, interactionist, critical, anarchist, critical race, and feminist, as well as postmodernist positions are presented here. Leroy Gould, Gary Kleck, and Marc Gertz begin by describing "Crime as Social Interaction" in chapter 6. Based on a development of their 1992 statement (Gould, Kleck, and Gertz 1992), they argue that rather than crime being an isolated event, it requires us to examine the interrelationship of several factors that allow crime to occur. Related to the interactionist view, in chapter 7, "Defining Crime in a Community Setting," Paul Schnorr takes a social constructionist approach to crime by exploring the competing claims made within a local community and how these are legitimized by the various agencies involved. In chapter 8, "The Media's Role in the Definition of Crime," Ray Surette and Charles Otto reflect concerns raised in previous work (Surette 1997) that explores the role of the mass media in shaping how we think about and define events as crime, and indeed what we then see as crime. Aspects of this are considered in chapter 9, "Racing Crime: Definitions and Dilemmas" by Katheryn Russell, who builds on her wider study of race and crime (Russell 1998). Further expanding the definition of crime as power is the affirmative postmodernist view of crime presented by Dragan Milovanovic and Stuart Henry in chapter 10, "Constitutive Definition of Crime: Power as Harm." Their argument, based on their developing constitutive criminological theory (Henry and Milovanovic 1996, 1999), is that power itself is the problem and that its exercise over others denies others their freedom of humanity: the ability to make a difference. They assert that such expressions of power are criminal whatever the particular dimension presently reflected in popular sentiment or contemporary law. They illustrate how this is manifest in subtle ways, particularly with regard to law and institutionalized racist tendencies of "petit apartheid."

Finally, in chapter 11, Larry Tifft and Dennis Sullivan present a "restorative justice" approach entitled "A Needs-Based Social Harms Definition of Crime." This argument, outlined in a previous work (Tifft 1995), stems from their fundamental belief that governmental power in defining crime is part of the problem rather than a neutral representative of popular sentiment. Moreover, the power of government reflects the power structure of society, and that power structure harbors and reflects gender, racial, and ethnic bias in seeing crime.

In the final part of the book, we go back to go forward. Here we suggest that integrating the diverse strains outlined in the previous two parts is essential to obtain a comprehensive understanding of the phenomenon. One of the first criminologists to recognize the need to integrate consensus, legalistic approaches, and critical conflict approaches to crime, John Hagan (1977, 1985), provided us with the inspiration for our prism of crime. In their contribution, Scott Greer and John Hagan replay this integrative approach of the study of crime in chapter 12, which they call "Crime as Disrepute." They begin by providing a useful summary of the previous diverse positions before outlining a synthesis of their argument in the innovative three-dimensional concept of the "crime pyramid." Building on Hagan's earlier contribution, our concluding chapter addresses how integrationists might attempt not only to synthesize the earlier conflict positions with the legalistic ones, but also to incorporate the new diverse critical perspectives' definitions into one model that simultaneously takes account of all the constitutive dimensions of the subject. This final chapter, "The Prism of Crime," represents what we believe should be a starting point, rather than a definitive statement, in future discussions about what counts and what is to count as crime.

Prior to evaluating the various authors' perspectives on what constitutes crime, it may be useful for students of crime to consider several issues. First, none of the works can be considered the final word on defining crime. Each is deficient in one way or another. As an academic exercise, identifying these deficiencies will help you clarify the central issues in this debate and also contemplate not just the differences but the similarities over what defines crime. Finally, always consider the context. Without contextualizing the issues, any discussion of what is crime is meaningless. We sincerely hope that this work will not be viewed simply as a philosophical debate. Rather, we hope that it will be taken as a serious reexamination of what crime *means*. Among other things, consider how crime is defined and how each version of what crime is has implications for policy and practice. It determines how we treat perpetrators and victims, and it impacts how we view ourselves and our social environment.

REFERENCES

Barak, Gregg. 1998. *Integrating Criminologies*. Boston: Allyn & Bacon.
Durkheim, Emile. [1893] 1984. *The Division of Labor in Society*. New York: Free Press.

Gibbons, Donald C. 1975. "Offender Typologies: Two Decades Later." *British Journal of Criminology* 15: 140–56.

Gibbons, Donald C. 1992. *Society, Crime and Criminal Behavior*. 6th ed. Englewood Cliffs, N.J.: Prentice Hall.

Gibbons, Donald C. 1994. *Talking about Crime and Criminals: Problems and Issues in Theory Development in Criminology*. Englewood Cliffs, N.J.: Prentice Hall.

Gould, Leroy, Gary Kleck, and Marc Gertz. 1992. "The Concept of Crime in Criminological Theory and Practice." *The Criminologist* 17: 1–6.

Hagan, John. 1977. *The Disreputable Pleasures*. Toronto: McGraw-Hill Ryerson.

Hagan, John. 1985. *Modern Criminology*. New York: McGraw-Hill.

Henry, Stuart, and Mark M. Lanier. 1998. "The Prism of Crime: Arguments for an Integrated Definition of Crime." *Justice Quarterly* 15(4): 609–27.

Henry, Stuart, and Dragan Milovanovic, eds. 1999. *Constitutive Criminology: Applications to Crime and Justice*. Albany: State University of New York Press.

Henry, Stuart, and Dragan Milovanovic. 1996. *Constitutive Criminology: Beyond Postmodernism*. London: Sage.

Lanier, Mark M., and Stuart Henry. 1998. *Essential Criminology*. Boulder, Colo.: Westview.

Michael, Jerome, and Mortimer J. Adler. 1933. *Crime, Law and Social Science*. New York: Harcourt Brace.

Michalowski, Raymond. 1985. *Order, Law and Crime*. New York: Random House.

Russell, Katheryn. 1998. *The Color of Crime*. New York: New York University Press.

Schwendinger, Herman, and Julia Schwendinger. 1970. "Defenders of Order or Guardians of Human Rights?" *Issues in Criminology* 5: 123–57.

Surette, Ray. 1997. *Media, Crime and Criminal Justice*. 2d ed. Pacific Grove, Calif.: Brooks/Cole.

Sutherland, Edwin H. 1940. "White-Collar Criminality." *American Sociological Review* 5(1): 1–12.

Sutherland, Edwin H. 1945. "Is 'White-Collar Crime' Crime?" *American Sociological Review* 10: 132–39.

Tappan, Paul W. 1947. "Who Is the Criminal?" *American Sociological Review* 12: 96–102.

Tifft, Larry L. 1995. "Social Harm Definitions of Crime." *The Critical Criminologist* 7: 9–13.

1

Crime in Context: The Scope of the Problem

Mark M. Lanier and Stuart Henry

Nearly fifty years ago, C. Ray Jeffery provided an illustration of the fundamental disagreement among criminologists concerning the basic question of "What is crime?" The illustration concerned a doctoral examination question in which the student was asked, "Would there be any crime tomorrow if the criminal law was repealed today?" (Jeffery 1956: 658). Professor Jeffery did not tell us how the student responded, but he did reveal that the professors present at the doctoral examination could "not agree among themselves as to what constituted a crime" (1956: 658). The illustration signifies one of criminology's more pressing issues: how to resolve the question of what constitutes crime? Much research on crime tends to take for granted that we know what "crime" means. So, why is defining crime important?

Research and theory suggest that it is very important to know what counts as crime, not only for criminologists but also for anyone studying and trying to understand the cause of the harm produced by crime. If the definition of crime is too narrow, harms that might otherwise be included are ignored. This was the case for years with domestic violence, racial hate, and much of what now counts as corporate and white-collar crime. Conversely, if the definition is too broad, then almost every deviation becomes a crime. This was the case with the old concept of sin, where anything that deviated from the norm could be prosecuted by the church as an offense against God.

A further consideration that makes defining crime important is that several policy decisions concerning social control are made based on a particular definition of crime. These include the selection of priorities in policing and what to police, budget allocations for measures such as crime prevention programs, how to "handle" offenders, and what a "crime-free" neighborhood actually looks like. For example, is a crime-free neighborhood one in which there are low rates of crimes known to the police or one with a low incidence of serious harm? What is the real level of crime when the incidence of serious crime, such as homicide, burglary, rape, and aggravated assault, is low but the level of crimes that disturb the public, such as prostitution, vandalism, public drunkenness, and panhandling, is high? Should the public or community define crime, or should this be a matter for legislators or the police? Despite the obvious importance of arriving at an appropriate definition of crime, no such agreement exists. Indeed, Robert Bohm (1999: 24) has observed that, "[a]n appropriate definition of crime . . . remains one of the most critical unresolved issues in criminal justice today."

In this book, we take the view that arriving at a single shared definition of crime is less important than incorporating the diversity of perspectives of what counts as crime into any definition. To do this, we have adopted a three-stage process. First, we identified classic statements in the controversy over defining crime. Second, we invited authors whose research has led them to define or redefine crime in a particular way to present their arguments. Third, we explored attempts that have been made to integrate the multiple dimensions that constitute crime. In this stage we are suggesting more than the simple idea that crime can be looked at in many different ways or through multiple lenses. Rather, we are asserting that we need to look at crime from a holistic perspective, in a way that integrates its multiple dimensions simultaneously. Ultimately, we aim at a synthesis of these diverse views, but not one that excludes their differences. We believe that such a definition needs to be sensitive to the multifarious ways that the actions of individuals and collective agencies can harm and victimize others.

Yet, we are not seeking a fixed definition, either. We aim instead for a continuously revisable definition that takes account of changing social and cultural contexts, while capturing in the contemporary time frame the harm and the pain that crime causes to its victims. To proceed, it is important to briefly outline the scope of the existing diverse definitions of the crime concept. We will begin this task by reviewing some of the more established views, starting with what might appear to be a perverse notion that crime is normal and functional. Crime is simply the inverse of the behavior that we desire. In other words, by defining what we desire, we simultaneously define what is undesirable.

CRIME AS NORMAL, NECESSARY, AND FUNCTIONAL

At a societal level, it has long been argued that crime serves several functions. The French sociologist Emile Durkheim ([1893] 1984), about whom we will have more to say later, pointed out that crime is not only normal but is also necessary to hold society together. First, crime serves to establish and clarify the moral boundaries of a society. By identifying those behaviors deemed unacceptable, the members of a society reaffirm and refine what is acceptable. Second, crime enhances solidarity by giving the law-abiding members of a society a common enemy, or source of resistance. Crime provides the opportunity to maintain the rules of society by offering occasions "to arouse and reaffirm public support and recognition of the moral boundaries of society. Only where there is a public pronouncement of the offence, drawing out its illegality and immorality, are moral boundaries reaffirmed and individually reinforced" (Box 1981: 38). Third, deviations from social norms (e.g., crime) promote innovative social change allowing social rules to be modified. According to Durkheim (1938 [1897]: 71), "Crime implies not only that the way remains open to necessary changes but that in certain cases it directly prepares for these changes. Where crime exists, collective sentiments are sufficiently flexible to take on a new form, and crime sometimes helps determine the form they will take." Crime, then, shows us ways to do things differently that might be more efficient or more suited to a changed environment. Finally, like pain for the individual patient, crime can serve as an indicator of a society's health; the more there is, the sicker the society. Yet Durkheim (1938 [1897]: 72) also makes the controversial point that too little crime is also a sign of a sick society: "Crime, for its part, must no longer be conceived as an evil that cannot be too much suppressed. There is no occasion for self-congratulation when the crime rate drops noticeably below the average level, for we may be certain that this apparent progress is associated with some social disorder."

In short, Durkheim is referring here to what we might call excessive repression. Since all societies have a "normal" rate of crime, a state of no crime indicates that the forces of crime control are excessive. While Durkheim's ideas have been criticized on numerous grounds (Cohen and Machalek 1994), if he is correct that crime serves these functions, a definition of crime would certainly seem warranted so that these functions can be empirically examined.

Historical Differences in Perception

Over several different historical eras, a debate has raged about what constitutes crime (Bohm 1993). This debate is founded on different philosophical traditions. Two centuries ago, classical theorists challenged the prevalent church and state-based views of crime as evil behavior, the product of meddlesome demons, demonic possession, or irrational thought (Beccaria [1764] 1963). Classicists instead saw crime as mere behavior, albeit outlawed by the state, but just like any other behavior, it was chosen by its perpetrators. The "positivists," who were proponents of the scientific method, challenged the narrow, legalistic definition of crime advocated by classicist philosophers. They believed that crime was very different from other behavior; rather, it was an extreme case of abnormal behavior, the product of defective bodies or minds.

In contemporary times, the debate over the nature of crime was reignited by Edwin Sutherland in his 1939 presidential address to the American Sociological Society (1940). Sutherland argued for extending the existing legal definition of crime to include "white-collar" offenders on the basis that the central issue was the social injury or harm caused, regardless of whether the acts themselves had been defined as crime in law. Paul Tappan (1947; see chap. 3 in this volume) entered the fray, forcefully arguing once more for a strict legal definition, since without adhering strictly to law, the concept of crime was open-ended and meaningless.

By the late 1950s, it seemed that the question of crime's definition had been settled. The law defined crime and, as Gibbons argued (see chap. 4 by Gibbons and Farr in this volume), the issue now was to identify the types of crimes and particularly the types of offenders who broke the law (Gibbons and Garrity 1959; Gibbons 1965, 1975). Indeed, he states that this was imperative "if progress is to be made toward the discovery of causal factors" (Gibbons 1979: 85).

In the late 1960s and early 1970s, radical and critical criminologists again challenged the legal definition (see chap. 5 in this volume). They argued that the problem of crime was indeed tied to the law, but only insofar as those who made the law criminalized the harmful behavior of some, the powerless, but not others, notably the powerful (Schwendinger and Schwendinger 1970; Platt 1975; Quinney 1977). This debate continues, although "most criminologists today act as if the debate is settled in favor of a 'legal' definition" (Bohm 1993: 3).

DIVERSITY OF DEFINITION

Most criminology texts include an explanation of what constitutes crime. We do not want to be redundant but do believe a summary of these different definitional approaches is warranted and worth presenting before a more in-depth approach is discussed by our contributors. Moreover, several of the contributing authors to this text also include brief summaries of varied crime definitions. While we do not want to preempt their comments, we feel justified in providing our interpretation of the perspectives and paradigms that serve to shape these definitions and ultimately our own definition of crime. In the following section, we discuss the influence of the more common of these windows to understanding.

The Classical and Modern Legal Definition

The classical approach to defining crime was based on a simplification and abstraction designed to counter the arbitrariness of the prevailing orthodoxy. In Europe, although the church had traditionally defined sin, and by extension crime, by the fifteenth century the state had not only largely supplanted the church in matters of criminal law but had also increased the scope of behaviors deemed serious crimes. In England, for example, by 1776 there were 160 offenses resulting in the death penalty; by 1819 this figure had increased to 223 (Hibbert

1966: 70–71). Added to the existing list of treason, murder, piracy, arson, rape, sodomy, and every sort of theft of money or goods, it was also a capital offense:

> To appear armed and disguised in a park . . . ; to cut down a tree . . . ; to set fire to an out-house; to send a letter demanding money signed with a fictitious name; to impersonate a Chelsea pensioner; to make false entry in the books of the Bank of England; to strike a Privy Councilor; to damage Westminster Bridge; to refuse to remain in quarantine; and to commit many other acts more or less reprehensible, some of which had not even been crimes, let alone capital ones, before. (Hibbert 1966: 71)

The reformist writings of eighteenth-century classical social philosophers such as Cesare Beccaria ([1764] 1963) and Jeremy Bentham ([1789] 1970), protested against the existing cruel, unjust, and arbitrary European justice systems, which in England, alone, saw roughly two death sentences a week. They argued that the administration of justice needed revising in order to minimize the punishments, and to improve the fairness of the system. A cornerstone of their philosophy reflected the emerging ideas of the time: that people (by which they meant men) are created equal, have the ability to exercise reason, and can rationally choose to pursue their own self-interests. To be effective, the control of crime would require clear laws defining crime, a minimal amount of discretion by judges so that the consequences of offending would be clear and certain. It also requires quick and equitable punishments for similar crimes, with punishments set proportionately to the harm caused by the offense. An emphasis on a clear legal definition of crime was required if people were to exercise the cost–benefit calculus of rational choice. To achieve these goals, people must know what counts as crime and what the consequences of committing it will be. The preference was for a minimal amount of clearly written statutory law to avoid both the "evils" of obscurity and interpretation by the judiciary.

As Einstadter and Henry (1995) point out, from the classicists' perspective, crime is defined by the legal code such that there is no crime without law, and law is based on the "injury" or "harm done to society." The concept of "harm," according to Beccaria, refers to restrictions on the freedom of individuals to accumulate wealth (Beirne 1991: 798). Thus, for Beccaria it was necessary "to restrain men from encroaching upon the freedom of one another defined and established by the terms (laws) of a social contract" (Monachesi 1955: 40).

Beccaria identified three categories of crimes based on the seriousness of their harm *to society*. Most serious of these crimes were those against the state, followed by crimes that injure the security and property of individuals; last in importance were crimes disruptive to the public peace. But for Bentham, harms were behaviors that caused pain rather than restrictions of freedom to accumulate wealth. As Einstadter and Henry (1995: 53) point out, Bentham discusses twelve categories of pain whose measurement was necessary to give legislators a basis on which to decide whether to prohibit an act. He believed that no act ought to be an offense *unless* it was detrimental to the community. An act is detrimental if it harms one or more members of the community. Bentham elaborated a list of categories of offenses which he considered to be of five classes: public offenses, semipublic offenses, self-regarding offenses (offenses detrimental only to the offender), offenses against the state, and multiform or anomalous offenses. Each should carry a punishment determined by the circumstances. Bentham declared that only harms to others should be criminal offenses; cases of public morality and transactional crimes where "consent has been given" should not be subject to the criminal law. In considering what is defined in law, therefore, there is no concern with those who commit crime, only with those acts that harm others (Einstadter and Henry 1995: 53). This version of the legal definition of crime formed the basis of our modern legal approach to crime.

The modern legal definition of crime refers to acts prohibited, prosecuted, and punished by criminal law. In fact, "most criminologists have traditionally relied on the legal conception, which defines crime as behavior in violation of criminal law and liable for sanctioning by the criminal justice system" (Kramer 1982: 34). In a seminal statement on the issue, Michael and Adler (1933: 5; see chap. 2 in this volume) assert that "criminal law gives behavior its quality of criminality." In other words, criminal law specifies the acts or omissions that constitute crime. The most extreme version of the legal definition was provided by Tappan (1947; see chap. 3 in this volume), who argued that the study of criminals should be restricted to those convicted by the courts. The strict legal definition, while supported by many, has come under criticism from criminologists representing several different theoretical perspectives.

Expansion from the Legal: Social, Historical, and Cultural Relativity

Many criminologists have argued that the legal definition is too restrictive. Walter Reckless was among the first to expand the definition sociologically. For Reckless (1940: 10), crime "is fundamentally a violation of conduct norms which contain sanctions, no matter whether found in the criminal law of a modern state or merely in the working rules of special social groups." Indeed, the first criminologists to seriously challenge the legal definition of crime were sociological positivists. Positivists sought to provide a value-free definition of crime that was objective and founded on scientific principles. For one thing, this mandated shifting emphasis from legal codes to criminals. The focus of the positivists was thus on why crimes occurred and who committed them. The legal definition was too restrictive since positivists were interested in causality (what caused crimes) and why certain people were more likely to engage in criminal acts. For some like Gibbons (see chap. 4 by Gibbons and Farr in this volume):

Typologies or classifications of offender patterns, types, syndromes, or role careers are required if progress is to be made toward the discovery of causal factors. Typological ventures were launched on the premise that no single theory can be uncovered to account for all of the diverse types of lawbreaking and lawbreakers. Instead, separate but perhaps interrelated causal hypotheses must be developed for each distinct offender type. (Gibbons 1979: 85)

Further definitional expansion occurs when other theoretical orientations are considered. According to Kramer (1982: 43), "[a]rguments over social versus legal definitions of crime should be grounded in the context of more fundamental paradigms of crime." In other words, says Kramer, definitions of crime will be based on acceptance of a particular theoretical paradigm. Thus, the philosophical views of the criminologist provide the first opportunity for a "value judgment" and the inclusion of bias. This challenge is strengthened by contemplation of hermeneutics, which forces us to take into account an understanding of how existing views and prejudices may shape one's definition of crime (Denzin and Lincoln 1994). In this light, Barak (1998: 21) has argued that "there are no purely objective definitions; all definitions are value laden and biased to some degree." If this is correct, then the theoretical bias and perceptual framework that society or individuals accept must be made clear when defining crime.

Another criticism of the strict legal definition of crime is that it ignores the cultural and historical relativity of law. What is defined as "crime" by the legal code varies from location to location and changes over time. In the United States, crimes such as gambling and pornography are generally illegal but may be legal in some states, counties, or sections of town. For example, several states now run gambling "lotteries" and casinos, and many towns restrict adult entertainment establishments to certain locations. Ironically, Tappan was among the first to acknowledge the cultural and historical variability of "crime" in society's norms but argued that this is why law's precision makes it the only certain guide. However, others have claimed that this is a false certainty, for what the law defines as crime "is somewhat arbitrary, and represents, a highly selective process" (Barak 1998: 21).

Clearly, what counts as a crime at one place in time, culture, or location may not be considered criminal at another time, in another culture, or even across the street! Nettler (1984: 1) sums up the relativity problems with a strict legal definition:

Because there are so many possible wrongs and because "crime" denotes only a select sample of all disapproved acts, the definition of crime varies from time to time and from place to place and there is continuing controversy about what should or should not be called "crime."

In addition, relying on a legal definition of crime presents other problems related to who defines the kinds of behavior labeled crime.

The Importance of Power and Ideology

Crimes are not produced by legislation alone. As even Beccaria recognized, judicial interpretation also determines what is, or is not, crime. Judicial effects on the law are still very evident today. Judicial decisions can be appealed, overturned, and revised. Consider, for example, the *Roe v. Wade* (1973) Supreme Court case that legalized abortion during the first three months of pregnancy, and the more recent limitations that recriminalize certain aspects of it.

Even where legislators make law, a significant problem is whose views they represent. Some critical criminologists argue that criminal actions by corporations and governments often go unrecognized because those who hold economic power in society are, in effect, those who make the law (Coleman 1997; Friedrichs 1996). People in positions of power deemphasize the importance of corporate crime or political corruption, while overemphasizing the significance of violent "street" offenses. For example, street crimes are deemed to be more harmful and newsworthy, although they are much less harmful to society as a whole compared to white-collar crime (Welch, Fenwick, and Roberts 1997). The primary reason for this disparity is found to be the media's overreliance on law enforcement officers to define crime. Understandably, law enforcement officials define the crimes that they are equipped and willing to handle. This becomes self-reinforcing, since the media receive information about crime from police reports, which in turn shape the kind of crime the public "sees," making it more likely that they will report such acts as "crime" rather than others that may be less visible but more harmful (see chaps. 6, 7, and 8, by Gould, Kleck, and Gertz; Schnorr; and Surette and Otto in this volume).

Feminists and critical race theorists argue that those who make the law and those who influence them through political action committees (PACs), and special interest lobbying groups, are not only economically and politically powerful but represent certain gender and ethnic groups; they are largely white males (see chap. 9 by Russell, in this volume).

In short, relying on a strict legal definition of crime may be appropriate for study at an elementary level, but it is sorely lacking for students of criminology or for the thinking criminal justice professional. The multiple facets of crime and its control require serious reflective consideration of what constitutes the action we call crime. One approach to accommodate the range of definitions outlined earlier is to divide them into one of two types depending on whether they reflect consensus or conflict in society.

CONSENSUS AND CONFLICT APPROACHES

In sociology and criminology, two prevalent theoretical paradigms are consensus and conflict. *Consensus* refers to definitions that reflect the values of society as a whole, assuming that these can be identified. Consequently, a consensus definition would reflect universal values and thus "ideals." The opposing theoretical argument is that definitions of crime are based on the idea that society is composed of competing individuals and groups. The conflict is most pronounced between the haves and have-nots, between the powerful and powerless, and between those with the will and ability to enact and enforce law against those less empowered. We will briefly consider each of these ways of defining crime.

Consensus

Historically and pragmatically, consensus theorists circumvent the problem of variations in the law by tying the definition of crime to social morality. French sociologist Emile Durkheim ([1893] 1984) argued that in the integrated communities that preceded industrialization, people were held together by common religious beliefs, traditions, and a similar worldview. The similarity between people acted as a "social glue" that bonded them to each other in a shared morality. Thus, the consensus position states that crimes are acts, which shock the common conscience, or collective morality, producing intense moral outrage among people. Durkheim stated that "an act is criminal when it offends the strong, well-defined states of the collective consciousness" ([1893] 1984: 39). Specifically, crime was a term used "to designate any act, which, regardless of degree, provokes against the perpetrator the characteristic reaction known as punishment" ([1893] 1984: 31). Michael and Adler (1933: 23), who argued that "the character of the behavior content of criminal law will be determined by the capacity of behavior to arouse our indignation," expressed a similar sentiment. More recently, Burgess (1950) argued that "a lack of public outrage, stigma, and official punishment, attached to social action indicates that such action is not a violation of society's rules, independent of whether it is legally punishable" (cited in Green 1990: 9). Current supporters of this position claim there is a "consensus" or agreement among most people of all economic, social, and political positions about what behaviors are unacceptable and what should be labeled criminal. Indeed, echoing Durkheim and Michael and Adler, some commentators, such as Roshier (1989: 76), have defined crime "as only identifiable by the discouraging response it evokes." This view of crime, however, is problematic. In particular, it ignores the importance of social context, social definition of the situation, and especially power.

The Problem of Context

Considering the social context of action deemed criminal presents a major challenge to the consensus definition. The context in which one views social action and events shapes whether the event is deemed criminal. While abstractly and superficially criminal behavior is specified by law, the reality of a situation, who is involved, and how they interpret the actions of others, shape what counts as crime (see Schnorr's chap. 7 in this volume). Consider the obvious example: If one man kills another, is it murder? If the offender kills the victim during a robbery, then the act is clearly murder. But if the offender is a soldier in an army and the victim is another soldier of the enemy during wartime, then the event is typically not seen as murder; it may even be honored. But what if a corporation illegally dumps toxic waste that contaminates drinking water and people die? Another major problem with the consensus view is the question of *whose* morality is important in defining the common morality? If harm affects a minority, will the majority be outraged? Is it any less harmful if they are not? Clearly, understanding the context is the first step toward defining crime.

Consider sexual behavior as an example. Sexual intercourse with a minor, or statutory rape, is in the United States universally agreed to be a crime—that is, until we consider the social context. On closer inspection, legally defined rape is not universally condemned. For example, sexually active boys and girls under the age of legal consent often do not consider themselves raped. In previous historical eras, adolescents of the same age were often married and shared the rights of adults. In this same period, husbands could not "rape" their spouses, though they could force themselves on unwilling wives. Under old German law, an act of sexual intercourse with a women would be considered "as rape only if it was committed against a respectable women, but not a 'vagrant woman' "(Hinckeldey 1981: 107). Whether the physical act is condemned depends on the social and historical context and on the definition of rape. For example, if parents give permission to marry, two sexually active teens are no longer committing "rape," though their physical actions (intercourse) and circumstances (age) are the same.

Consider the rape scenario again. If religious leaders and parents define the crime of statutory rape, then the age of consent may be much older than if sexually active youth were empowered enough to shape legislation. Though some children have successfully "divorced" their parents, more power is generally granted to adults than adolescents in our society. Rape laws have historically had a gender bias as well. Young girls have traditionally been treated much more harshly "by the law" than are young boys (Edwards 1990). The social reaction to sexual activity and prowess continues to reflect gender bias.

Conflict Approaches

Conflict theory is based on the idea that rather than being similar, society is composed of various interest groups in competition with one another over scarce, or limited, resources and ultimately in a struggle over power. The conflict between different interest groups produces differing definitions of crime, each biased to reflect the interests and standards of their own group. These definitions are determined by the group in power and are used to further their needs and consolidate their power. Richard Quinney (1970: 15–16) has expressed this position: "crime is a definition of human conduct created by authorized agents in a politically organized society. . . . [It describes] behaviors that conflict with the interests of the segments of society that have the power to shape public policy."

Interest groups form around many issues. As well as wealth, these may include power, culture, prestige, status, morality/ethics, religion, ethnicity, gender, race, ideology, human rights, the right to own guns, and so forth. Often groups will overlap and share certain beliefs, values, and needs. The earliest definitions of crime from the conflict perspective were based on economic differences reflecting class divisions in society. More recently, gender and racial differences (see chap. 9 by Russell in this volume) have been recognized as shaping definitions of what counts as crime and harms (Gelsthorpe and Morris 1990; Schwartz and Milovanovic 1996).

When power is determined by wealth, the conflict is considered class based. Analysis of this type of conflict is founded on principles outlined by nineteenth-century social philosopher Karl Marx and the Dutch criminologist Willem Bonger. Crime is rooted in the vast differences of wealth and power associated with class divisions. In the late 1970s, Quinney (1977: 31) expanded the study of crime to include economic inequality resulting from the "contradictions of capitalism" expressed as "poverty, inequality, unemployment, and the economic crisis." Groups that acquire economically based political power exert legal constraints on those without power. This helps them retain and consolidate their power. A definition of crime based on economic interests emphasizes that "crime and deviance are the inevitable consequences of fundamental contradictions within society's economic infrastructure" (Farrell and Swigert 1988: 3). Under this version of conflict theory, crime is defined as the activities of those who threaten the powerful. Such a view explains why crimes committed by "street" offenders are seen as serious, while those of corporate or white-collar "suite" offenders are considered less serious. This perception exists despite the fact that white-collar crimes cost thirteen times more per year than street crimes, while producing a greater number of avoidable physical harms (Friedrichs 1996).

Critical criminologists continue to expand the range of crime, suggesting that the *harm* of crime should become central. They assert that the definition of crime should be expanded to include the socially injurious activities of powerful groups against the powerless and behavior that violates or intrudes on others' *human rights* (see chap. 5 by Schwendinger and Schwendinger in this volume). They argue that criminal harm can come not just from individuals but also from social conditions such as imperialism, racism, sexism, and poverty.

The idea of crime as a violation of human rights has become a major theme of critical humanist criminologists. As Quinney and Wildeman (1991: 5) note, "The notion of crime as social injury, social harm, or a violation of human rights is, in effect, basic to those who strive to improve the human condition, for it provides the intellectual and practical tools for the reconstruction of society."

Other criminologists want to extend crime definitions even further by arguing that harm to animals is a crime (Beirne 1994). In summary, in contrast to the narrow, strictly defined legal definition of crime, conflict theorists go much farther in defining crime. They argue that any behavior that intentionally or negligently causes harm is crime (Reiman 1979).

BEYOND CONSENSUS AND CONFLICT

Beyond legal/consensus and conflict definitions, some criminologists have begun to redefine crime even more broadly. For example, instead of seeing established groups as significant, Gould, Kleck, and Gertz (chap. 6 in this volume) expand the social definitional view into one emphasizing the situational context and its constituent players as important. Here crime is defined as a *social event*, involving many players, actors, and agencies. Thus, crimes

> involve not only the actions of individual offenders, but the actions of other persons as well. In particular, they involve the actions of such persons as victims, bystanders and witnesses, law enforcement officers, and members of political society at large. A crime, in other words, is a particular set of interactions among offender(s), crime target(s), agent(s) of social control and society. (Gould et al. 1992: 4)

This broader view of crime highlights the complexities associated with defining crime by recognizing its socially constructed nature, a point developed by Paul Schnorr in his constructionist approach to community definitions of crime (see chap. 7 in this volume).

Another recent reassessment of the definition of crime that takes account of the total context of powerful relations and the situational context comes from postmodernist-influenced *constitutive criminologists*. Postmodernism is a perspective that rejects claims that any body of knowledge is true or can be true. Instead, its advocates believe that "claims to know" are simply power plays by some to dominate others. Constitutive criminologists seek anarchy of knowledge whereby the oppressed, marginalized, and excluded are given their own voice to define what harms them, rather than have others claim to know how to protect them. For example, consistent with the important place given to power, Henry and Milovanovic (see chap. 10 in this volume) see *constitutive criminology* as "the framework for reconnecting crime and its control with the society from which it is conceptually and institutionally constructed by human agents. . . . Crime is both *in* and *of* society" (1991: 307). They define crime as an agency's ability to make a difference to others that reduces or represses the other. Thus, they assert:

> [C]rimes are nothing less than moments in the expression of power, such that those who are subjected to them are denied their own contribution to the encounter and

often to future encounters. . . . Crime then is the power to deny others . . . in which those subject to the power of another agency suffer the pain of being denied their own humanity, the power to make a difference. (Henry and Milovanovic 1994: 116)

Perhaps the most dramatic call to expand the definition of crime comes from Larry Tifft and Dennis Sullivan (see chap. 11 in this volume), who argue that the hierarchical structure and social arrangements of society produce harm that evades the legal definition and that these harms must be included. They recognize that doing so will render many contemporary legal modes of production and distribution criminal, as will many of our criminal justice system's response to crime, based on the harms that they produce. They call for a "needs-based" system of justice based on the concept of equality of well being as the objective.

These increasingly broader definitions of crime have not been made without criticism (see Henry and Milovanovic 1999). Nor have these definitions been accepted by, much less, incorporated into, the criminal justice system or legal doctrine (Lanier and Henry 1998). However, some have argued that "definitions of the content of crime are undergoing constant changes and subtle modifications, and even though the laws themselves may not be changed, the meanings given to the law may shift in their emphasis" (Phillipson 1974: 69).

CONCLUSION

In this introductory chapter, we have provided snapshot views of the major approaches to defining crime. We have illustrated the critical consideration of historical, social, and cultural context and drawn attention to the importance of philosophical and ideological orientation. We have also shown how crime definitions have evolved from a specifically focused legal definition to include virtually everything that causes harm. We have intentionally tried not to integrate these differing aspects, yet this will be our ultimate goal. Before beginning that task, in each of the following chapters the leading advocates of different definitional approaches present their own arguments and justifications.

Finally, although the divisions between consensus/legal and social/conflict definitions are helpful to gain an overall sense of different dimensions that constitute crime and also serve as an organizing mechanism, these divisions do not by themselves present an integrated approach. In the final chapters, we present two interrelated attempts to achieve this integration, the first from Scott Greer and John Hagan and the second, our own development of Hagan's pioneering analysis.

REFERENCES

Barak, Gregg. 1998. *Integrating Criminologies*. Boston: Allyn & Bacon.
Beccaria, Cesare. [1764] 1963. *On Crimes and Punishments*. Trans. Henry Paolucci. Indianapolis: Bobbs-Merrill.

Bentham, Jeremy. [1789] 1970. *An Introduction to the Principles of Morals and Legislation.* London: Pickering.

Beirne, Piers. 1991. "Inventing Criminology: The 'Science of Man' in Cesare Beccaria's *Dei Delitti e Delle Pene* (1764)." *Criminology* 29: 777–820.

Beirne, Piers. 1994. "The Law Is an Ass: Reading E. P. Evans' 'The Medieval Prosecution and Capital Punishment of Animals.'" *Animals and Society* 21: 27–46.

Bohm, Robert M. 1993. "Social Relationships That Arguably Should Be Criminal although They Are Not: On the Political Economy of Crime." In *Political Crime in Contemporary America: A Critical Approach,* ed. Kenneth Tunnell. New York: Garland.

Bohm, Robert M., and Keith N. Haley (1999). *Introduction to Criminal Justice.* 2d ed. New York: McGraw-Hill.

Box, Steven. 1981. *Deviance, Reality and Society.* 2d ed. New York: Holt, Rinehart & Winston.

Burgess, Ernest. 1950. "Comment to Hartung." *American Journal of Sociology* 56: 25–34.

Cohen, Lawrence, and Richard Machalek. 1994. "The Normalcy of Crime: From Durkheim to Evolutionary Ecology." *Rationality and Society* 6: 286–309.

Coleman, James W. 1997. *The Criminal Elite.* New York: St. Martin's.

Denzin, Norman, and Yvonna S. Lincoln 1994. *Handbook of Qualitative Research.* Thousand Oaks, Calif.: Sage.

Durkheim, Emile. [1893] 1984. *The Division of Labor in Society.* New York: Free Press.

———. [1897] 1938. *The Rules of the Sociological Method.* New York: Free Press.

Edwards, Susan. 1990. "Violence against Women: Feminism and the Law." In *Feminist Perspectives in Criminology,* ed. L. Gelsthorpe and A. Morris. Milton Keynes, U.K.: Open University Press.

Einstadter, Werner, and Stuart Henry. 1995. *Criminological Theory: An Analysis of Its Underlying Assumptions.* Fort Worth, Tex.: Harcourt Brace.

Farrell, Ronald A., and Victoria Lynn Swigert. 1988. *Social Deviance.* 3d ed. Belmont, Calif.: Wadsworth.

Friedrichs, David. 1996. *Trusted Criminals: White Collar Crime in Contemporary Society.* Belmont, Calif.: Wadsworth.

Gelsthorpe, Loraine, and Allison Morris, eds. 1990. *Feminist Perspectives in Criminology.* Milton Keynes, U.K.: Open University Press.

Gibbons, Don C. 1965. *Changing the Lawbreaker.* Englewood Cliffs, N.J.: Prentice Hall.

———. 1975. "Offender Typologies—Two Decades Later." *British Journal of Criminology* 15: 140–56.

———. 1979. *The Criminological Enterprise: Theories and Perspectives.* Englewood Cliffs, N.J.: Prentice Hall.

Gibbons, Don C., and Donald L. Garrity. 1959. "Some Suggestions for the Development of Etiological and Treatment Theory in Criminology." *Social Forces* 38: 51–58.

Gould, Leroy, Gary Kleck, and Marc Gertz. 1992. "The Concept of 'Crime' in Criminological Theory and Practice." *The Criminologist* 17: 1–6.

Green, Gary S. 1990. *Occupational Crime.* Chicago: Nelson-Hall.

Henry, Stuart, and Dragan Milovanovic. 1991. "Constitutive Criminology: The Maturation of Critical Theory." *Criminology* 29: 307–15.

———. 1994. "The Constitution of Constitutive Criminology: A Postmodern Approach to Criminological Theory." In *The Futures of Criminology,* ed. David Nelken. London: Sage.

Henry, Stuart, and Dragan Milovanovic. 1996. *Constitutive Criminology: Beyond Postmodernism*. London: Sage.

———, eds. 1999. *Constitutive Criminology: Applications to Crime and Justice*. Albany: State University of New York Press.

Hibbert, Christopher. 1966. *The Roots of Evil: A Social History of Crime and Punishment*. London: Weidenfeld & Nicholson.

Hinckeldey, Christoph. 1981. *Criminal Justice through the Ages*. Rothenburg, Germany: Mittelalterliches Kriminal Museum.

Jeffery, C. Ray. 1956. "The Structure of American Criminological Thinking." *Journal of Criminal Law, Criminology, and Police Science* 46: 658–72.

Kramer, Ronald C. 1982. "The Debate over the Definition of Crime: Paradigms, Value Judgments, and Criminological Work." In *Ethics, Public Policy, and Criminal Justice*, ed. Frederick Elliston and Norm Bowie. Cambridge, Mass: Oelgeschlager, Gunn, & Hain.

Lanier, Mark, and Stuart Henry. 1998. *Essential Criminology*. Boulder, Colo.: Westview.

Michael, Jerome, and Mortimer J. Adler. 1933. *Crime, Law and Social Science*. New York: Harcourt Brace & Jovanovich.

Monachesi, Elio D. 1955. "Cesear Beccaria." *Journal of Criminal Law, Criminology and Police Science* 46: 439–49.

Nettler, Gwynn. 1984. *Explaining Crime*. 3d ed. New York: McGraw-Hill.

Phillipson, Michael. 1974. *Understanding Crime and Deviance*. Chicago: Aldine.

Platt, Tony. 1975. "Prospects for a Radical Criminology in the USA." In *Critical Criminology*, ed. I. Taylor, P. Walton, and J. Young. London: Routledge & Kegan Paul.

Quinney, Richard. 1970. *The Social Reality of Crime*. Boston: Little, Brown.

———. 1977. *Class, State, and Crime*. New York: Longman.

Quinney, Richard, and John Wildeman. 1991. *The Problem of Crime: A Peace and Social Justice Perspective*. 3d ed. London: Mayfield.

Reckless, Walter C. 1940. *Criminal Behavior*. New York: McGraw-Hill.

Reiman, Jeffrey. 1979. *The Rich Get Richer and the Poor Get Prison*. New York: Wiley.

Roshier, Bob. 1989. *Controlling Crime: The Classical Perspective in Criminology*. Philadelphia: Open University Press.

Schwartz Martin, and Dragan Milovanovic, eds. 1996. *Race, Gender and Class in Criminology: The Intersections*. New York: Garland.

Schwendinger, Herman, and Julia Schwendinger. 1970. "Defenders of Order or Guardians of Human Rights?" *Issues in Criminology* 5: 123–57.

Sutherland, Edwin H. 1940. "White-Collar Criminality." *American Sociological Review* 5: 1–12.

Tappan, Paul W. 1947. "Who Is the Criminal?" *American Sociological Review* 12: 96–102.

Welch, Michael, Melissa Fenwick, and Meredith Roberts. 1997. "Primary Definitions of Crime and Moral Panic: A Content Analysis of Experts' Quotes in Feature Newspaper Articles on Crime." *Journal of Research in Crime and Delinquency* 34: 474–94.

Part I

Classic Statements

2

The Nature of Crime

Jerome Michael and Mortimer J. Adler

Such words as *crime* and *criminal*, *delinquent* and *delinquency*, are currently used with a variety of meanings in technical as well as in popular discussions of crime. It is therefore necessary at the very threshold of this discussion that we should precisely state the meanings with which we shall employ them. It is important for purposes of discourse and exposition that these words should be defined as precisely as possible; it is even more important, as we shall see, for purposes of the study of crime and criminals. It is, for example, impossible to observe and study criminal behavior unless it can be defined in such a way as sharply to distinguish it from non-criminal conduct. So, too, unless the class of criminals can be defined in such a manner as to distinguish them from the class of non-criminals, we shall be unable to identify criminals in the general population and, hence, unable to observe and study them. In brief, we cannot make empirical investigations of crime and criminals unless we have some basis for differentiating criminal from other behavior and criminals from other persons, which is so precise and definite that we will not confuse them in our observations. Attempts have been made to define crime in moral terms and in social terms. The definition of crime as behavior which is immoral lacks precision and clarity. Opinions on questions of morals are notoriously diverse and confused. If there was ever a time when the population of a community was single-minded in their moral judgments, that time has long since passed. There is no moral code to which all men or even all men in a single community subscribe.

The definition of crime as antisocial behavior is hardly more precise or less ambiguous although it does shift the emphasis somewhat from what is thought of as the intrinsic quality of conduct to its social consequences. But we do not know and can seldom discover more than the initial and immediate effects of any behavior, and even these we can often know only in a superficial way. Moreover, here, again, values with respect to which there is no general agreement intrude themselves; again we are confronted with the necessity of evaluating behavior by standards which are necessarily largely personal. It is not enough to know the consequences of behavior; we must pass judgment upon them as social or antisocial. The most precise and least ambiguous definition of crime is that which defines it as behavior which is prohibited by the criminal code.[1] The criminal law describes many kinds of behavior, gives them names such as murder and arson and rape and burglary, and proscribes them. If crime is defined in legal terms, the only source of confusion is such ambiguity as may inhere in the legal definitions of specific crimes. It is sometimes difficult to tell whether specific conduct falls within the legal definition, whether, for example, a specific homicide is murder or what degree of murder, as that offense is defined by law. But even so, the legal rules are infinitely more precise than moral judgments or judgments with regard to the antisocial character of conduct. Moreover, there is no surer way of ascertaining what kinds of behavior are generally regarded as immoral or antisocial by the people of any community than by reference to their criminal code, for in theory, at least, the criminal code embodies social judgments with respect to behavior and, perhaps, more often than not, fact conforms to theory. Most of the people in any community would probably agree that most of the behavior which is proscribed by their criminal law is socially undesirable.

Questions as to the immoral or antisocial character of behavior thus enter into the question whether a specific kind of behavior shall be prohibited, that is, shall be made criminal; they are, as we shall see, questions for the legislator. But they do not enter into the question whether specific kinds of behavior are criminal. To answer that question one need ascertain only whether the conduct in question is prohibited by the criminal law. In other words, a crime is merely an instance of behavior which is prohibited by the criminal law. It is in this sense that we shall use the term *crime* throughout this discussion (italics added).

It follows that a criminal is a person who has behaved in some way prohibited by the criminal law; and he is a criminal whether or not he has been convicted of his crime or, indeed, whether his crime is known either to himself or to anyone else. However, unless criminality has been officially determined by the legal processes established for that purpose, it must nearly always remain in doubt. The most certain way, therefore, to distinguish criminals from non-criminals is in terms of those who have been convicted of crime and those who have not. It would obviously be most difficult in any other way to identify the immoral or antisocial persons in the population or to distinguish between criminals and non-criminals. We do not mean to say either that all persons convicted of crime are criminals or that all criminals are convicted of their crimes; we mean to say only that both for practical purposes and for theoretical purposes we must proceed as if that were true. However inadequate conviction of crime may be as a test of criminality, in no other way can criminality be established with sufficient certainty for either practical or scientific purposes. The criminologist is therefore quite justified in making the convict population the subject of his studies, as he does.

In the same way and for the same reasons we shall use the word *delinquency* to mean the criminal behavior of a person below some age prescribed by law, and the term *delinquent* to refer to a person whose delinquency has been officially determined. The legal definition of delinquents often includes young persons who are neglected or whose conduct and environment seem to point to a criminal career. Words such as these are too vague and indefinite to enable us to distinguish between young persons who are delinquent and those who are not. Throughout this discussion we shall therefore use *crime* and *delinquency* as identical terms, except that by the former we shall mean the criminal behavior of adult, and by the latter the criminal behavior of juvenile, offenders. Delinquency often precedes criminality in the case of the same individual, and delinquency is commonly regarded as a step in the development of criminality. Indeed, as will later appear, a very large proportion of all criminological research has been concerned with delinquency and delinquents rather than with crime and criminals. In this discussion we must therefore take delinquency as well as crime into account. However, in large part the problems of crime and delinquency are identical. It will therefore not be necessary as a rule to consider delinquency as such or to distinguish between criminals and delinquents. We shall use the word *offense* to refer indiscriminately to criminal and delinquent behavior, and the term *offender* to refer in the same way to criminals and delinquents. As they exist in the general population, the class of potential offenders includes those who have as well as those who have never offended. However, we shall find it necessary to distinguish between those who have and those who have never committed crimes or delinquencies and we shall refer to the former as actual, and to the latter as potential, offenders, criminals, or delinquents.[2]

Actual criminality or delinquency thus has reference to behavior which has occurred in the past; potential criminality or delinquency to that which may occur in the future. We shall therefore use the term *criminal* or *delinquent behavior* to refer both to actual and potential criminality or delinquency, to crimes and delinquencies that have been committed in the past and to those which may be committed in the future. There are other reasons for defining crime and criminals and delinquency and delinquents as we have defined them. The empirical studies which have heretofore been made of criminals and delinquents have almost invariably been studies of persons whose criminality and delinquency have, in the first place, taken the form of behavior which is prohibited by the criminal law, and have, in the next place, been established by legal processes. Obviously, criminals and delinquents cannot as a rule be studied until they have come into official custody and have in this way been segregated from the rest of the population.[3] To define crime and delinquency, criminals and delinquents, in other than legal terms, would therefore be to ignore the conditions of past as well as of future research in the field of criminal behavior.

If crime is merely an instance of conduct which is proscribed by the criminal code, it follows that the criminal law is the formal cause of crime. That does not mean that the law produces the behavior which it prohibits, although, as we shall see, the enforcement or administration of the criminal law may be one of the factors which influence human behavior; it means only that the criminal law gives behavior its quality of criminality. Without a criminal code there would be no crime, however much immoral or socially undesirable behavior might survive its repeal. From this point of view, the question involved in the formulation or amendment of a criminal code can be stated as what crimes do we wish to cause. As we shall see, this is a useful way for the lawmaker to state his problem. . . .

WHAT BEHAVIOR SHALL BE MADE CRIMINAL?

The retributive and retaliative aim of criminal justice is probably the most primitive end of criminal justice. . . . Retributive punishment proceeds upon the theory that the amount of suffering inflicted upon a criminal should somehow be proportionate to the enormity of his offense and to the public indignation which it arouses.

If, therefore, retributive punishment is to be the final purpose of criminal justice, the character of the behavior content of the criminal law will be determined by the capacity of behavior to arouse our indignation. The question what behavior shall be made criminal, will be answered in terms of our likes and dislikes. If our dislike for any conduct is sufficiently strong, we will make it criminal, and the seriousness or magnitude of the resulting crime can be measured only by the intensity of our dislike for that type of conduct. We may dislike behavior either because of what we know or believe to be its consequences, or without regard to its consequences. It may not arouse our indignation although its results are detrimental to the common welfare, and, on the other hand, it may arouse our indignation although its consequences are not known or even believed to be inimical to the common good. It may be quite enough that behavior rails counter to strong and deep-seated prejudices. We may, for example, make the expression of certain ideas criminal because we do not like them. In a punitive system of criminal justice, therefore, the question what behavior shall be made criminal seems to resolve itself into the question what behavior arouses our indignation.

The first question that arises in a non-punitive system of criminal justice is likewise what behavior shall be made criminal. Since the ultimate end of a non-punitive system is the defense of social interests against antisocial behavior, to answer that question in such a system we have to determine, first, what are the social interests to be protected and, next, what behavior is incompatible with them. Dean Pound (1930) has very generally classified the numerous social interests which we now endeavor to protect by criminal justice as the general security, the security of social institutions, the general morals, the conservation of social resources, the general progress, and the individual life. Whether we agree with this classification or not, it is clear that whatever the social interests which we attempt to safeguard by criminal justice may be, they will represent values, and our determination of those interests will represent a choice among values. Thus, the question as to the social interests to be protected by criminal justice, like the problem of the ultimate ends of criminal justice, is a practical problem.[4]

Having fixed upon the social interests which we desire to secure by criminal justice, the next question which confronts us in our effort to decide what behavior shall be made criminal, is what types of behavior are incompatible with those interests. Unless we know the consequences of behavior and their compatibility with what we conceive to be the common good, we may prohibit some behavior which is not socially undesirable and which, indeed, may be socially desirable; and we may fail to prohibit other conduct which is in fact antisocial.[5] Unless we have rather precise knowledge of the characteristics of those kinds of behavior which we wish to prohibit, we may not describe them in the criminal law with sufficient definiteness for our practical purposes. It must be remembered that the proscription of behavior is an intermediate and not a final end; it is a means as well as an end. Criminal laws are made to be enforced. They should describe the behavior which they prohibit with sufficient precision to insure both that they will be applied by the officials who administer them to the types of behavior at which they are directed, and that they will not be applied to similar but innocuous forms of conduct.[6] Ignorance of the nature of conduct which we wish to prohibit or the careless formulation of our prohibitions may defeat our purpose.[7]

We do not mean to say that we shall always find it difficult to know the characteristics and consequences of behavior with sufficient precision for our practical purposes. The characteristics and at least the immediate consequences of many kinds of behavior are quite apparent; and, whatever their other consequences may be, it is clear that they are inimical to the common good, as we conceive it.[8]

In other cases the problem is not so simple. We can refer to the types of behavior which in common speech are known as racketeering and to those which in the language of the law are known as larceny, as examples of behavior whose characteristics it is difficult to know and describe with precision;[9] and to traffic in intoxicating liquors as an example of conduct whose consequences it is difficult to ascertain and evaluate in terms of social interests.[10] Social values are not entirely static and human behavior and its consequences take myriad shifting forms. There are fashions in criminal behavior, especially in that of the so-called professional or habitual criminals. Moreover, new non-criminal behavior patterns, some of which are quite obviously inconsistent with the common welfare, develop with changes in the social and economic structure. It appears to be desirable that the behavior content of the criminal law should keep abreast of changes in behavior patterns or, at least, that it should not lag too far behind.

We do not mean to suggest that it is expedient that all behavior which is known to be incompatible with the common good be made criminal in a non-punitive system. A further question is involved, namely, whether the administration of the criminal law is likely to be an effective device for preventing such behavior, either alone or in connection with other preventive devices. It can operate as a preventive device only by reforming actual offenders and by deterring potential offenders. The question, therefore, is whether the persons who are behaving in a particular way which is regarded as inimical to the common good are likely to be deterred from behaving in that way if it is made criminal to do so.[11] This is obviously a question as to the influence of the administration of the criminal law upon the behavior of actual and potential offenders, a problem which we are about to consider.

Nor do we mean to suggest that criminal laws are in fact enacted as the result of a consideration of social interests, of the compatibility of behavior with those interests, and of the probable efficiency of the criminal law as a device to prevent such behavior. We suggest only that a rational legislative technique in a non-punitive system would be based upon such considerations.

The theoretical aspects of the practical problem what behavior shall be made criminal are thus seen to be questions regarding the characteristics and consequences of behavior and the efficiency of the criminal law as a device to prevent behavior which is hostile to the common good.

NOTES

Reprinted from Jerome Michael and Mortimer J. Adler, *Crime, Law and Social Science* (New York: Harcourt Brace, 1933), 1–5, 23–26. Copyright International Library of Psychology, Philosophy, and Scientific Method.

1. Not only is the legal definition of crime precise and unambiguous, but it is the *only possible* definition of crime. This is what is meant by the subsequent statement that the criminal law is the formal cause of crime. The definition of particular crimes by the criminal law may be inadequate in the sense that it may not make criminal all the types of behavior which *should* be made criminal.

2. As we have said, the most certain way in which to differentiate between those who have and those who have never offended in fact is in terms of the official determination of their criminality or delinquency. It is thus possible that one who must be classified as an actual offender because his 'guilt' has been officially determined, may never in fact have committed any crime. It is also very likely that many persons who are offenders in fact will be classified as potential offenders merely because their criminality has not been officially established. The distinction is thus in many cases merely a distinction between those who have been convicted of crime and those who have not. This enormously complicates the problems of the criminologist, as we shall see, but there seems to be no practicable way at present of avoiding the complication. If the distinction between actual and potential offenders is one which must be made in the study of criminal behavior, greater efficiency in the detection of crime and in the apprehension and prosecution of criminals is of scientific as well as of practical importance.

3. There are exceptional studies of potential offenders as, for example, Locard's study

of the organization of street gangs, or Reiss' observations of professional prostitutes and their role in burglaries.

4. We shall later consider whether this problem has any theoretical aspects.

5. Of course, the argument applies as well to existing, as to proposed, legislation. The existing criminal laws may be formulated in indefinite terms or they may be directed at behavior which is not socially deleterious.

6. One of the purposes of criminal justice seems to be the definition and delimitation of the authority of officials to interfere by the processes of criminal justice with the freedom of the individual to behave as he pleases. The individual is to be left free to act in any way which is not prohibited by the criminal law. Of course, the civil law may further limit his freedom of action. Lack of knowledge of the characteristics of behavior or careless drafting of legislation may result in giving officials an authority which it was never intended that they should possess, as well as in inefficient administration.

7. This is only one example of how the criminal law may itself make for inefficiency in its enforcement. We shall subsequently refer to others.

8. This is particularly true of the consequences and, to a less extent, of the characteristics, of some of the so-called common law felonies, that is, of the kinds of conduct which we call murder or rape or burglary or arson.

9. In common speech racketeering is a name given to many forms of conduct; and one has only to refer to the maze of judicial precedents to see how many and what diverse kinds of behavior are given such names as homicide and larceny. Frequently the criminal law describes the behavior, which it prohibits in very gross terms. The problem of drafting criminal legislation is obviously a very difficult and important practical problem to which we shall revert.

10. To know this to be true, one has only to follow current discussions of the Eighteenth Amendment and of the National Prohibition Act or, indeed, to read the Report on the Enforcement of the Prohibition Laws of the United States by the National Commission on Law Observance and Enforcement.

11. The behavior which made a criminal will usually be behavior which is already familiar in society. Rarely, if ever, does the criminal law prohibit a type of behavior of which there have not theretofore been frequent manifestations. And, of course, instead of making it criminal to behave in a certain way, we may make it criminal to fail to behave in a certain way. That is, we may employ the criminal law as a device either to prevent or to induce behavior. However, whether we do the one thing or the other, we are using the criminal law as a device for controlling behavior and both the practical and the theoretical problems which ensue, are largely the same. Therefore, we shall find it unnecessary to emphasize this distinction.

REFERENCES

Pound, Roscoe.1930. *Criminal Justice in America*. New York: Holt.

3

Who Is the Criminal?

Paul W. Tappan

What is crime? As a lawyer–sociologist, the writer finds perturbing the current confusion on this important issue. Important because it delimits the subject matter of criminological investigation. A criminologist who strives to aid in formulating the beginnings of a science finds himself in an increasingly equivocal position. He studies the criminals convicted by the courts and is then confounded by the growing clamor that he is not studying the real criminal at all, but an insignificant proportion of nonrepresentative and stupid unfortunates who happened to have become enmeshed in technical legal difficulties. It has become a fashion to maintain that the convicted population is no proper category for the empirical research of the criminologist. Ergo, the many studies of convicts which have been conducted by the orthodox, now presumably outmoded criminologists, have no real meaning for either descriptive or scientific purposes. Off with the old criminologies, on with the new orientations, the new horizons!

This position reflects in part at least the familiar suspicion and misunderstanding held by the layman sociologist toward the law. To a large extent it reveals the feeling among social scientists that not all antisocial conduct is proscribed by law (which is probably true), that not all conduct violative of the criminal code is truly antisocial, or is not so to any significant extent (which is also undoubtedly true). Among some students the opposition to the traditional definition of crime as law violation arises from their desire to discover and study wrongs which are absolute and eternal rather than mere violations of a statutory and case law system which vary in time and place; this is essentially the old metaphysical search for the law of nature. They consider the dynamic and relativistic nature of law to be a barrier to the growth of a scientific system of hypotheses possessing universal validity.[1]

Recent protestants against the orthodox conceptions of crime and criminal are diverse in their views: they unite only in their denial of the allegedly legalistic and arbitrary doctrine that those convicted under the criminal law are the criminals of our society and in promoting the confusion as to the proper province of criminology. It is enough here to examine briefly a few of the current schisms with a view to the difficulties at which they arrive.

A number of criminologists today maintain that mere violation of the criminal law is an artificial criterion of criminality, that categories set up by the law do not meet the demands of scientists because they are of a "fortuitous nature" and do not "arise intrinsically from the nature of the subject matter" (Sellin 1938: 20–21). The validity of this contention must depend, of course, upon what the nature of the subject matter is. These scholars suggest that, as a part of the general study of human behavior, criminology should concern itself broadly with all antisocial conduct, behavior injurious to society. We take it that antisocial conduct is essentially any sort of behavior which violates some social interest. What are these social interests? Which are weighty enough to merit the concern of the sociologist, to bear the odium of crime? What shall constitute a violation of them?—particularly where, as is so commonly true in our complicated and unintegrated society, these interests are themselves in conflict? Roscoe Pound's suggestive classification of the social interests served by law is valuable in a juristic framework, but it solves no problems for the sociologist who seeks to depart from legal standards in search of all manner of antisocial behavior.

However desirable may be the concept of socially injurious conduct for purposes of general normation or abstract description, it does not define what is injurious. It sets no standard. It does not discriminate cases, but merely invites the subjective value-judgments of the investigator. Until it is structurally embodied with distinct criteria or norms—as is now the case in the legal system—the notion of antisocial conduct is useless for purposes of research, even for the rawest empiricism. The emancipated criminologist reasons himself into a cul-de-sac: having decided that it is footless to study convicted offenders on the ground that this is an artificial category—though its membership is quite precisely ascertainable—he must now conclude that, in his lack of standards to determine antisociality, though this may be what he considers a real scientific category, its membership and its characteristics are unascertainable. Failing to define antisocial behavior in any fashion suitable to research, the criminologist may be deluded further into assuming that there is an absoluteness and permanence in this undefined category, lacking in the law. It is unwise for the social scientist ever to forget that all standards of social normation are relative, impermanent, variable. And that they do not, certainly the law does not, arise out of mere fortuity or artifice.[2]

In a differing approach certain other criminologists suggest that "conduct norms" rather than either crime or antisocial conduct should be studied (Sellin 1938: 25). There is an unquestionable need to pursue the investigation of general conduct norms and their violation. It is desirable to segregate the various classes of such norms, to determine relationships between them, to understand similarities and differences between them as to the norms themselves, their sources, methods of imposition of control, and their consequences. The subject matter of this field of social control is in a regrettably primitive state. It will be important to discover the individuals who belong within the several categories of norm violators established and to determine then what motivations operate to promote conformity or breach. So far as it may be determinable, we shall wish to know in what way these motivations may serve to insure conformity to different sets of conduct norms, how they may overlap and reinforce the norms or conflict and weaken the effectiveness of the norms.

We concur in the importance of the study of conduct norms and their violation and, more particularly, if we are to develop a science of human behavior, in the need for careful researches to determine the psychological and environmental variables which are associated etiologically with nonconformity to these norms. However, the importance of the more general subject matter of social control or "ethology" does not mean that the more specific study of the law-violator is nonsignificant. Indeed, the direction of progress in the field of social control seems to lie largely in the observation and analysis of more specific types of nonconformity to particular, specialized standards. We shall learn more by attempting to determine why some individuals take human life deliberately and with premeditation, why some take property by force and others by trick, than we shall in seeking at the start a universal formula to account for any and all behavior in breach of social interests. This broader knowledge of conduct norms may conceivably develop through induction, in its inevitably very generic terms, from the empirical data derived in the study of particular sorts of violations. Too, our more specific information about the factors which lie behind violations of precisely defined norms will be more useful in the technology of social control. Where legal standards require change to keep step with the changing requirements of a dynamic society, the sociologist may advocate—even as the legal profession does—the necessary statutory modifications, rather than assume that for sociological purposes the conduct he disapproves is already criminal, without legislative, political, or judicial intervention.

Another increasingly widespread and seductive movement to revolutionize the concepts of crime and criminal has developed around the currently fashionable dogma of "white collar crime." This is actually a particular school among those who contend that the criminologist should study antisocial behavior rather than law violation. The dominant contention of the group appears to be that the convict classes are merely our "petty" criminals, the few whose depredations against society have been on a small scale, who have blundered into difficulties with the police and courts through their ignorance and stupidity. The important criminals, those who do irreparable damage with impunity, deftly evade the machinery of justice, either by remaining "technically" within the law or by exercising their intelligence, financial prowess, or political connections in its violation. We seek a definition of the white collar criminal and find an amazing diversity, even among those flowing from the same pen, and observe that characteristically they are loose, doctrinaire, and invective. When Professor Sutherland launched the term, it was applied to those individuals of upper socioeconomic class who violate the criminal law, usually by breach of trust, in the ordinary course of their business activities (Sutherland 1941). This original usage accords with legal ideas of crime and points moreover to the significant and difficult problems of enforcement in the areas of business crimes, particularly where those violations are made criminal by recent statutory enactment. From this fruitful beginning the term has spread into vacuity, wide and handsome. We learn that the white collar criminal may be the suave and deceptive merchant prince or "robber baron," that the existence of such crime may be determined readily "in casual conversation with a representative of an occupation by asking him, 'What crooked practices are found in your occupation?' " (Sutherland 1940: 1).

Confusion grows as we learn from another proponent of this concept that, "There are various phases of white-collar criminality that touch the lives of the common man almost daily. The large majority of them are operating within the letter and spirit of the law" and that "In short, greed, not need, lies at the basis of white-collar crime"(Barnes and Teeters 1943: 42–43). Apparently the criminal may be law obedient but greedy; the specific quality of his crimes is far from clear.

Another avenue is taken in Professor Sutherland's (1945: 132) more recent definition of crime as a "legal description of an act as socially injurious and legal provision of penalty for the act." Here he has deemed the connotation of his term too narrow if confined to violations of the criminal code; he includes by a slight modification conduct violative of any law, civil or criminal, when it is "socially injurious."

In light of these definitions, the normative issue is pointed. Who should be considered the white collar criminal? Is it the merchant who, out of greed, business acumen, or competitive motivations, breaches a trust with his consumer by "puffing his wares" beyond their merits, by pricing them beyond their value, or by ordinary advertising? Is it he who breaks trust with his employees in order to keep wages down, refusing to permit labor organization or to bargain collectively, and who is found guilty by a labor relations board of an unfair labor practice? May it be the white-collar worker who breaches trust with his employers by inefficient performance at work, by sympathetic strike or secondary boycott? Or is it the merchandiser who violates ethics by undercutting the prices of his fellow merchants? In general these acts do not violate the criminal law. All in some manner breach a trust for motives which a criminologist may (or may not) disapprove for one reason or another. All are within the framework of the norms of ordinary business practice. One seeks in vain for criteria to determine this white-collar criminality. It is the conduct of one who wears a white collar and who indulges in occupational behavior to which some particular criminologist takes exception. It may easily be a term of propaganda. For purposes of empirical research or objective description, what is it?

Whether criminology aspires one day to become a science or a repository of reasonably accurate descriptive information, it cannot tolerate a nomenclature of such loose and variable usage. A special hazard exists in the employment of the term, "white-collar criminal," in that it invites individual systems of private values to run riot in an area (economic ethics) where gross variation exists among criminologists as well as others. The rebel may enjoy a veritable orgy of delight in damning as criminal most anyone he pleases; one imagines that some experts would thus consign to the criminal classes any successful capitalistic business man; the reactionary or conservative, complacently viewing the occupational practices of the business world might find all in perfect order in this best of all possible worlds. The result may be fine indoctrination or catharsis achieved through blustering broadsides against the "existing system." It is not criminology. It is not social science. The terms "unfair," "infringement," "discrimination," "injury to society," and so on, employed by the white-collar criminologists cannot, taken alone, differentiate criminal and noncriminal. Until refined to mean certain specific actions, they are merely epithets. Vague, omnibus concepts defining crime are a blight upon either a legal system or a system of sociology that strives to be objective. They allow judge, administrator, or—conceivably— sociologist, in an undirected, freely operating discretion, to attribute the status "criminal" to any individual or class which he conceives nefarious. This can accomplish no desirable objective, either politically or sociologically.[3]

Worse than futile, it is courting disaster, political, economic, and social, to promulgate a system of justice in which the individual may be held criminal without having committed a crime, defined with some precision by statute and case law. To describe crime the sociologist, like the lawyer–legislator, must do more than condemn conduct deviation in the abstract. He must avoid definitions predicated simply upon state of mind or social injury and determine what particular types of deviation, in what directions, and to what degree, shall be considered criminal. This is exactly what the criminal code today attempts to do, though imperfectly of course. More slowly and conservatively than many of us would wish: that is in the nature of legal institutions, as it is in other social institutions as well. But law has defined with greater clarity and precision the conduct which is criminal than our antilegalistic criminologists promise to do; it has moreover promoted a stability, a security and dependability of justice through its exactness, its so-called technicalities, and its moderation in inspecting proposals for change.

Having considered the conceptions of an innovating sociology in ascribing the terms "crime" and "criminal," let us state here the juristic view: Only those are criminals who have been adjudicated as such by the courts. Crime is an intentional act in violation of the criminal law (statutory and case law), committed without defense or excuse, and penalized by the state as a felony or misdemeanor. In studying the offender there can be no presumption that arrested, arraigned, indicted, or prosecuted persons are criminals unless they also be held

guilty beyond a reasonable doubt of a particular offense.[4] Even less than the unconvicted suspect can those individuals be considered criminal who have violated no law. Only those are criminals who have been selected by a clear substantive and a careful adjective law, such as obtain in our courts. The unconvicted
offenders of whom the criminologist may wish to take cognizance are an important but unselected group; it has no specific membership presently ascertainable.
Sociologists may strive, as does the legal profession, to perfect measures for more
complete and accurate ascertainment of offenders, but it is futile simply to rail
against a machinery of justice which is, and to a large extent must inevitably
remain, something less than entirely accurate or efficient.

Criminal behavior as here defined fits very nicely into the sociologists' formu-
lations of social control. Here we find *norms* of conduct, comparable to the
mores, but considerably more distinct, precise, and detailed, as they are fashioned through statutory and case law. The *agencies* of this control, like the norms
themselves, are more formal than is true in other types of control: the law depends for its instrumentation chiefly upon police, prosecutors, judges, juries, and
the support of a favorable public opinion. The law has for its *sanctions* the specifically enumerated punitive measures set up by the state for breach, penalties
which are additional to any of the sanctions which society exerts informally
against the violator of norms which may overlap with laws. *Crime* is itself simply
the breach of the legal norm, a violation within this particular category of social
control; the criminal is, of course, the individual who has committed such acts
of breach.

Much ink has been spilled on the extent of deterrent efficacy of the criminal
law in social control. This is a matter which is not subject to demonstration in
any exact and measurable fashion, any more than one can conclusively demonstrate the efficiency of a moral norm.[5] Certainly the degree of success in asserting
a control, legal or moral, will vary with the particular norm itself, its instrumentation, the subject individuals, the time, the place, and the sanctions. The efficiency of legal control is sometimes confused by the fact that, in the common
overlapping of crimes (particularly those *mala in se*) with moral standards, the
norms and sanctions of each may operate in mutual support to produce conformity. Moreover, mere breach of norm is no evidence of the general failure of a
social control system, but indication rather of the need for control. Thus the
occurrence of theft and homicide does not mean that the law is ineffective, for
one cannot tell how frequently such acts might occur in the absence of law and
penal sanction. Where such acts are avoided, one may not appraise the relative
efficacy of law and mores in prevention. When they occur, one cannot apportion
blame, either in the individual case or in general, to failures of the legal and
moral systems. The individual in society does undoubtedly conduct himself in
reference to legal requirements. Living "beyond the law" has a quality independent of being nonconventional, immoral, sinful. Mr. Justice Holmes has shown
that the "bad man of the law"—those who become our criminals—are motivated

in part by disrespect for the law or, at the least, are inadequately restrained by its taboos.

From introspection and from objective analysis of criminal histories one can not but accept as axiomatic the thesis that the norms of criminal law and its sanctions do exert some measure of effective control over human behavior; that this control is increased by moral, conventional, and traditional norms; and that the effectiveness of control norms is variable. It seems a fair inference from urban investigations that in our contemporary mass society, the legal system is becoming increasingly important in constraining behavior as primary group norms and sanctions deteriorate. Criminal law, crime, and the criminal become more significant subjects of sociological inquiry, therefore, as we strive to describe, understand, and control the uniformities and variability in culture.

We consider that the "white-collar criminal," the violator of conduct norms, and the antisocial personality are not criminal in any sense meaningful to the social scientist unless he has violated a criminal statute. We cannot know him as such unless he has been properly convicted. He may be a boor, a sinner, a moral leper, or the devil incarnate, but he does not become a criminal through sociological name-calling unless politically constituted authority says he is. It is footless for the sociologist to confuse issues of definition, normation, etiology, sanction, agency, and social effects by saying one thing and meaning another.

To conclude, we reiterate and defend the contention that crime, as legally defined, is a sociologically significant province of study. The view that it is not appears to be based upon either of two premises: (1) that offenders convicted under the criminal law are not representative of all criminals and (2) that criminal law violation (and, therefore, the criminal himself) is not significant to the sociologist because it is composed of a set of legal, nonsociological categories irrelevant to the understanding of group behavior and/or social control. Through these contentions to invalidate the traditional and legal frame of reference adopted by the criminologist, several considerations, briefly enumerated below, must be met.

1. Convicted criminals as a sample of law violators:
   a. Adjudicated offenders represent the closest possible approximation to those who have in fact violated the law, carefully selected by the sieving of the due process of law; no other province of social control attempts to ascertain the breach of norms with such rigor and precision.
   b. It is as futile to contend that this group should not be studied on the grounds that it is incomplete or nonrepresentative as it would be to maintain that psychology should terminate its description, analysis, diagnosis, and treatment of deviants who cannot be completely representative as selected. Convicted persons are nearly all criminals. They offer large and varied samples of all types; their origins, traits, dynamics of development, and treatment influences can be studied profitably for

purposes of description, understanding, and control. To be sure, they are not necessarily representative of all offenders; if characteristics observed among them are imputed to law violators generally, it must be with the qualification implied by the selective processes of discovery and adjudication.

   c. Convicted criminals are important as a sociological category, furthermore, in that they have been exposed and respond to the influences of court contact, official punitive treatment, and public stigma as convicts.

2. The relevance of violation of the criminal law:

   a. The criminal law establishes substantive norms of behavior, standards more clear cut, specific, and detailed than the norms in any other category of social controls.

   b. The behavior prohibited has been considered significantly in derogation of group welfare by deliberative and representative purpose of establishing such norms; nowhere else in the field of social control is there directed a comparable rational effort to elaborate standards conforming to the predominant needs, desires, and interests of the community.

   c. There are legislative and juridical lags which reduce the social value of the legal norms; as an important characteristic of law, such lag does not reduce the relevance of law as a province of sociological inquiry. From a detached sociological view, the significant thing is not the absolute goodness or badness of the norms but the fact that these norms do control behavior. The sociologist is interested in the results of such control, the correlates of violation, and in the lags themselves.

   d. Upon breach of these legal (and social) norms, the refractory are treated officially in punitive and/or rehabilitative ways, not for being generally antisocial, immoral, unconventional, or bad, but for violation of the specific legal norms of control.

   e. Law becomes the peculiarly important and ultimate pressure toward conformity to minimum standards of conduct deemed essential to group welfare as other systems of norms and mechanics of control deteriorate.

   f. Criminals, therefore, are a sociologically distinct group of violators of specific legal norms, subjected to official state treatment. They and the noncriminals respond, though differentially, of course, to the standards, threats, and correctional devices established in this system of social control.

   g. The norms, their violation, the mechanics of dealing with breach constitute major provinces of legal sociology. They are basic to the theoretical framework of sociological criminology.[6]

NOTES

This essay first appeared in the *American Sociological Review* (1947) 12: 96–112.

1. The manner in which the legal definition of the criminal is avoided by prominent sociological scholars through amazingly loose, circumlocutory description may be instanced by this sort of definition:

> Because a collective system has social validity in the eyes of each and all of those who share in it, because it is endowed with a special dignity which merely individual systems lack altogether, individual behavior which endangers a collective system and threatens to harm any of its elements appears quite different from an aggression against an individual (unless, of course, such an aggression hurts collective values as well as individual values). It is not only a harmful act, but an objectively evil act [*sic!*], a violation of social validity, an offense against the superior dignity of this collective system. . . . The best term to express the specific significance of such behavior is crime. We are aware that in using the word in this sense, we are giving it a much wider significance than it has in criminology. But we believe that it is desirable for criminology to put its investigations on a broader basis; for strictly speaking, it still lacks a proper theoretic basis. . . . Legal qualifications are not founded on the results of previous research and not made for the purpose of future research; therefore they have no claim to be valid as scientific generalizations—nor even as heuristic hypotheses. (Znaniecki 1928: 207)

2. An instance of this broadening of the concept of the criminal is the penchant among certain anthropologists to equate crime with taboo. See, especially, Malinowski 1926, 1944). Compare Seagle (1937, 1941) and Llewellyn and Hoebel (1941) and Hoebel (1946).

3. In the province of juvenile delinquency we may observe already the evil that flows from this sort of loose definition in applied sociology. In many jurisdictions, under broad statutory definition of delinquency, it has become common practice to adjudicate as delinquent any child deemed to be antisocial or a behavior problem. Instead of requiring sound systematic proof of specific reprehensible conduct, the courts can attach to children the odious label of delinquent through the evaluations and recommendations of overworked, undertrained case investigators who convey to the judge their hearsay testimony of neighborhood gossip and personal predilection. Thus these vaunted "socialized tribunals" sometimes become themselves a source of delinquent and criminal careers as they adjudge individuals who are innocent of proven wrong to a depraved offender's status through an administrative determination of something they know vaguely as antisocial conduct. See Pound (1937) and also Tappan (1946, 1947).

4. The unconvicted suspect cannot be known as a violator of the law: to assume him so would be in derogation of our most basic political and ethical philosophies. In empirical research it would be quite inaccurate, obviously, to study all suspects or defendants as criminals.

5. For a detailed consideration of the efficacy of legal norms, see Jerome Michael and Herbert Wechsler, "A Rationale of the Law of Homicide," *Columbia Law Review* 37 (1937): 701, 1261.

6. For other expositions of this view, see Hall (1936, 1941, 1945).

REFERENCES

Barnes, Harry Elmer, and Negley K. Teeters. 1943. *New Horizons in Criminology*. New York: Prentice Hall.

Hall, Jerome. 1936. "Criminology and a Modern Penal Code." *Journal of Criminal Law and Criminology* 27 (May–June): 1–16.

———. 1941. "Prolegomena to a Science of Criminal Law." *University of Pennsylvania Law Review* 89: 549–80.

———. 1945. "Criminology." In *Twentieth Century Sociology*, ed. Georges Gurvitch and Wilber Moore. New York: Philosophical Library, pp. 342–65.

Hoebel, E. Adamson. 1946. "Law and Anthropology." *Virginia Law Review* 32: 835–54.

Llewellyn, Karl, and E. Adamson Hoebel. 1941. *The Cheyenne Way*. Norman: University of Oklahoma Press.

Malinowski, Bronislaw. 1926. *Crime and Custom in Savage Society*. London: Kegan, Paul, Trench & Trubner.

———. 1944. "A New Instrument for the Study of Law—Especially Primitive." *Yale Law Journal* 51: 1237–54.

Michael, Jerome, and Herbert Wechsler. 1937. "A Rationale of the Law of Homicide." *Columbia Law Review* 37.

Pound, Roscoe. 1937. "Introduction." In *Social Treatment in Probation and Delinquency*, ed. Pauline V. Young. New York: McGraw-Hill.

Seagle, William. 1937. "Primitive Law and Professor Malinowski." *American Anthropologist* 39: 275.

———. 1941. *The Quest for Law*. New York: Knopf.

Sellin, Thorsten. 1938. *Culture Conflict and Crime*. New York: Social Science Research Council.

Sutherland, Edwin H. 1940. "White-Collar Criminality." *American Sociological Review* 5: 1–12.

———. 1941. "Crime and Business." *Annals of the American Academy of Political and Social Science*. 217: 112–18.

———. 1945. "Is 'White-Collar Crime' Crime?" *American Sociological Review* 10: 132–39.

Tappan, Paul W. 1946. "Treatment without Trial." *Social Forces* 24: 306–11.

———. 1947. *Delinquent Girls in Court*. New York: Columbia University Press.

Znaniecki, Florian. 1928. "Social Research in Criminology." *Sociology and Social Research* 12: 307–22.

4

Defining Patterns of Crime and Types of Offenders

Don C. Gibbons and Kathryn Ann Farr

Over the many decades of criminological inquiry from the 1800s to the present, criminologists have grappled with the question "What is crime?" and have given considerable attention to the sorting out of types or patterns of criminality. Then, too, they have often attempted to identify distinct "types" or kinds of lawbreakers, such as "armed robbers," "serial killers," or "white-collar criminals." These are matters with which this chapter is concerned.

In his classic "legalistic" position regarding the nature of crime and criminality, criminologist Paul Tappan (1960) insists that crime consists solely of violations of criminal laws and that "offenders" are properly identified as persons who engage in these law violations. Furthermore, he suggests that only those persons who have been convicted of lawbreaking should be labeled as "criminals," largely because of the special restrictions and liabilities that are associated with criminal status—that is, with having been legally declared to be guilty of a criminal act or acts. As Tappan (1960: 10) argues, *"Crime is an intentional act or omission in violation of a criminal law (statutory or case law) committed without defense or justification, and sanctioned by the state as a felony or misdemeanor"* (emphasis in the original).

Although many criminologists have taken a similar legalistic position on the definitions of crime and criminals, a small number of theorists have argued for one or another "social definition" of crime, in which acts that are not proscribed in the criminal laws but that are viewed by criminologists or some other group as socially harmful are identified as crimes (Gibbons 1992: 71–74). A number of these "social" or "sociological" perspectives are discussed in succeeding chapters of this book.

Our position is a legalistic one: crime is defined by the criminal law. "Criminal offenders" are persons who violate criminal laws, whether or not they become

37

officially identified as lawbreakers. However, we hasten to add that this "legalistic" versus "social" distinction is somewhat misleading. *All* crime definitions are social in nature in that they are all created by social actors. Clearly, social processes are in play when legislators go about enacting prohibitions against marijuana use, sex acts between adults and children, or myriad other kinds of behavior. Parenthetically, lawmakers also occasionally go about "decriminalizing" behavior by expunging a statute that previously prohibited some kind of human activity. In the same way, social processes are involved when criminologists put forth an argument that "violations of basic human rights" should be regarded as crimes or when a group of citizens claim that crime should rest on "the word of God" or the teachings of some other supreme being about right and wrong.

The legalistic perspective is broad in its sweep. Crime and criminals include a rich and variegated bundle of activities and persons; as a result, many criminologists have argued that classification systems that make sense out of forms of crime or types of criminal actors are required as a first step toward explaining these phenomena. In an earlier essay (Farr and Gibbons 1990: 223), we expressed this theme in the following passage:

> Imagine what etymology might look like if it were composed of two groups of scientists—one engaged in the study of "reddish bugs," "greenish bugs," or "brownish bugs," with the other one studying "all bugs, whatever their color." It would represent a field in a primitive state of development—much like contemporary criminology—since an adequate system for making sense of its subject matter would be lacking. In the case of plants or animals, a taxonomy refers to a classification scheme that sorts these forms into phyla, species, etc. In criminology, taxonomies are classification systems that place crimes or offenders into homogeneous types.

This chapter reports on efforts that have been made to develop theoretically meaningful taxonomies of crime forms or offender types. As noted elsewhere (Gibbons 1992: 195–96), two different lines of activity have been pursued by criminologists, one being *crime centered* and the other, *criminal centered*. Crime-centered activities attempt to identify distinct forms of crime, while criminal-centered endeavors search for relatively distinct patterns or types into which real-life offenders can be sorted.

Perhaps criminologists will ultimately identify a number of crime forms and a number of types of offenders as well. Or, it may turn out that distinct patterns of lawbreaking can be identified, but persons who specialize in these patterns may rarely be encountered. For example, burglary may exhibit a recurrent form (occurring most often during the daytime, etc.), but few if any "burglars" who specialize in that kind of criminality may exist in the real world. Finally, it is possible that it will turn out that there are no distinctive patterns, in the case of either crime or criminal offenders.

Considerably more effort has been directed at the identification of types of criminals (and/or delinquents) than at uncovering crime types. However, our discussion begins with the latter and then turns to the results of efforts to develop offender typologies or taxonomies.

CRIMINAL LAW AND CRIMINOLOGY

The reach of the criminal law in modern society is long and wide. When they speak of "crime," laypersons probably have in mind murder, assault, robbery, burglary, and a few other acts, but the scope of the criminal law is much broader. For example, in the United States, Oregon's criminal code prohibits the "sale of a drugged horse," "failure to maintain a metal purchase record," "unlawful transportation of hay," "transportation of coniferous trees without a bill of sale," and myriad other acts. In all, the Oregon code contains several hundred criminal acts, classified as various kinds and degrees of felonies and misdemeanors. Moreover, other bodies of law such as the Fish and Game Code and the Motor Vehicle Code identify still other forms of criminality, often termed "violations," which carry lesser penalties than those in the main body of criminal laws in Oregon. These various bodies of law exist in other states as well. Little wonder, then, that criminologists have often argued that crime must be broken down into meaningful categories and that separate theories or hypotheses must be developed to account for them.[1] For example, in an essay on criminological theory, Gibbs (1987: 830) argues, "Each theory should be limited to one type of crime if only because it is unlikely that any etiological or reactive variable is relevant for all crimes."

THE SEARCH FOR CRIMINAL TYPES

Sutherland's Views

The fact that *crime* is an umbrella term for a large variety of acts of omission or commission has been recognized for many decades. A number of criminologists have asserted that attention should focus on the development of classification systems that sort crime forms or types of criminals into theoretically meaningful types. Even so, we have not progressed very far from the situation described by Sutherland (1924: 22) in the first edition of his textbook: "A great deal of effort has been devoted to the attempt to classify crimes. Most of the results must be regarded as useless." In a later edition, Sutherland (1939: 218) wrote:

> Most of the scientific work in criminology has been directed at the explanation of crime in general. Crime in general consists of a great variety of criminal acts. These acts have very little in common, except that they are all violations of the law. They differ among themselves in the motives and characteristics of the victims, the situations in which they occur, the techniques that are used, the damages which result,

and the reactions of the victims and of the public. Consequently it is not likely that a general explanation of all crimes will be sufficiently specific or precise to aid greatly in understanding or controlling crime. In order to make progress in the explanation of crime it is desirable to break crime into more homogeneous units. In this respect crime is like a disease. Some general theories of disease have been stated and are useful. The germ theory of disease is a very useful general theory, but even this theory does not apply to all diseases. Progress in the explanation of disease is being made principally by studies of specific diseases. Similarly, it is desirable to concentrate research in criminology on specific crimes.

Sutherland argued that criminologists should study "behavior systems," which he said are "sociological units." Behavior systems are "integrated units" made up of individual acts, codes, traditions, esprit de corps, social relations among the direct participants, and indirect participation of other persons. In addition, the behavior is not unique to any individual; rather, it is "common behavior." Unlike psychiatric notions of behavior systems which center on cognitive patterns, Sutherland emphasized behavior shared by group participants. A third characteristic of the behavior system is that it grows out of a unified causal process, or, in other words, those who engage in it all share a common social background. According to Sutherland, kidnapping is not a behavior system, but professional theft does qualify as an example. At least at the time that Sutherland wrote, kidnapping was usually carried out by lawbreakers operating alone, although this appears to be less true today. By contrast, professional thieves, then and now, are part of a criminal network or subculture.

Even though the concept of behavior systems continued to turn up in subsequent editions of Sutherland's text (Sutherland, Cressey, and Luckenbill 1992: 269–75), it failed to stimulate efforts by other criminologists to uncover other behavior systems, in addition to professional theft.

Other Views

Sutherland was not alone, in either (1) his concern about the limitations of taxonomies based *solely* on legal categories or (2) his efforts to develop theoretically meaningful crime categories. For example, Sellin (1938) argued that the criminal law is an inadequate foundation for criminological theorizing and that attention should focus instead on "conduct norms," but that suggestion did not take hold.

In their classificatory scheme, Clinard and Quinney (1973) identified the following types of crime: violent personal, occasional property, public order, conventional, political, occupational, corporate, organized, and professional. The classification is organized around five dimensions: legal aspect of selected offenses, criminal career of the offender, group support for criminal behavior, correspondence between criminal and legitimate behavior, and societal reaction and legal processing.

However, the notion of "criminal career of the offender," as used in an of-
fense-based typology, implies that types of crime and types of offenders are
closely related: burglaries are performed by burglars, auto thefts by car thieves,
and so on. However, the evidence does not support this hypothesis about crime
specialists (Chaiken and Chaiken 1982). Behavioral versatility rather than specialization in particular crimes is most common among repeat offenders. Clinard
and Quinney also distinguished between such types as "occasional property criminal behavior" and "conventional criminal behavior," but both of these involve
larcenies of one kind or another; thus, this is actually a distinction based on the
frequency of criminal acts on the part of *persons* rather than the identification of
distinct kinds of crime.

EFFORTS TO IDENTIFY SPECIFIC CRIME TYPES

Some other efforts to identify sociologically meaningful types of crime have zeroed in on one particular crime form, rather than on a host of them.

Folk/Mundane Crime

Ross (1960–61, 1973) invented the term *folk crime* to designate certain relatively petty, socially invisible, yet frequently encountered forms of crime, such
as moving traffic violations, that have often been overlooked by criminologists.
Along the same line, Gibbons (1983) offered "mundane crime" as another type
that ought to receive attention. *Mundane crime* refers to a collection of criminal
activities that includes Ross's folk crimes. However, no one else has apparently
been impressed with these categories, for virtually no other work has been done
on either folk or mundane crime (although for a review of studies of lawbreaking
that seems to fit these categories, see Gibbons 1992: 341–61).

White-Collar Crime

Sutherland's attempt to limit the contours of "white-collar crime" was a particularly important venture. However, his term *white-collar crime* was more evoca-
tive than precise and more useful in drawing attention to an overlooked area in
criminality than it was a clear conceptual category. Sutherland offered inconsistent observations on what he meant by the term, for on some occasions, he focused on white-collar *crime* and, at other times, on white-collar *criminals*. Also,
he sometimes suggested that embezzlement falls into this category but at other
times implied that it did not.

Some criminologists have tried to clear up the confusion regarding white-collar crime. Schrager and Short (1978) have suggested that we ought to zero in on
"organizational crime," which they believe is also what Sutherland had in mind.

Organizational offenses are illegal, serious, and harmful acts of an individual or group of persons in a legitimate, formal organization, carried on in the pursuit of the goals of the organization. In other words, it is crime carried on *for* the organization, as contrasted with embezzlement, which involves crimes *against* organizational ends.

A different position was staked out by Coleman (1987: 407), who opted for an omnibus definition of white-collar crime, asserting that "white collar crimes . . . are violations of law committed in the course of a legitimate occupation or financial pursuit by persons who hold respectable positions in their communities" and also that they are "committed for the benefit of the individual criminal without organizational support and organizational crimes committed with support from an organization that is, at least in part, furthering its own ends."

In the opinion of some criminologists, offenses that serve organizational ends should be examined separately from those by organizational members solely for their own benefit and from "fringe" violations by professionals, such as commingling of funds by lawyers, Medicare fraud by doctors, and the like (Gibbons 1992: 284–317; Schrager and Short 1978). Organizational crime involves law violations for the benefit of the organization, while embezzlers are "enemies within" whose acts are detrimental to the goals of the firm.

Political Crime

Political crime has been proposed as another significant category of criminality. In the past several decades, we have been confronted with numerous examples of hijacking and kidnapping, political coups, assassinations, bombings, and the like; thus, the idea of political crime is "in the air." But, how are we to throw a conceptual net around this activity? Turk (1982) has made a serious attempt to bring order to this topic, but even so, conceptual ambiguities in the notion of political crime persist.

Turk (1982) restricts political crime to illegal activities on the part of "subjects," reserving the term *political policing* for the criminal acts of the "authorities." Many other criminologists, however, regard illegal acts by the authorities as political crime, particularly since many of them are proactive; that is, they are illegal acts used by governmental agents to prevent persons who are thought to be politically dangerous from acting.

Another difficulty with the notion of political crime is that it bleeds into other kinds of criminality that are not viewed by some citizens as political in nature, such as the bombing of abortion clinics by right-to-life zealots. Clearly, what is or is not "political" is in the eye of the beholder. On this point, many feminists contend that attacks on abortion clinics, as well as numerous other efforts that have been made over the last two centuries in the United States, through either legislative actions or acts of terror, to deny women the right to control their own bodies are political in nature. On this same point, crimes are usually identified as political or otherwise, not because of the distinctive properties of certain illegal acts but rather on the basis of the motives that are assumed to lie behind the acts. For example, some homicides are viewed as "political assassinations," while others are seen as "garden variety" or routine killings.

CRIME PATTERNS AND CRIMINOLOGICAL PRACTICE

Although a number of criminologists have attempted to develop crime categories to be used for theorizing about crime, these efforts have not had much impact on criminological practice or the research efforts of criminologists. The most common crime type in research studies is "index offenses," sometimes broken down into "property" and "violent" subcategories, taken from FBI Uniform Crime Reports. Murder and nonnegligent manslaughter, aggravated assault, forcible rape, armed robbery, motor vehicle theft, burglary, theft, and arson are lumped together because they are for the most part serious crimes that are likely to be reported when they occur. However, it would be hard to argue that they group together in another clearly apparent way or that this is a sociologically relevant rubric.

Toward a New Crime Classification

In a 1990 essay (Farr and Gibbons 1990), we identified some major dimensions that ought to be involved in a crime taxonomy and also sketched out the rough outlines of some of the crime categories generated by these basic dimensions.

Because crime is identified by the legal/political community as behavior that produces or results in some societal harm (or, conversely, goes against the public good), our starting point for identifying crime forms was to distinguish between the harms to which particular criminal acts are tied. We employed the term *harm* in the legalistic sense—that is, various consequences of behavioral acts that have been defined by lawmaking bodies as having a negative impact on social interests. For example, burglary is a harm because it is an attempt to deprive owners of their property and it also threatens general social interests.

Harm is a core concept in the legal codes. For example, Oregon statutes identify seven classes of harms: harms against property; harms involving fraud or deception; harms against the person; harms against public order; harms against the state or public justice; harms against public health, decency, and animals; and controlled substance harms. Modifying these somewhat, we identified seven crime categories that are sufficiently broad to accommodate most of the specific felonies, misdemeanors, and violations that appear in federal, state, and local statutes.

Under property harm crimes, we distinguished between (1) *property-predatory crime* (e.g., burglary, robbery, auto theft, and larceny) and (2) *property-fraudulent crime* (e.g., embezzlement, forgery, fraud, and bribery). Both predatory and fraudulent crimes are generally engaged in for instrumental rather than expressive or ideological gain. In predatory crime, persons are involved in taking or attempting to take directly, without permission, the personal property of others. In fraudulent crimes, the offenders are involved in deceit or manipulation with the purpose of converting property or services (including information) of others to their own use. In fraudulent crimes, unlike predatory offenses, the victim may be unaware that he or she is involved in a fraudulent transaction.

We drew a distinction between two kinds of personal harm. The first, *interpersonal violence—general*, includes such offenses as homicide, assault, and kidnapping, while the second, *interpersonal violence—sexual*, involves rape, sexual abuse, incest, and other crimes that include some form of sexual conduct. It is important to note that rape and sexual abuse often contain elements of criminal assault resulting in physical injury to the victim. Moreover, victims are not infrequently subjected to rape, assault, kidnapping, and even homicide as part of the same criminal event.

Another important caveat is that our sexual violence category centers on *behavioral acts* that are widely regarded as sexual in form (e.g., vaginal-genital penetration, forcible oral copulation, etc.) and leaves open the question of motivation. Regarding rape, the evidence suggests that it is often motivated more by the desire to control and degrade females than it is by erotic interests (Groth and Birnbaum 1979). Even so, this distinction between general and sexual violence serves a theoretical purpose in that there is evidence that the etiology of many sex offenses is different from that of garden-variety assaults or homicides.

We identified three categories of social order/social values harm-related offenses. *Transactional vice* refers to "victimless" offenses involving a willing exchange of goods or services (e.g., prostitution, gambling, and drug sales), while *order disruption* includes escape, resisting arrest, disorderly conduct, riot, loitering, and firearms offenses. While there are no direct victims in these cases, public concern is raised about potential victims in some instances (e.g., an offender carrying a concealed weapon eventually harming someone; resisting arrest leading to an assault on a police officer). The final category, *folk/mundane crime*, is a broad rubric that includes relatively minor rule violations (e.g., not purchasing a fishing license, jaywalking), along with more serious ones, such as weight and load regulations concerning commercial trucks. There is considerable public ambivalence about many of these violations. Although such rules have been justified in the name of order, efficiency, or effectiveness, much of the public regards one or another of them as a nuisance or inconvenience, without moral import, and/or as not really crime.

The identification of these crime forms is only a first step, for they neither constitute crime *patterns* nor inform us theoretically. Standing alone, they are unexceptionable categories. Their value lies in the fact that they are based on a single criterion, rather than on a shifting mixture of criteria: characteristics of offenders, organizational context, nature of offender involvement, social stigma, and the like. To illustrate, organized crime is often defined in terms of the organizational context in which crimes occur, rather than by certain forms of crime, such as fraud or vice. These acts occur both inside and outside criminal organizations. Differently, conceptions of political crime frequently emphasize the motives of the offenders, rather than the acts in which they engage. Political crime is often defined in terms of the ends being pursued by offenders, rather than by the criminal acts that they commit.

Our classification of crime patterns is not simply a restatement of the criminal laws, for we have identified five theoretically meaningful dimensions of crime additional to the harms they involve. There is considerable agreement on the importance of the first of these—namely, the *organizational level* at or around which crime(s) take place. A number of criminologists have argued that it is important to distinguish between offenses carried on within organizational settings and those that are the work of small offender networks or of individuals acting alone and outside organizational settings. Accordingly, we distinguished between criminal activities carried on by formal or complex organizations (i.e., by a substantial number of organizational members), by offender networks (both within and outside large-scale organizations), and by individuals acting alone (but again, either inside or outside large organizations). For example, both organizational/white-collar crime and organized crime are engaged in by members of relatively large and/or formal organizations. By contrast, street hustling involves small, loosely knit organized networks, as do crime–partner associations among predatory offenders.

Although we took note of crimes occurring both inside and outside organizations, we refrained from speaking of "criminal organizations." Persons who engage in law violations within complex organizations often believe that their actions are likely to achieve "company goals," and in this sense, these actions qualify as organizational crime. At the same time, it would be difficult to argue that the organization per se is a criminal one. For example, in the case of a pharmaceutical company engaged in violating FDA regulations, it might be difficult or impossible to show that all of the employees shared the view that such violations are an acceptable form of conduct.

Our second domain, *legitimacy continuum*, refers to variations in public definitions of the organizational structures in which some crimes occur. Although there is considerable ambiguity about the criminal or noncriminal nature of some organizational activities and therefore of the organizations themselves, many businesses and corporations are viewed by the general public as being at the legitimate pole on the scale, while the Mafia is assigned to a highly illegitimate point on the legitimacy continuum, as are many criminal networks. New car dealerships qualify as an example of organizations that are at an intermediate point on this scale—since many of them are perceived by the general public to be engaged in both shady practices as well as more legitimate activities.

A number of business firms engage entirely in legitimate business activities, while many others are involved in some blend of legal and illegal endeavors. Drug firms that violate FDA regulations or rental car agencies that charge customers inflated sums for repairs to damaged rental cars are two examples of the latter. Less often recognized is that "organized crime" may also refer to organizations that engage both in such illegal activities as loan sharking and in legal businesses such as dry cleaning. However, our legitimacy dimension refers to how organizations are *perceived* by the general public rather than to the actual balance of legal and illegal activities in which they engage.[2]

The legitimacy/illegitimacy distinction is separate from the issue of the perceived seriousness of specific crimes in the eyes of the general public. There is a modest research literature on public perceptions regarding the criminal or noncriminal status of various crimes and citizens' judgments of the seriousness of these specific acts, but relatively little data regarding public evaluations of organizations or the seriousness of offenses attributed to them (Gibbons 1992: 69–71). Moreover, the links between public perceptions of the criminality of individuals and of the organizations that they represent require further probing. For example, doctors who engage in Medicare fraud may be held in low regard by citizens, at the same time that the medical organizations within which these persons work are viewed favorably. Citizens may believe that miscreant doctors are "rotten apples" in an otherwise legitimate organization. Since the legitimacy domain refers to the status of organizations or networks, it is not applicable to crime patterns in which individuals act alone.

A third dimension involves the *organizational alignment of offenders*, which includes (1) individuals or networks within an organization who engage in illegal acts while pursuing ends that they perceive to be among the goals of the organization, (2) individuals or networks within an organization who direct illegal acts *at* those organizations (e.g., embezzlers), and (3) offenders who are outside and thus not aligned with a conventional organization.

A fourth dimension is *range of crime forms*, with specialized patterns at one end and diversified ones at the other. Range of crime forms is a version of the harms we identified earlier, although in table 4.1, our entries involve more specific forms of the seven harms in a number of instances.

Finally, we took note of the *primary victim(s)*. Victim categories include specific persons, organizations, the general population or subgroups of it, and the social fabric, which is another way of speaking of diffuse harms with unspecified victims.

These five contextual domains may be useful in the identification of distinct crime patterns. Table 4.1 presents a crime classification that employs these five defining dimensions. The first column, labeled "Crime Type," refers to the summarizing label we attached to the various crime patterns that were generated using the variables identified. In most cases, we employed the crime type terminology that has become common in the criminological literature, but in a more precise fashion.

Some subtypes, as well as major forms of criminal activity, are identified in the table. We singled out five forms of workplace crime, largely because the criminological evidence suggests that considerable variability exists within this broad category. Additionally, we separated a pattern of diversified street crime, in which offenders are involved in a variety of "hustles," as well as some violent criminal activities, from a second form of relatively specialized street crime, in which offenders are focused primarily on one type of criminal activity, most commonly for instrumental gain.

Table 4.1 could profit from a good bit of fine-tuning. In its current form, this scheme serves a heuristic function more than anything else. Our classification is an exercise in conceptualization, involving identification of some dimensions that may be useful in bringing some order to the seeming heterogeneity of lawbreaking. Some indication that we may be on the right track can be found in a study of the offenses of a large sample of federal offenders, conducted by Weisburd, Wheeler, Waring, and Bode (1991). These investigators indicated that most of the offenses fell into eight categories: antitrust violations, securities fraud, mail fraud, false claims, bribery, tax fraud, credit fraud, and bank embezzlement. Because they appeared to be diverse crimes, the researchers were moved to try to find some patterns into which they might be sorted.

Weisburd et al. settled on *organizational complexity* and the *consequences of the crimes to the victims* as dimensions for sorting offenses into groupings. Offenses that are high on organizational complexity are those in which a discernible offense pattern is apparent, organizational resources are employed to commit crimes, and the acts take place over a lengthy time period. The crime consequences variable centered on the number of victims, the size of their losses, and the breadth of the area over which victimization was spread.

Weisburd et al. indicate that the eight offenses can be combined into three relatively distinct types, forming a rough hierarchy of offense complexity, with antitrust and securities fraud at the top and fraud and embezzlement at the bottom.

OFFENDER TYPOLOGIES

The belief that criminals and delinquents can be placed into relatively distinct types dates back to the origins of criminology. For example, Cesare Lombroso (1836–1909) argued that there were three kinds of lawbreakers: born criminals, insane criminals, and criminaloids. According to Lombroso, the latter constituted over half of all offenders and were persons of normal physical and psychological makeup who committed crimes because of stressful life experiences.

The proposition that there are a number of distinctive criminal types also sur-

Table 4.1   A Preliminary Classification of Crime Patterns

Crime Type	Organizational Level at Which Crime Occurs	Legitimacy of Organizational Context	Organizational Alignment of Offender	Range of Crime Forms	Primary Victims
Organizational (white-collar) crime	Formal/complex organization	Legitimate	With organization	Fraudulent (diverse or specialized)	General public, groups, other complex organizations
Organized crime	Formal/complex organization	Illegitimate	With organization	Fraudulent (transactional vice) Violence—general	General public, groups, social fabric
Workplace crime	Network or individual	Legitimate	Against organization	(a) Fraudulent (e.g., fraud against legal clients)	Individuals, groups
				(b) Fraudulent (e.g., embezzlement)	Organization
				(c) Predatory (e.g., employee theft)	Organization
				(d) Transactional vice (e.g., physician drug sales)	Social fabric
				(e) Violence—general (e.g., assault by police officers)	Individuals, groups

"Street" crime	Network or individual	Illegitimate	Outside conventional organization	(a) Diversified (predatory, fraudulent, violence—general, violence—sexual, transactional vice)	Individuals, groups, organizations, social fabric
				(b) Specialized (e.g., a ring that buys and sells stolen property)	Individuals, groups, organizations, social fabric
Social protest (political crime)	Network or individual (may be indirect link to organization)	Legitimate or quasilegitimate	Outside conventional organization or with organization	Order disruption Violence—general	Groups, organizations, social fabric
Violent crime	Individual	NA	Outside conventional organization	(a) Violence—general	Individuals, groups
				(b) Violence—sexual	Individuals, groups
Folk/mundane crime	Individual	NA	Outside conventional organization	Folk/mundane crimes	Organizations, social fabric

Source: Kathryn Ann Farr and Don C. Gibbons. 1990. Observations on the Development of Crime Categories. *International Journal of Offender Therapy and Comparative Criminology* 34 (December): 234.

faced in nineteenth-century England, where many citizens became convinced that they had much to fear from "the dangerous class." For example, Patrick Colquhoun, a Scottish social philosopher and police reformer, estimated that there were at least 115,000 members of "the dangerous and criminal class" engaged in full-time crime (Low 1982: 25–27). He identified twenty-four separate groups of lawbreakers, including "professed and known receivers of stolen goods" and "a class of suspicious characters, who live partly by pilfering and passing base money—ostensibly costar mongers, ass drivers, dustmen, chimney sweepers, rabbit sellers, fish and fruit sellers, flash coachmen, bear baiters, dog keepers (but in fact dog stealers), etc., etc."

A few decades later, social reformer Henry Mayhew listed over one hundred criminal types that were said to make up "the criminal class" in late nineteenth-century England. His list included such types as "stook buzzers" (persons who steal handkerchiefs) and "snow gatherers" (individuals who steal clothes off the hedges) (Tobias 1967: 622–25).

In the 1950s, considerable criminological interest centered on offender typologies, with a number of persons arguing that lawbreakers are so varied that they must be sorted into behavioral types. According to this view, offender typologies are required in order that (1) explanations of lawbreaking can be clarified and (2) effective treatment for offenders can be developed.

The causal argument was that no single theory can account for such diverse types of offenders as embezzlers, rapists, arsonists, or white-collar criminals; rather, separate causal theories must be developed for each of them. The case for typologies and diagnostic classifications in correctional treatment closely paralleled the etiological argument. The basic claim was that "different strokes for different folks" were in order. Specific tactics such as psychotherapy, group counseling, reality therapy, or behavioral modification should be matched to particular offender types. Treatment would be tailored to the offender, thereby bringing about more effective rehabilitation (Gibbons 1965).

How should we go about classifying offenders? Most sociological classifications of persons or social phenomena are imposed on the facts of social life rather than being drawn directly from observations. Stated another way, offender "types" such as naive check forgers or white-collar criminals are identified by criminologists. The real-life offenders who are assigned to these types may be unaware that they have been categorized.

One way to sort offenders would be on their specific instant offenses—that is, the crimes for which they were most recently arrested or convicted. However, the practice of "plea copping," in which many persons plead guilty to reduced charges, means that the legal charges often do not accurately mirror the offenses actually committed. Even more important, legal-offense categories often fail to reflect dimensions of lawbreaking that may be of theoretical significance. For example, the legal category of rape includes several patterns of deviant behavior: Some rapes involve extreme violence and the totally unwilling participation of the victim; others, such as statutory rape, involve quite different elements, including a lesser degree of coercion. Another problem with legal-offense categories is that many offenders exhibit versatility in the criminal acts they commit. A person who is a burglar today may be a larcenist the next week and an assaulter the following week; thus, it is doubtful that meaningful types of offenders can be identified solely on the basis of legal offenses.

When we sort offenders into behavioral types, we invent conceptual schemes that allow us to see common threads or characteristics that identify groups of similar offenders. Again, these threads may not be apparent at first glance, to either the lawbreakers or other criminologists. Violators can be classified in many different ways: sex, hair color, race, urban or rural residence, psychological profiles, and so on. When criminologists settle on one scheme from the many that might be used, they hope they have selected one that will allow them to place offenders into clear-cut categories that are also causally significant. Let us turn to some of the typologies that have been put forth, to see how criminologists have approached this classificatory task.

Juvenile Offenders

In American society, many misbehaving youngsters manage to escape public attention and thus are "hidden delinquents" (Gibbons and Krohn 1991: 41–48). Also, a goodly number of suspected youthful offenders who come to the attention of the police are handled informally, so that only a relatively small number of them end up in juvenile court. But regardless of how far juveniles are drawn into the juvenile justice machinery, most of them have been suspected of or charged with violations of the criminal law. At the same time, it would be an error to assume that all juvenile offenders are simply "junior criminals," in that juvenile courts in the United States also have jurisdiction over "status offenders"—that is, youngsters who have been sent to the court on such charges as "ungovernability," "waywardness," or being "in danger of leading an idle, dissolute, lewd, or immoral life."

Because of these "omnibus clauses" that put juveniles at risk of court processing for conditions or behaviors that do not apply to adults, and also because of common assumptions that juveniles (usually defined as persons under eighteen years of age) are less sophisticated and less blameworthy than adults, criminologists have commonly divided their attention, with some focusing mainly on juveniles and others on adult offenders. Then, too, theorists and researchers who have zeroed in on juvenile offenders have engaged in a number of efforts to sort these persons into "types" or behavior patterns (Gibbons and Krohn 1991: 61–73).

For example, many years ago, Jenkins and Hewitt (1944) argued that child guidance clinics and juvenile courts commonly are called on to deal with two distinct types of offenders, adaptive and maladaptive ones. The former are relatively well-socialized youngsters, while the latter are poorly socialized children who often engage in violence. Along this same line, Reiss (1952) drew attention to three psychological types of delinquents that had been identified by juvenile court workers in Chicago.

Sociologists who have been involved in the study of juvenile gangs have suggested that some urban gangs are "conflict oriented," while others are "criminalistic"; or, in other words, some gangs specialize in violence directed at other gangs, while others concentrate upon predatory, "instrumental" behavior (Cloward and Ohlin 1960). However, subsequent research on gangs has failed to confirm this characterization and instead has indicated that *behavioral versatility* is more common than is offense specialization among gangs.

Most recently, attention has been directed at the identification of serious and/ or violent juvenile offenders, as well as to "chronic" ones (Loeber, Farrington, and Waschbusch 1998). Youngsters have been labeled as serious and/or violent offenders on the basis of specific criminal offenses they have committed, while the "chronic delinquent" tag has been attached to juveniles who have been involved in some specific number of offenses. It should be apparent that these types are useful for a number of purposes but are also relatively crude in form. For example, it may well be that some truly violent behavior is not captured by these schemes.

Adult Offenders

One comprehensive typology of adult offenders was created by Glaser (1972: 28–66), who identified ten patterns, including "adolescent recapitulators," "subcultural assaultists," "vocational predators," "crisis-vacillation predators," and "addicted performers."[3] His scheme was based on what he called "offense-descriptive" and "career-commitment" variables. The former separated predatory from nonpredatory offenses, personal from property crimes, and so forth; career-commitment variables had to do with recidivism, criminal-group contacts maintained by offenders, and related factors. Glaser used these variables to identify *adolescent recapitulators* as "adults who periodically repeat the pattern of delinquency begun in adolescence—or even childhood" (1972: 28), while *subcultural assaulters* were described as persons who "live in a subculture emphasizing violence as a value more than does the rest of our society" (1972: 32).

It may be that many real-life offenders resemble the profiles sketched by Glaser. However, he also offered some pithy remarks about problems with offender classifications, noting that many lawbreakers show diversity rather than specialization in the offenses they commit, making it difficult to sort them into clearcut types. According to Glaser (1972: 14), "The difficulty arises from the fact that a large variety of offenses are found in most separate criminal careers, and the combinations occur in all possible proportions." We would also do well to keep in mind his related comment (Glaser 1972: 14): "In the real world, the gradations and mixtures of characteristics in people are so extensive that most of our categories must be given very arbitrary boundaries if everyone in a cross-section of the population is to be placed in one empirical type—or another. Most real people do not fall neatly into uniform patterns."

We may make another observation about Glaser's typology. Although his classificatory dimensions make sense, the offender categories that he offered, such as *adolescent recapitulator*, were not spelled out in sufficient detail to be amenable to research scrutiny. Instead, he endeavored to give specificity to his types principally through examples of lawbreakers who might be said to exemplify one or another of the types. But absent detailed instructions on how real persons should be sorted into types, it probably would be difficult to carry out research on actual offenders and to assign them to Glaser's types.

Criminologists who have developed typologies of lawbreakers have often pointed to research reports on specific offender types as support for their schemes. For example, in a study of inmates in a District of Columbia reformatory, Roebuck (1966) sorted them into such groups as "Negro armed robbers," "Negro drug addicts," and "Negro 'short con' men." His typology was based on the inmates' crime records as revealed in their official records. Thirteen criminal patterns in all were identified.

The list of specific offender patterns identified in research studies is fairly large and includes Conklin's (1972: 59–78) classification of types of robbers, as well as Lemert's (1953, 1958) reports on naive check forgers and systematic forgers. Also, more recent work by Knight, Carter, and Prentky (1989), sorting child molesters into relatively homogeneous types, is promising, as is true of the attempt by Knight and Prentky (1990) to sort forcible rapists into a set of subtypes. The message is that criminologists ought to be aware of these taxonomic efforts and ought to build on them.

Gibbons's Role–Career Typology

One of us has developed a comprehensive typology of adult offenders (Gibbons 1965), which bears more than a little similarity to Glaser's scheme. The typology was based on social roles and statuses—concepts that have been applied most often by sociologists to prosocial positions such as student, teacher, or physician. However, criminal conduct can also be examined within such a perspective. For example, Irwin's (1970) account of the typical careers of felons constitutes a persuasive application of social role analysis to lawbreakers.

Gibbons's scheme describes offender types in terms of the offenses they commit and the social contexts in which they commit them. Additional to behavioral acts, role conceptions (self-image patterns and role-related attitudes) of offenders are also identified. For example, some deviants view their misbehavior as atypical of their "real selves," while others utter self-reference statements of the sort "I am a hype" or "I am a badass." In all, twenty offender types are outlined in this scheme. Detailed descriptions of these twenty alleged types can be found in *Changing the Lawbreaker* (Gibbons 1965).

What about Female Offenders?

Until recently, little attention was given to patterns of crime or gender types among adult female lawbreakers. Early efforts at typing were most prevalent in the literature on female delinquents. Beginning with Thomas's (1928) "unadjusted girl," characterizations of delinquent girls reflected the belief that female delinquency was largely sexual delinquency, engaged in by relationally impoverished and emotionally disturbed girls. Emergent profiles played on these themes, as in Vedder and Somerville's (1970) types—"the runaway," "the incorrigible girl," and "the sex-delinquent girl"—or Cowie, Cowie, and Slater's (1968) "beyond control girl."

Perhaps the best-known early example of adult female offense typing was Cameron's (1964) portrayal of women shoplifters. Cameron captured the role diversification in female shoplifting with her descriptions of the "booster" and the "snitch." While this research dealt only with shoplifting, it did highlight the predominance of minor property offenses in women's lawbreaking activity.

Female lawbreaking has always been more circumscribed than that of men. While women do engage in the full range of criminal offending, they most frequently commit minor property crimes, prostitution, and drug-related offenses. In regard to arrests, the only categories consistently showing a higher percentage of females than males are "prostitution and commercialized vice" and, for juveniles, "runaway." Additionally, women are less likely than men to have extensive criminal careers, to be integrated into criminal subcultures (Steffensmeier and Allan 1998), or to show a strong commitment to crime (Arnold 1989; Miller 1986).

Like their male counterparts, women who come into contact with the criminal justice system are likely to be poor and unemployed or underemployed; minorities, particularly African Americans, are overrepresented (Richie 1996; Chesney-Lind and Shelden 1992; Gilfus 1992). However, in contrast to men, women are unlikely to be found in the upper echelons of crime—be it in corporate, organized, or drug crime hierarchies (Steffensnmeier and Allan 1996; Inciardi, Lockwood, and Pottieger 1993). In fact, relative to that of men, women's involvement in corporate or organized crime at any level is minimal (Steffensmeier and Allan 1998; Daly 1989).

Also, incarcerated women are more likely than their male counterparts (and than *non*incarcerated women) to have a history of victimization from childhood sexual abuse and domestic violence (Richie 1996; Miller 1986; Chesney-Lind and Rodriguez 1983; Morash, Bynum, and Koons 1998; although see Maher [1997], who warns against an uncritical acceptance of a direct cause-and-effect relationship here).

Moreover, drugs appear to figure more prominently in women's criminal connections and lifestyles than men's (Inciardi et al. 1993; Pettiway 1987). Indeed, more incarcerated women than men are under the influence of alcohol or other drugs at the time of their crime (Greenfeld and Minor-Harper 1991).

Finally, women's involvement with drugs and crime commonly occurs or escalates through an association with a criminal, often a violent (toward her as well as others) man (Daly 1992; Gilfus 1992), whereas this situation is rare for male offenders.

Given these contours of female lawbreaking, along with a preference of many feminist researchers for a life history approach, examinations of female lawbreaking patterns have focused heavily on routes or pathways through which women enter into crime and, sometimes, a criminal career. Arguably the most frequently identified careerlike pattern of female crime is that of the "street woman" or "hustler," who engages in myriad forms of minor lawbreaking, usually as a means of survival. In her book *Street Woman*, Eleanor Miller (1986) reports on the research that led her to identify three routes of recruitment into street hustling networks: involvement in criminally oriented familial or domestic networks, running away, and drug use. Once connected to deviant networks, the women Miller studied engaged in a variety of street hustles, including property crimes, prostitution, and drug sales. Miller (1986: 117) also found race differences in these routes, concluding:

> It is the *organization* of households among poor blacks into domestic networks that promotes the recruitment of young black women directly to deviant street networks. It is often a situation of household *disorganization*, at least as it is indicated by intense conflict between young women and their caretakers, that is most likely to promote the recruitment of white and Hispanic women to deviant street networks, however, via running away and drug use.

Miller points out that some number of black women are also recruited into deviant networks through the runaway and drug routes. She further acknowledges problems with placing all cases in one or another category, due to a "blurring" of conditions shaping the experiences of some women. That is, she recognizes that her categories are not necessarily mutually exclusive or a perfect fit.

Corroboration for Miller's findings comes from Kathleen Daly's (1992) study of female pathways to felony court. Daly's research confirms the prominence of the "street woman" type, as described by Miller. Daly classifies the women felons she studied into one of four types (and an "other" category, into which four of her sample of forty women fell). The first of her types was *harmed and harming women*, with subtypes: (1) history of violence and alcohol—common offense is assault; (2) history of violence and drugs—common offenses are property crimes stemming from drug addictions; (3) psychological problems and inability to cope with current circumstances. Daly's second type was *battered women*, identified as persons whose relationship with a violent man is the source of the crime for which they appeared in felony court; the third group was *street women*, characterized by hustling for survival, a relatively extensive prior criminal record, and, sometimes, drug addiction; the last type was *drug-connected women*, whose relationship with a boyfriend or family member was the source of using and selling drugs.

A third such effort came from Beth Richie's (1996) interview study of battered black women (along with control groups of nonbattered black and battered white women) incarcerated in a New York correctional facility. She elaborates a gender-entrapment argument that attributes these women's lawbreaking to the interaction of culturally determined gender roles and social disadvantages stemming from their racial and ethnic positions, along with more specific conditions prevailing in African American communities, and biased practices within the criminal justice system.

Richie identifies six "paths" through which the women in her study were "compelled to crime." Some had been held hostage by an abusive partner who had also killed their child. These women had been arrested and tried as codefendants in the homicide. Others were battered black women who had been arrested for violent crimes toward men other than their abuser, while a third group involved battered women from varied racial backgrounds who had been arrested for illegal "sex work," primarily prostitution for money or drugs. A fourth group consisted of battered women who had been arrested for arson or other property damage and for assaults on their abusers during a battering incident. The fifth group consisted of black women, both battered and not battered, who had been arrested for property and other economically motivated crimes. The final group was made up of battered women of varying racial backgrounds who had been arrested for drug-related crimes.

Mary Gilfus's (1992) research offers still another view of pathways into street crime. Her subjects all had prior arrest records, often for prostitution, shoplifting, fraud, or drug violations. The routes to crime for these women uniformly began as "survival strategies" (e.g., running away, using drugs, etc.), in an attempt to escape the physical and sexual violence in their childhood environments. Racism and racial violence are prominent themes in the narratives of many women. Their transition to adulthood involved illegal street work and revictimization on the street and ultimately to eventual "immersion in street crime."

There is a dearth of research on crime patterns or careers of violent female offenders. Women account for only a small portion of violent offenders, and when they do engage in violence, their victims are overwhelmingly family members or intimate others, frequently an abusive husband or boyfriend (Browne 1987). Women who assault or even kill a batterer typically have no prior criminal record or only a very minor one. In short, they have no criminal career to study!

The scant literature comparing female and male patterns of violence indicates that women's violent acts are much less likely to be repeated and that their violence stops at earlier ages (Steffensmeier and Allan 1998; Weiner 1989). However, in their research, Baskin and Sommers (1998) provide a window into the careers of the relatively small number of women who *do* become immersed in violent street crime. They argue that some women have active careers in myriad forms of lawbreaking. These careers are not solely the result of their prior victimization; rather, community disorder and increased opportunities for crime, along with situational and personal factors, propel women into violent street crime. Baskin and Sommers found two routes among the women they studied: one involved early participation in violent and other criminal acts, as well as deviant lifestyles; the other began at a later age, and it included heavy drug involvement and was preceded by participation in a number of nonviolent street crimes, including prostitution and minor theft.

Further research on pathways in female offending is much needed, not only to fill a gap in basic criminological knowledge but for practical considerations as well. To date, most decisions with regard to the processing of women offenders in the criminal justice machinery have paid little heed to important differences between male and female offenders, to the detriment of the latter. For example, violent women offenders have often been overclassified. That is, decision makers have assumed that these women represent the same degree of dangerousness and the like as do violent males; thus, they have received inappropriately harsh treatment in the correctional system (e.g., they have been placed in maximum or medium security even though they only require minimum supervision). Then, too, because important differences between male and female prisoners have been slurred over, women have been deprived of correctional services that might have been beneficial in getting them disentangled from lawbreaking (Burke and Adams 1991; Brennan 1998; Pollock 1998).

Offender Types and Real People

If it were possible to sort lawbreakers into a relatively small number of clearcut types, we might then be able to throw considerable light on the causes of criminality. But how accurate are typological descriptions? How closely do offenders fit these types? How comprehensive are typologies? Do most real-life lawbreakers fit within a typology, or, instead, are there large numbers of them who cannot be placed within existing schemes?

Returning to Glaser's typology for a moment, probably a number of persons look more or less similar to his "subcultural assaulters," "crisis-vacillation predators," "addicted performers," or other types. But it is also true that we would probably have a good bit of difficulty in reliably sorting offenders into Glaser's types, given the anecdotal nature of his descriptions of them.

Next, consider the role–career description of the semiprofessional property offender in Gibbons's (1965: 104–6) typology. A sizable body of evidence on offender behavior is broadly supportive of this description; indeed, Shover's (1991) review of a variety of data on burglary and burglars contains a portrayal that is similar to this type description.

The question regarding the accuracy of typologies involves two separate but related aspects: *inclusiveness* and *closeness of fit*. A classification scheme is inclusive insofar as most real-life offenders can be placed within its categories, while closeness of fit refers to the degree to which specific persons resemble the descriptions or categories in a typology. Consider a fourfold table of possibilities, the most desirable one being a typology that is both inclusive and characterized by closeness of fit, with every real-life lawbreaker placed precisely in one type or another. By contrast, a typology might be inclusive but not precise, it might be relatively precise but with many individuals falling outside of it, or, in the worst case, it might be neither inclusive nor accurate.

There is evidence that bears on the accuracy of typologies. Let us briefly scrutinize some of it, beginning with reports by Schrag (1961) and Sykes (1958) on inmate types in prison. According to these criminologists, prisoners exhibit social role patterns identified in prison argot (inmate language) by such labels as "Square John," "right guy," "hipster," and "outlaw." These roles are structured around loyalty attachments to other prisoners: the "right guy," for example, is a loyal member of the inmate subculture, while the "Square John" is an outsider who has little or no awareness of the prisoners' rule-violating activities in the underlife of the institution.

If distinct social roles exist among inmates, they may also be found among criminals at large. However, Schrag's and Sykes's observations are relatively impressionistic; hence, we might wonder whether these types can be easily and consistently identified. Some indication of the loose fit between typologies and the real world is found in Garabedian's (1964) study, conducted in the same prison studied by Schrag. Garabedian identified social-role incumbents through inmate responses to a series of questionnaire items. While two-thirds of the convicts did fall into types, about one-third were unclassified. Moreover, although various presumed social correlates of the role types were observed (e.g., long arrest histories on the part of "right guys"), many of these associations were weak. This study suggested that social types exist but also that there is less regularity of inmate behavior than Schrag and Sykes implied.

Even more damaging evidence came from a study by Leger (1979), who employed a number of different techniques to uncover inmate social types. He used Garabedian's attitude items, and he also asked inmates to indicate the social type, if any, to which they belonged. Furthermore, he obtained judgments from guards about which convicts were members of particular types. Finally, he sorted inmates by the social backgrounds that are supposed to characterize the different types. There was very little agreement in the findings—very few prisoners were consistently identified as "Square Johns" or some other type.

When investigators begin to examine some specific type of offender in detail, subtypes commonly proliferate, as the researcher attempts to capture the variability of behavior encountered among actual offenders. For example, one project in a federal probation office (Adams, Chandler, and Neithercutt 1971) classified probationers by their present offenses, along with their ages, prior records, and scores on a personality inventory. Fifty-four possible types of offenders were noted, and probationers were found in all of these categories.

Somewhat similarly, McCaghy (1967) found it necessary to sort child molesters into six types, and Conklin (1972) contended that there are four types of robbers: professional, opportunist, drug-addicted, and alcoholic.

Two studies have been conducted on Gibbons's role–career scheme. In one of these (Hartjen and Gibbons 1969), probation officers in a California probation department attempted to sort probationers into the typology categories, but slightly less than half of the offenders were classifiable, even when relatively relaxed guidelines were used. Subsequently, Hartjen and Gibbons sifted through the records of the unassigned cases and managed to place most of them into seven types, such as "nonsupport offenders" or "petty property offenders." However, these ad hoc types did not differ markedly from one another in terms of commitment to deviance, social backgrounds, or other variables.

McKenna (1972) also investigated the role–career typology. Inmates in a state correctional institution were classified into types through examination of their arrest records, and 87 percent were placed in twelve offense types. He then sought to determine whether the combinations of these characteristics said to identify particular role-careers actually occurred among offenders, but only in one of the twelve types did the definitional pattern emerge. His findings indicate that many real-life offenders cannot be assigned to the categories of the role–career scheme with much precision.

Finally, a set of studies conducted by the Rand Corporation provided evidence on behavioral regularities among offenders. The first (Petersilia, Greenwood, and Lavin 1977) involved forty-nine "armed robbers" in a California prison—offenders who had been singled out as robbers because their current prison commitments were for that crime. Most were in their late thirties and had been criminally involved for some time. Asked to report the number of times they had committed any of nine specific crimes since becoming involved in lawbreaking, they confessed to over 10,000 offenses, or an average of 214 per person! More important, they admitted collectively to 3,629 drug sales, 2,331 burglaries, 1,492 auto thefts, 995 forgeries, 993 grand thefts, and 855 robberies. Clearly, these were not specialists in armed robbery; instead, they were "jack-of-all-trades" offenders.

The second study (Peterson, Braker, and Polich 1980) involved over six hundred prison inmates who were asked to indicate the number and kinds of crimes they had committed during the three years prior to their present incarceration. For each type of crime, most of those who reported doing it said they did so infrequently, but a minority confessed to engaging in the crime repeatedly. The researchers concluded that there are two major types of offenders: occasional criminals and broadly active ones. Few prisoners claimed to have committed a single kind of crime at a high rate; thus, *there appeared to be few career specialists in prison.*

The third study (Chaiken and Chaiken 1982) involved 2,200 jail and prison inmates in Texas, Michigan, and California who were given a lengthy questionnaire that included self-report crime items. They were asked to report the number of times they had committed robberies, assaults, burglaries, forgeries, frauds and thefts, and drug deals. About 13 percent of the prisoners said they had committed none of the offenses during the previous two years, while the remainder reported involvement in one or more of the offenses but, most commonly, at relatively low rates. In other words, most of them had dabbled in crime and were not career criminals, but a sizable minority admitted having committed one or more crimes extremely frequently prior to incarceration. Many of the prisoners reported offense versatility (crime switching); hence, criminal specialization was not common among them.

Some criminologists—most prominently, Gottfredson and Hirschi (1990)— have suggested that the evidence indicates that, having committed one offense, lawbreakers are equally likely to commit any of the myriad acts defined as criminal in the statutes. In other words, persons who have committed a burglary, for example, may commit rape, embezzlement, arson, drug sales, misrepresentation in advertising, or virtually any other crime as a second one. Indeed, the Gottfredson and Hirschi thesis is that many of these offenders may also engage in other forms of deviance or become involved in accidents. In short, some have contended that involvement in particular kinds of lawbreaking or deviance is random and unpredictable. However, most of the evidence noted earlier points in a different direction. Although offenders engage in a varied repertoire of illegal acts, most do *not* range across the entire body of criminal statutes. For example, the Chaiken and Chaiken (1982) data suggest that persons who commit robberies often engage in assaults, other predatory offenses, and drug sales as well, but they do not indicate that drug-selling robbers commonly engage in homicide, white-collar crimes, sexual assaults, or various other crimes.

OFFENDER TYPOLOGIES: AN ASSESSMENT

What can be said, in conclusion, about offender classifications? Skepticism is in order regarding simple systems that assign offenders to a relatively small number of types. Most of these schemes are fuzzy and ambiguous, so they are difficult if not impossible to verify through research. By contrast, the role–career scheme is relatively clear and explicit. However, as we have seen, the degree of patterning of offense behavior and other definitional characteristics in it (and in others noted in this discussion) is greater than what exists in the world of criminality.

A few lawbreakers closely resemble the portrayals in typologies, but they are mixed in with a much larger number of offenders who defy classification.

CONCLUDING COMMENTS

Media discussions of lawbreaking often involve observations about one or another allegedly distinct type of crime or offender; thus, laypersons often appear to believe that "street crime," "road rage–related crime," and "hate crime," among others, are easily recognizable forms of lawbreaking and also that "serial killers," "hard-core criminals," and "burglars," among others, are clearly identifiable. However, the evidence reviewed in this chapter has indicated that crime patterns and/or offender types are less often observable in the real world. Moreover, it appears that the development of crime classifications has become a low-priority task for many contemporary criminologists. Then, too, while the typological approach enjoyed considerable popularity in the 1950s and 1960s, much less has been heard about offender typologies in the past several decades. Perhaps criminological classification is an idea whose time has passed.

NOTES

This chapter is a revised and expanded version of material that first appeared in Don C. Gibbons, *Talking about Crime and Criminals* (Englewood Cliffs, N.J.: Prentice Hall, 1994), pp. 45–68.

1. Not all contemporary criminologists agree that separate theories are required in order to account for the myriad forms of lawbreaking. The most detailed statement of an opposite view has been made by Gottfredson and Hirschi (1990: 16), who contend that "the vast majority of criminal acts are trivial and mundane affairs that result in little loss or gain." Additionally, they argue that criminality has much in common with accidents and other forms of deviant behavior. According to these theorists, criminals, deviants, and persons who are prone to accidents all exhibit low self-control, which is the major cause of their behavior.

2. The savings and loans collapse and the demise of brokerage firms such as Drexel Burnham Lambert in the 1980s are examples of another point—to wit, public perceptions of "legitimate organizations" may change independent of the activities of the organizations themselves. The misconduct of Don Dixon, Charles Keating, Ivan Boesky, Dennis Levine, and Michael Milken preceded their "fall from grace" in the public eye.

3. Another version of this scheme has been put forth by Glaser (1992), in which he discusses five patterns of criminality: adolescence-transition criminality, vice-propelled criminality, professional criminality, legitimate-occupation criminality, and passion-driven criminality. These categories have the ring of plausibility but are not explicitly defined.

REFERENCES

Adams, William P., Paul M. Chandler, and M. G. Neithercutt. 1971. "The San Francisco Project." *Federal Probation* 35 (December): 45–53.

Arnold, Regina. 1989. "Processes of Criminalization from Girlhood to Womanhood." In *Women of Color in American Society*, ed. Maxine Baca Zinn and Bonnie T. Dill. Philadelphia: Temple University Press, pp. 88–102.

Baskin, Deborah R., and Ira B. Sommers. 1998. *Casualties of Community Disorder: Women's Careers in Violent Crime*. Boulder, Colo.: Westview.

Brennan, Tim. 1998. "Institutional Classification of Females: Problems and Some Proposals for Reform." In *Female Offenders: Critical Perspectives and Effective Interventions*, ed. Ruth T. Zaplin. Gaithersburg, Md.: Aspen, pp. 179–204.

Browne, Angela. 1987. *When Battered Women Kill*. New York: Free Press.

Burke, Peggy, and Linda Adams. 1991. *Classification for Women Offenders in State Correctional Facilities: A Handbook for Practitioners*. Washington, D.C.: National Institute of Corrections.

Cameron, Mary Owen. 1964. *The Booster and the Snitch*. New York: Free Press.

Chaiken, Jan, and Marcia B. Chaiken. 1982. *Varieties of Criminal Behavior*. Santa Monica, Calif.: Rand.

Chesney-Lind, Meda, and Noelle Rodriguez. 1983. "Women under Lock and Key: A View from the Inside." *Prison Journal* 63: 47–65.

Chesney-Lind, Meda, and Randall G. Shelden. 1998. *Girls, Delinquency, and Juvenile Justice*. 2d ed. Belmont, Calif.: Wadsworth.

Clinard, Marshall B., and Richard Quinney. 1973. *Criminal Behavior Systems*. 2d ed. New York: Holt, Rinehart & Winston.

Cloward, Richard A., and Lloyd Ohlin. 1960. *Delinquency and Opportunity*. New York: Free Press.

Coleman, James William. 1987. "Toward an Integrated Theory of White-Collar Crime." *American Journal of Sociology* 93 (September): 406–39.

Conklin, John. 1972. *Robbery and the Criminal Justice System*. Philadelphia: Lippincott.

Cowie, John, Valerie Cowie, and Eliot Slater. 1968. *Delinquency in Girls*. London: Heinemann.

Daly, Kathleen. 1992. "Woman's Pathways to Felony Court: Feminist Theories of Lawbreaking and Problems of Representation." *Southern California Review of Law and Women's Studies* 2: 11–52.

———. 1989. "Gender and Varieties of White-Collar Crime." *Criminology* 27: 769–94.

Farr, Kathryn Ann, and Don C. Gibbons. 1990. "Observations on the Development of Crime Categories." *International Journal of Offender Therapy and Comparative Criminology* 34 (December): 223–37.

Garabedian, Peter G. 1964. "Social Roles in a Correctional Community." *Journal of Criminal Law, Criminology and Police Science* 55 (September): 338–47.

Gibbs, Jack P. 1987. "The State of Criminological Theory." *Criminology* 25 (November): 821–40.

Gibbons, Don C. 1965. *Changing the Lawbreaker*. Englewood Cliffs, N.J.: Prentice Hall.

———. 1983. "Mundane Crime." *Crime and Delinquency* 29 (April): 213–27.

———. 1992. *Society, Crime, and Criminal Behavior*. 6th ed. Englewood Cliffs, N.J.: Prentice Hall.

Gibbons, Don C., and Marvin D. Krohn. 1991. *Delinquent Behavior*. 5th ed. Englewood Cliffs, N.J.: Prentice Hall.

Gilfus, Mary E. 1992. "From Victims to Survivors to Offenders: Women's Routes of Entry and Immersion into Street Crimes." *Women and Criminal Justice* 4: 63–89.

Glaser, Daniel. 1972. *Crime and Social Policy*. Englewood Cliffs, N.J.: Prentice Hall.

Gottfredson, Michael R., and Travis Hirschi. 1990. *A General Theory of Crime*. Stanford, Calif.: Stanford University Press.

———. 1992. "Preconceiving Some Confounding Domains in Criminology: Issues of Terminology, Theory, and Practice." In *Facts, Frameworks, and Forecasts*, ed. Joan Mc-Cord. New Brunswick, N.J.: Transaction, pp. 23–46.

Greenfeld, Lawrence, and Stephanie Minor-Harper. 1991. *Women in Prison*. Washington, D.C.: U.S. Department of Justice.

Groth, A. Nicholas, and H. Jean Birnbaum. 1979. *Men Who Rape: The Psychology of the Offender*. New York: Plenum.

Hartjen, Clayton A., and Don C. Gibbons. 1969. "An Empirical Investigation of a Criminal Typology." *Sociology and Social Research* 54 (October): 56–62.

Inciardi, James A., Dorothy Lockwood, and Anne E. Pottieger. 1993. *Women and Crack Cocaine*. New York: Macmillan.

Irwin, John. 1970. *The Felon*. Englewood Cliffs, N.J.: Prentice Hall.

Jenkins, Richard L., and Lester E. Hewitt. 1944. "Types of Personality Structure Encountered in Child Guidance Clinics." *American Journal of Orthopsychiatry* 14 (January): 84–94.

Knight, Raymond A., Daniel Lee Carter, and Robert Alan Prentky. 1989. "A System for the Classification of Child Molesters: Reliability and Applicability." *Journal of Interpersonal Violence* 4 (March): 3–24.

Knight, Raymond A., and Robert Alan Prentky. 1990. "Classification of Sex Offenders: The Development and Corroboration of Taxonomic Models." In *Handbook of Sexual Assault*, ed. W. L. Marshall, D. R. Laws, and H. E. Barbee. New York: Plenum, pp. 23–54.

Leger, Robert G. 1979. "Research Findings and Theory as a Function of Operationalization of Variables: A Comparison of Four Techniques for the Construct, Inmate Type." *Sociology and Social Research* 63 (January): 346–65.

Lemert, Edwin M. 1953. "An Isolation and Closure Theory of Naive Check Forgery." *Journal of Criminal Law, Criminology and Police Science* 44 (September–October): 296–307.

———. 1958. "The Behavior of the Systematic Check Forger." *Social Problems* 6 (Fall): 141–49.

Loeber, Rolf, David P. Farrington, and Daniel A. Waschbusch. 1998. "Serious and Violent Juvenile Offenders." In *Serious and Violent Juvenile Offenders*, ed. Rolf Loeber and David P. Farrington. Thousand Oaks, Calif.: Sage, pp. 13–29.

Low, Donald A. 1982. *Thieves' Kitchen*. London: Dent.

Maher, Lisa. 1997. *Sexed Work: Gender, Race and Resistance in a Brooklyn Drug Market*. New York: Oxford University Press.

McCaghy, Charles H. 1967. "Child Molesters: A Study of Their Careers as Deviants." In *Criminal Behavior Systems*, ed. Marshall B. Clinard and Richard Quinney. New York: Holt, Rinehart & Winston, pp. 75–88.

McKenna, James J. 1972. "An Empirical Testing of a Typology of Adult Criminal Behavior." Ph.D. dissertation, University of Notre Dame.

Miller, Eleanor M. 1986. *Street Woman*. Philadelphia: Temple University Press.

Morash, Merry, Timothy S. Bynum, and Barbara A. Koons. 1998. *Women Offenders: Programming Needs and Promising Approaches*. Washington, D.C.: U.S. Department of Justice, Office of Justice Programs, National Institute of Justice.

Petersilia, Joan, Peter W. Greenwood, and Marvin Lavin. 1977. *Criminal Careers of Habitual Felons*. Santa Monica, Calif.: Rand.

Peterson, Mark A., Harriet B. Braker, and Suzanne M. Polich. 1980. *Doing Crime*. Santa Monica, Calif.: Rand.

Pettiway, Leon E. 1987. "Participation in Crime Partnerships by Female Drug Users." *Criminology* 25 (August): 741–67.

Pollock, Jocelyn M. 1998. *Counseling Women in Prison*. Thousand Oaks, Calif.: Sage.

Reiss, Albert J., Jr. 1952. "Social Correlates of Psychological Types of Delinquents." *American Sociological Review* 17 (December): 710–18.

Richie, Beth E. 1996. *Compelled to Crime: The Gender Entrapment of Battered Black Women*. New York: Routledge.

Roebuck, Julian B. 1966. *Criminal Typology*. Springfield, Ill.: Thomas.

Ross, H. Laurence. 1960–61. "Traffic Law Violation: A Folk Crime." *Social Problems* 9 (Winter): 231–41.

———. 1973. "Folk Crime Revisited." *Criminology* 11 (May): 41–85.

Schrag, Clarence C. 1961. "A Preliminary Criminal Typology." *Pacific Sociological Review* 4 (Spring): 11–16.

Schrager, Laura Shill, and James F. Short, Jr. 1978. "Toward a Sociology of Organizational Crime." *Social Problems* 25 (April): 407–19.

Sellin, Thorsten. 1938. *Culture Conflict and Crime*. New York: Social Science Research Council.

Shover, Neal. 1991. "Burglary." In *Crime and Justice*, ed. Michael Tonry. Chicago: University of Chicago Press, pp. 71–113.

Steffensmeier, Darrell J., and Emilie Allan. "The Nature of Female Offending: Patterns and Explanations." In *Female Offenders: Critical Perspectives and Effective Interventions*, ed. Ruth T. Zaplin. Gaithersburg, Md.: Aspen, pp. 5–29.

Sutherland, Edwin H. 1924. *Criminology*. Philadelphia: Lippincott.

———. 1939. *Principles of Criminology* 3d ed. Philadelphia: Lippincott.

Sutherland, Edwin H., Donald R. Cressey, and David F. Luckenbill. 1992. *Principles of Criminology*. 11th ed. Dix Hills, N.Y.: General Hall.

Sykes, Gresham M. 1958. *Society of Captives*. Princeton, N.J.: Princeton University Press.

Tappan, Paul W. 1960. *Crime, Justice and Correction*. New York: McGraw–Hill.

Thomas, William I. 1928. *The Unadjusted Girl*. Boston: Little, Brown.

Tobias, J.J. 1967. *Crime and Industrial Society in the 19th Century*. London: Batsford.

Turk, Austin T. 1982. *Political Criminality*. Beverly Hills, Calif.: Sage.

Vedder, Clyde B., and Dora B. Somerville. 1970. *The Delinquent Girl*. Springfield, Ill.: Thomas.

Weiner, Neil. 1989. "Violent Criminal Careers and Violent Career Criminals." In *Violent Crime, Violent Criminals*, ed. Neil Weiner and Marvin Wolfgang. Newbury Park, Calif.: Sage, pp. 35–138.

Weisburd, David, Stanton Wheeler, Elin Waring, and Nancy Bode. 1991. *Crimes of the Middle-Class*. New Haven, Conn.: Yale University Press.

5

Defenders of Order or Guardians of Human Rights?

Herman Schwendinger and Julia Schwendinger

NEW INTRODUCTION

The article "Defenders of Order or Guardians of Human Rights" appeared decades ago, at the height of the Vietnam War, when political movements were scourging American institutions; when endemic causes of gender, racial, and class inequality were being laid bare; when crimes against humanity and violations of constitutional law were being exposed at the highest levels of government; and when popular rage over the carnage produced by the U.S. government in Southeast Asia, Latin America, and Africa had ruptured the political fabric of the United States.

These events shaped our inquiry into a forgotten debate over the relation between criminology, the law, and the state. This long-lost debate raised a limited number of issues; yet, when examined critically, it opened a Pandora's box and let loose fundamental questions about the nature and aims of American criminology. We became convinced that criminology was the only discipline whose object of inquiry was imposed by the state. While church and state in the Middle Ages had defined the parameters of astronomy and physics, they could now no longer confine these scientific fields to a cage. Crime, on the other hand, was behavior defined by the law and sanctioned by the state.

Yet, this object of inquiry was problematic. If "crime" was considered socially harmful conduct, what about crimes that lawmakers did not consider crimes because they were designed to repress human rights? And what about the popular usage of the word *crime* for great social harms that are not crimes by law simply because powerful groups or classes determine what will be defined as crime? If these great harms are produced by systemic characteristics of a social system, is that system criminal?

The operational interpretation of the legal definition of crime was also prob-lematic. Students at the University of California—Berkeley School of Criminol-ogy, who were writing papers in courses taught by law school professors, were criticized if they condemned Nixon and Kissinger as war criminals. Their profes-sors insisted that they were using the word *crime* unprofessionally because its definition was established legally. (Nixon and Kissinger, in this view, were not war criminals until they had actually been found guilty in a court of law.) How-ever, this view, we discovered, had also been expressed in the long-lost debate by a legal scholar, Paul Tappan, who contended that Edwin Sutherland, a crimi-nologist, had no right to use the term *white-collar crime* to classify corporations that had not been found guilty of violating the law. Consequently, the Berkeley professors who shared Tappan's opinion were further tightening the bonds that tied criminology to the state and its definitions of crime.

The political struggles at Berkeley convinced us that despite Sutherland's ob-jections, the old debate had never departed from certain taken-for-granted as-sumptions. We felt that grounding definitions of crime in historically evolving conceptions of human rights (which are not necessarily accepted by a govern-ment even though the violations of these rights caused grievous harms) might prove useful in making this break.

When the Cambodian invasion occurred, we had already drafted our article on the definition of crime, and the invasion had noticeably elevated its impor-tance. Students across the nation flew into a rage: one-third of the colleges in the United States were shut down by demonstrations and walkouts. Ohio Na-tional Guardsmen killed four student protesters at Kent State, and two Missis-sippi students were killed at Jackson State. Nevertheless, even though Congress subsequently repealed the Gulf of Tonkin Resolution and passed the Cooper–Church Amendment, prohibiting the use of troops outside South Vietnam, Nixon continued to bomb Cambodia until 1973. An estimated one hundred thousand peasants died in the bombing, and two million people were left home-less. The suffering and devastation rallied the Cambodian peasantry to Pol Pot and, by assuring his success, set the stage for his "killing fields."

In the days following "Herman's talk," the lecture "got around," and the edi-tors of *Issues in Criminology* asked us to publish the article we had been writing in our student journal.

THE ORIGINAL ARTICLE

Crime, most modern sociologists agree, is behavior which is defined by the legal codes and sanctioned by the institutions of criminal justice. It is generally agreed, moreover, that legal definitions of crime and the criminal are ultimate standards for deciding whether a scholarly work should be considered crimino-logical.[1] Because of this, the contention that imperialist war and racism are crimes is not only considered an unjustifiable imposition of values, but also an incompetent use of the notion of crime. In order to challenge this prevailing judgment, it is necessary to critically review some of the complex issues involved in a thirty-year-old controversy about the definition of crime.

The Thirty-Year-Old Controversy

Toward the end of the great depression, sociologists became involved in a controversy about legal definitions of crime and criminals. At least two developments stimulated the issue raised at the time: the rapid growth of a corporate liberal sociological empiricism and the socially critical interest in white-collar crime. The former gave rise to what was primarily a scientific, methodological critique of the traditional legal definition. The second generated a substantive and ethical criticism. The positivist, reformist, and traditionalist aspects of this controversy will be selectively reviewed, as they were represented by three of the chief participants: Thorsten Sellin (1938), Edwin Sutherland (1945), and Paul Tappan (1947).

Positivism and the Definition of Crime

In the controversy, American sociologists and lawyers argued furiously about definitions which would distinguish crimes from other types of behavior and criminals from other types of persons. It was observed that traditionally, criminologists used definitions provided by the *criminal law* and, as a result, the domain of criminology was restricted to the study of behavior encompassed by that law. However, one sociologist, Thorsten Sellin, declared in 1938 that if the criminologist is interested in developing a science of criminal behavior, he must rid himself of the shackles forged by criminal law. Criminologists, Sellin added, should not permit nonscientists (e.g., lawyers or legislators) to fix the terms and boundaries of the scientific study of crime. Scientists have their own unique goals which include the achievement of causal theories of criminal behavior. In evaluating the usefulness of legal definitions for scientific purposes, Sellin noted that such definitions merely denote "external similarities" rather than "natural properties" of criminal behavior. The legal definitions, therefore, do not arise from the "intrinsic nature" of the subject matter at hand. They are, in Sellin's view, inappropriate as *scientific* definitions of crime (1938: 20–21).

How can scientific definitions be developed? In an effort to answer this, Sellin pointed out that scientists are interested in universal relationships. Since "conduct norms" represent such relationships (they "are found wherever groups are found"), studies of conduct norms "afford a sounder basis for the development of scientific categories than a study of crime as defined by the criminal law." "Such a study," Sellin added, "would involve the isolation and classification of norms into *universal categories*, transcending political and other boundaries, a necessity imposed by the logic of science." Conduct norms transcend any concrete group or institution such as the State, in Sellin's opinion, because "they are not the creation of any normative group; they are not confined within political boundaries; they are not necessarily embodied in the law" (1938: 30).

Sellin's argument, it should be noted, was organized around the assumption that scientific definitions are determined by the goals and methods of the scientist qua scientist. The limits of Sellin's critique, consequently, focused primarily on the achievement of *scientific* explanation. Moreover, his scientific *standards* for constructing definitions of crime, including his preference for universal, and obviously formal categories and generalizations, are apparently devoid of any moral content: they coldly reflect allegedly intrinsic "natural properties" of human behavior and the "necessity imposed by the logic of science." Sellin's approach to the definition of crime is therefore ostensibly *value-free*.

A Reformist Definition in Which the State Still Reigns Supreme

For many years European and American sociologists incorporated specific references to the ethical properties of criminal behavior in their definitions of crime. William A. Bonger (1936: 5) for example, referred to crime as "a serious antisocial act to which the State reacts consciously by inflicting pain. . . ." Other terms such as "social injury" were also used for this purpose (in the sense that crime involved socially injurious behavior). In some cases these ethical defining criteria provided an implicit warrant for defining unethical practices as crimes, even though these practices might not have been covered by the criminal law. Because these ethical defining criteria have implications for social policy, we shall regard statements embodying their usage as *reformist* definitions.

In 1945, another sociologist, Edwin Sutherland, added fuel to the controversy over the legal definition of crime. His research (1940, 1941) into unethical practices among businessmen and corporation managers produced evidence that, even though very injurious to the public, these practices were considered violations of the civil rather than criminal law. (Consequently, penalties for petty thieves resulted in imprisonment while businessmen who defrauded the public of large sums of money were given insignificant fines.) Sutherland asserted that some of these unethical business practices, while unlawful, were being classified as civil violations because legislators were subservient to powerful interest groups who wanted to avoid the social stigma and penal sanctions imposed under criminal law.

Other consequences followed official subservience. Since criminologists were traditionally limited to behavior prescribed and proscribed by the criminal law, it followed that they were not assured of finding direct legal precedents[2] for the study of the unethical practices by groups powerful enough to fashion the law to their own advantage *no matter how socially injurious their practices might be*. In order to rectify this arbitrary restriction, Sutherland justifiably brushed aside the criteria used by legal scholars to differentiate between criminal and civil violations. He suggested (1945) that social scientists define crime on the basis of the more abstract notions of "social injury" and "legal sanctions." The legal sanctions he had in mind were not restricted to criminal law but were to include those in civil law. And although legal scholars traditionally contended that civil violations were viewed as injuries to individual persons, Sutherland's definition of "white collar" *crime* obviously designated some civil violations as crimes because they were *social* injuries rather than private wrongs. Sutherland's use of the terms "social injury" and "legal sanctions" for defining crime was understandably not wholly endorsed by legal scholars.

Sutherland's argument, it should be noted, made no reference to scientific goals and standards. Unlike Sellin's ostensibly value-free approach, moreover, Sutherland's solution to the problem assumed that there exist *moral* criteria of social injury which can be used to formulate definitions of crime. However, when Sutherland insisted that the abstract notion of "sanctions" be interpreted to mean legal sanctions, his conception of the relevant laws conjoined both criminal and civil laws. The domain of criminological inquiry, therefore, was extended beyond the limits of criminal law.

On the other hand, this domain still continued to reside within the limits of whatever was deemed socially injurious and sanctionable by the *State*. Although Sutherland never delineated his criteria of social injury in any organized manner, it can be inferred from comparisons between his different definitional statements that these criteria cannot exceed those legitimated by agents[3] of the State. In a definition, therefore, Sutherland (1949: 31) stated, "The essential characteristic of crime is that it is behavior which is prohibited by *the State* as an injury to *the State* and against which the State may react, at least as a last resort, by punishment" (our emphasis).

The Traditionalist Approach to the Definition of Crime

In 1947, Paul Tappan indignantly exclaimed that the criminal law contained the only justifiable definition of crime. Those who wanted to abandon this definition were saying, in his opinion: "Off with the old criminology, on with the new orientations . . ." (1947: 96). Since these laws also referred to procedural rules, Tappan added that a person could not be considered criminal until he was adjudicated and found guilty of a crime by the State. Were the new trends allowed to triumph, he foresaw potential hazards in that "the rebel may enjoy a veritable orgy of delight in damning as criminal most anyone he pleases; one imagines that some experts would thus consign to the criminal classes any successful capitalistic businessman." Such an approach to the definition of crime, Tappan explained, "is not criminology. It is not social science." Sutherland's approach, therefore, received methodological denunciation because the "terms 'unfair,' 'infringement,' 'discrimination,' 'injury to society,' and so on, employed by the white collar criminologists cannot, taken alone, differentiate criminal and non-criminal. Until redefined to mean certain actions, they are merely epithets" (1947:99).

Tappan criticized Sellin's and Sutherland's universal concepts for the absence of criteria defining such terms as "injurious." Furthermore, he felt these concepts served to delude the sociologist into assuming that "there is an absoluteness and permanence in this undefined category, lacking in the law." "It is unwise," Tappan added, "for the social scientist ever to forget that all standards of social normation are relative, impermanent, variable. And that they do not, certainly the law does not, arise out of mere fortuity or artifice" (1947:97). As a consequence, he condemned Sellin's and Sutherland's "vague, omnibus concepts defining crime" as "a blight upon either a legal system or a system of sociology that strives to be objective" (1947: 99). Indeed, he suspected subversive motives and attacked the critics of the legal definition for attempting to "revolutionize" its concepts and infiltrate it with terms of "propaganda." He expressed fears that in the end "the result may be fine indoctrination . . ." (1947: 99).

Also, carrying his logic to an extreme, Tappan flatly stated that the only persons who could be *scientifically* studied as criminals were those found guilty by the judicial system. He recommended that sociologists study prison inmates because these persons were truly representative of the total population of criminal offenders. By this logic, persons who had committed a robbery, rape or murder but had not been adjudicated were not criminals; therefore, they could not be part of a representative sample of criminals. Although there were, without question, more persons who had violated laws and had not been adjudicated for their violations, Tappan stubbornly argued that the traditional legal definitions of crime were more precise and objective than other definitions. Tappan's argument is obviously unjustified. However, it verges on the absurd when we add to the roster of criminals at large, those who have been falsely imprisoned. In the case of these guiltless victims, Tappan's argument, in its practical effects, is also pernicious: according to this argument Dreyfus and other less celebrated individuals should have been counted and considered among the criminal population merely because they had been adjudicated and found guilty by the institutions of criminal justice, for the duration of their lives, or at least until the State admits that it has allowed a miscarriage of justice.

Although Tappan also characterized crime as social injury, he made no explicit attempt to follow up his criticism of others by indicating the nature of its defining criteria. He merely deferred to the officials of the State as the only persons who could legitimately decide this question and write it into law. Their decisions, therefore, in addition to determining the specific populations of criminals to be studied by criminologists, also determined the scientific definitions of crime and criminals. Any scientific convention contradictory to this rule was considered illegitimate.

The Legalistic Compromise between Traditionalists and Reformists

The definition of crime and the criminal cannot be wholly separated on an abstract level because the criminal cannot be defined without a definition of crime. The sharp differentiation between definitions of crime and criminals has arisen because of the objections to the legal operational criteria which are part of the traditionalist definition of crime. Sutherland, as we have seen, objected to these operational criteria. He suggested that researchers can consider persons as criminals even though they have not been found guilty of a crime by legal procedures.[4]

It has been indicated recently (Quinney 1970: 4) that Sutherland's definition of crime as a violation of the *criminal law* has been the most acceptable to sociologists in this country. But Sutherland proposed more than one definition of crime. In various places he suggested that crime encompasses the concepts of "social injury," "injury to the State," and both the civil and criminal law. If his reformist preference is distinguished by the insistence that criteria such as "social injury" be explicitly used to define crime, then it is more accurate to say that traditionalist definitions of crime are generally used by sociologists today. In regard to the definition of *crime*, therefore, Tappan has won the day.[5] On the other hand, as we shall see, Sutherland's less restrictive definition of the *individual* criminal prevails over the traditionalist approach. In a sense, sociologists have made an ambiguous compromise between the traditionalist and reformist solutions to the definitional problem.

Nevertheless, although phrased differently, almost all American criminologists today define crime and the criminal by specific or abstract references to definitions and/or sanctions administered by *the State*.[6] Because of this, the term "legalistic" will be used to refer to the variety of legal definitions; and "legalists" refers to those social scientists assuming the legal definition, however reformist or traditional it may be. It has been observed that definitions of crime are ultimate standards for deciding whether a scholarly work should considered criminological. By extension, therefore, it can be claimed that the domain of the science of criminology is still, in spite of Sellin and the reformist approaches, determined by agents of the political state because legalistic definitions of crime are formulated by these agents.

Scientific Standards for Evaluating Legalistic Definitions

Each one of the scholars involved in the thirty-year-old controversy preferred particular defining criteria. Sellin, for example, indicated that "universal" or "causal" relationships should be signified by the definition of crime. Sutherland noted that criteria based on the notion of "social injury" and "sanction" were adequate. Tappan argued for procedural criteria which included reference to the rules by which the criminal law is instituted. He also contended that the legal definition is more precise than others. In order to evaluate these different critical attributes of the definition of crime, it will be shown that it is necessary to distinguish standards held useful by philosophers of science for scientific concept formation.[7] Since criminology is, above all, the *scientific* study of the causes, characteristics, prevention, and control of the incidence of criminal behavior, it is necessary to further note why scientific standards must take precedence over legal standards in evaluating the definition of crime.

Scientists Have Many Definitions of Crime

When their definitional usages are examined, it is found that social scientists are not bound by a single definition of crime; whatever definition is employed depends upon the types of activity the scientist is engaged in, or the kinds of relationships he is interested in.[8] Some of these activities require replication by other scientists and the definitions produced for this purpose operate like a manual of instructions which specifies the procedures for measuring phenomena. When a scientist is concerned with choosing among procedures for measuring crime, whether based on personal observation, self-report questionnaires, interview responses, or administrative processes involving police, judges, and juries, he becomes involved in making a choice of an *operational* definition of crime.[9]

Operational definitions, however, do not exhaust the kinds of definitions used by scientists. There are times when it is helpful to explicate the meaning of categories such as "social control," "anomie," "predatory crimes," or "crimes against property." In this case, a second or *analytic* definition might be in order.

In formulating useful, parsimonious and workable theories of empirical relationships, scientists have also found it necessary to use abbreviated forms of already understood meanings or to single out a particular property, relationship or function for convenient reference. Definitions of this type are called *nominal* definitions, and are even used in textbooks where crime is abstractly but not causally defined by reference to such properties or relations as "social injury," "sanction" or the "actor's relation to the State."

Finally, among the very most important definitions used by scientists are the *real* definitions which signify diachronic and synchronic relationships between variables.[10] Only one member of this class, causal definitions, which signify the necessary and sufficient conditions for the existence of a phenomenon, are real definitions. Causal definitions may be very complex and actually consist of a general theory of the phenomena in question. This may not be apparent in such statements as "anomie is the contradiction of all morality" (Durkheim [1893] 1933: 431), "crime is a symptom of social disorganization" (Sutherland and Cressey 1960: 23), or delinquency is an expression of "unsocialized aggression" (Jenkins and Hewitt 1944). However, these statements are actually abbreviated expressions of general theories of criminal behavior such as social disorganization theories or psychoanalytic theories.

The operational, analytic, nominal, and real definitions by no means exhaust the variety of definitional statements which characterize the work of scientists but they do indicate that the problem of selecting an appropriate definition of crime is not as simple as the legal scholars might suggest in their desire to achieve a universal definition of crime.

Historically, scholars involved in the study of theoretical explanations of human relationships have justifiably developed new modes of thought which depart greatly from customary ways of thinking in other professions. Perhaps the single most important feature of this perspective is the requirement that scientific categories must lead directly or indirectly to the formulation of empirically testable relationships. In light of this injunction, analytic or nominal categories may not be arbitrary; they must be heuristic and accurately descriptive and ultimately refer to accurate assumptions about the nature of the real world.

Sellin apparently challenged the notion that the *real* definition of crime must be derived from legal statutes however narrowly or loosely this mandate is defined. To our knowledge, however, no modern sociologist has fully considered the degree to which the empirical thrust of his challenge resides most importantly within the principle of the *autonomy of scientific inquiry.*[11] This principle was first raised and named by John Dewey (1938) as the "autonomy of inquiry." In developing this principle, Dewey was primarily concerned with encroachments by logicians and philosophers of science in the "logic in use" developed by scientists (Kaplan 1964: 3–11). However, as Abraham Kaplan (1964: 3–6) has indicated the act of encroachment can have its sources in other professions as well. For example, the insistence by members of the legal profession that the law provides the only possible definitions of crime is an unjustifiable encroachment by lawyers on the autonomy of science. But this disregards the fact that legal definitions do not meet standards of scientific inquiry. Legal definitions have questionable heuristic value when used nominally or analytically. Operationally, these definitions are unreliable and invalid. Legalistic real definitions are sheerly descriptive; they play a trivial and commonsensical role in advancing theories of criminal behavior. To demonstrate the validity of these evaluations, we will systematically compare defining criteria based on the notions of "precision," "procedural law," and "sanctions," with the standards regulating the proper use of operational, real, analytic, and nominal definitions.

What Is Precision? Or . . . "Is There a Lawyer in the House?"

In light of the variation in types of scientific definitions, it is difficult to comprehend from a scientific point of view what is meant when lawyers or sociologists claim that the legal definition of crime is the only "precise" or appropriately "technical" term available for defining crime.[12] What definitional usage is being referred to? If crime is to be defined in terms of its causal relationships, then it is important to reiterate that these real definitions which may consist of such abbreviated terms as "anomie" or "maladjustment" are actually theories of crime or criminals. The notion of "precision" in relation to this kind of definition has little meaning because in a causal inquiry, sensitizing concepts and hypothetical constructs[13] are not only permissible but are often absolutely necessary for achievement of explanations with high systematic (theoretical) import.

Legal scholars may agree on the importance of standardizing a *single* legal definition for every type of crime and criminal, but it can be flatly stated that the standardization of causal definitions in this manner would destroy the free marketplace of scientific ideas and the ability of scientists to advance the state of knowledge in the field.[14]

Are the Legalists Referring to Precise, Operational Definitions?

For purposes of scientific inquiry, the legal definition is a curious formulation which mixes normative, descriptive, and operational meanings without regard to their very different functions. But the plain fact is that even if we differentiated these meanings and employed them separately, they would still be inadequate for scientific purposes. To illustrate this, let us assume, for example, that legalists are actually talking about the use of the legal definition for operational purposes when they insist on its "precise" characteristics.[15] If used for operational purposes, then the key meaning of the legal definition would be the stipulation that administrative rules (i.e., procedural law), supply the procedures by which the amount of crime is to be measured. It should be noted that the only possible measurements which are permitted by these rules take the form of official enumerations of adjudicated cases. When criminologists derive their statistical rates from these enumerations, they operationalize criminal behavior in the *only way made possible by the law*.

Although the legality of a proposed definition of crime may be determined by a majority in a parliamentary situation (and, therefore, as we shall see later, subsuming the activity of social scientists under the prevailing dominant ideology), operational definitions cannot be considered appropriate by a majority vote from an empiricist's point of view. Instead, standards based on the concepts of scientific reliability and validity are used to evaluate their worthiness. On the basis of these standards, social scientists have for decades[16] criticized the use of officially adjudicated data as invalid and unreliable measures of criminal behavior. As a result, some research scientists have, in practice, abandoned the operative meanings contained in the legalistic definitions of crime irrespective of their own explicit commitments to these definitions. Even the substantive contents of these categories, which are stipulated in the legal code, are not used in the operational definitions in present practice. All that remains of legalistic definitions is the formal acquiescence, on the part of researchers, to such conceptual categories as robbery, rape or homicide.[17]

Political Power as a Determinant of Precision

Recent works on "crimes without victims" (Schur 1965) or "crimes of consumption" (Glaser 1970: 138) are good indicators of the considerable disagreement regarding *ethical* standards to be used in the definition of crime and criminals. (These standards are usually subsumed under such categories as "social injury.") As an outcome, in practice, administrative procedures and sanctions preempt "social injury" by default. In comparison with this ethical category, these standards are allegedly *relatively* more precise because they are operationally more reliable. (At least scholars *know* what is meant by the terms, procedures, and sanctions, but there may exist little understanding of "social injury.") But even though this is undoubtedly the case it should not obscure the fact that the degree of linguistic precision (i.e., social determinacy and usage) of the meanings of "procedures" and "sanctions," in this case, is actually dependent upon political processes. Ultimately, legal definitions assume certain political conditions for optimum operational precision. These conditions can be *best* fulfilled by a *totally* controlled society such as Orwell's "Oceania" in *1984*. The "reliability" of the measurements or descriptive relationships which are directly or indirectly defined by reference to administrative procedures and sanctions is dependent upon administrative purpose and expertise; but the completeness of its execution is dependent on political power. This is why it can be assumed that with regard to the legal definition: political power determines the precision of the definition and the measurement of the phenomena.

The Real Definitions of Legal Definitions and Legal Definitions as Real Definitions

Toward the beginning of criminology textbooks, a legalistic-nominal definition is usually offered. In this statement the authors single out certain ethical properties of criminal behavior and/or limit themselves to consideration of the relationships between criminal behavior and sanctioning agencies. Although these nominal definitions are sometimes treated as real or causal definitions, there are a number of reasons why they are merely nominal. Behavior which is legally defined as crime, according to the views of most persons trained in an empiricist tradition, had existed *before* its legal definition was formulated.[18] The *behavior*[19] can, therefore, be justifiably regarded as a determinant and as such, it is not the law which determines crime, but *crime which determines the law*.[20] In light of this, it is again highly misleading to use legalistic definitions (which refer, for example, to sanctions) as real definitions, in spite of the fact that sanctioning processes feed back and influence this behavior over time.

Sociologists are explicating and redefining the legal definition for purposes that are quite foreign to its original, legalistic usage. One reason for this is that, once formed, legally established sanctioning processes do influence criminal behavior. And the nature of this influence is being inquired into by sociologists today. The reworking of the definition is necessary because complex, and often discretionary, operational processes, which influence ongoing characteristics of criminal behavior, are very inadequately symbolized in the original legal statement.[21]

Are legal definitions real, i.e., causal definitions? In the process of ascertaining the effects of the institutions of criminal justice on criminals, it has become imperative to differentiate criminals who have been sanctioned by law from those who have avoided sanctions. But this is not the only reason why this differentiation is important. The certain knowledge that there are vast numbers of criminals "at large" has long generated serious questions about the adequacy of those theories which have only been confirmed by the use of official statistics. In light of this, scientists are fully justified in rejecting the logic of the argument that a criminal's status can only be defined legalistically. They are justified in viewing this matter as an *empirical* question in order to settle outstanding issues in their field. In the view of these scientists, the efficacy of calling "criminal" those who have acted as such but who have not been adjudicated and found guilty of their violations can be substantiated by empirical test. Canons of logic cannot be substituted for empirical criteria in making this assessment.[22]

Criminologists interested in the study of the *institutions of criminal justice* often use the notion of sanction to define crime. This notion is particularly plausible as a defining criterion because it is easily related to everyday experiences. One illustration of this is Austin T. Turk's explication of "the sanctioning process" as "generic"[23] to the word *criminal*. Turk (1969: 22) indicates that the sanctioning process is observed when "Somebody asserts a right-wrong; someone fails to conform; and some mode of coercion is used in the course of defining a violator and depriving him of something, even if it is little more than a few minutes spent in sending a lawyer to bat." It is suggested here, however, that if social scientists are interested in real definitions of the institutions of criminal justice, that they organize their defining criteria with reference to a *general theory* of the State (particularly in capitalist and socialist societies) rather than simple properties of microscopic and often contractually governed interpersonal relationships.

In constructing real definitions of the causes or control of crime, therefore, there is no absolute necessity for utilizing the notion of sanction as a defining criterion. In light of this a general definition, which identifies crime as behavior which is sanctioned by the State, is highly misleading. Just as misleading, however, is the notion that sanction is intrinsically necessary for any type of scientific definition of crime.

Are Sanctions Generic?

As we have noted, neither positivistic nor legalistic arguments can provide adequate explanations for the existence of a generally accepted notion that sanction is generic for defining crime. This notion, as we have seen, is certainly not necessary for scientific operational definitions of criminals. Nor is it necessarily essential to real definitions. It may be useful for defining particular kinds of relationships between the criminal and the State but there are undoubtedly instances where sanctions are an incidental aspect of this relationship. If we think in terms of the general relationship between the State and crime, rather than the State and the individual criminal, sanctions may be even less significant than other kinds of relationships. To some extent this fact has been obscured by the unanalyzed, metaphorical use of the term *sanction* to symbolize the extremely complex relationships between crime and the State.

Regardless of this unsubstantiated claim, authors of most textbook definitions identify crime by singling out sanctioning processes. To argue that crime must be defined in terms of sanction, however, is to insist that sanctions are absolutely necessary for understanding, predicting, preventing and/or controlling crime. Studies in the sociology of law and criminal behavior indicate that this necessity may exist in some cases,[24] but it has never been demonstrated that it holds as a general rule.

Humanistic scholars, including scientists and nonscientists, have long been tantalized by the possibility that behavior which is injurious to the great majority of persons in society can be prevented or controlled by means other than punishment of individuals. Psychologists and psychiatrists have asked whether there are other reeducative or rehabilitative procedures which can replace sanctioning processes as we have traditionally come to understand them. Sociologists, from their perspective, have asked whether the radical restructuring of social institutions or systems can eliminate crime more effectively and fairly than traditional and repressive forms of social control. Whatever one may think of the efficacy of any one specific proposal in this respect, it is quite clear that most run counter to the legislative definitions regarding the treatment of crime. They, more often than not, also contradict standards which legislators currently employ in defining criminal behavior. By contending that sanctions are generic to the definition of crime, legalists discourage the possibility of viewing crime from very different points of view and limit the definitions of crime to those established by the current occupants of the houses of political power. Political power, as we have seen, makes procedural criteria allegedly more "precise" for scientific purposes than ethical criteria. As a parallel to this, power also seems to make sanctions generic to the definition of crime.

The differentiation of the empirical properties of social relationships is strongly dependent upon the theoretical intentions of the social scientist. Because of this, it can be said that just as the knowledge of the empirical properties of social phenomena does *not* arise (as Sellin contends) "intrinsically from the nature of the subject matter," sanctioning processes are not more intrinsic to the definition of crime than any other possible relationship. This does not mean that sanctions are extraneous to all theoretical purposes. *This will always depend upon the theoretical perspective involved.*

The Critical Role of Ethical Criteria in Relation to Sanctions

Sellin was concerned with developing a general strategy for explaining crime while Sutherland was interested in explaining a particular type of crime (i.e., white collar crime). When Sellin's proposals in the controversy over the definition of crime are compared with Sutherland's, therefore, it can be shown that the differences between these scholars are due less to their general orientation than to their different purposes; they were concerned with problems on disparate levels of specificity. In other writings, Sutherland did propose a general, "normative conflict"[25] theory of crime, which was derived from the same metatheoretical assumptions underlying Sellin's "culture conflict" theory. The similarities in orientation between these scholars also become salient when it is realized that Sutherland was not alone in singling out sanctions as an essential feature of the phenomena he was interested in. Sellin, it is true, was concerned with more inclusive normative phenomena than legally codified norms, but in turning his attention to the concrete problem of comparing legal and non-legal norms, he suggested that the degree of *sanction* be used as a *universal* standard of comparison (1938: 23–45).

Perhaps the most revealing part of the controversy about the legal definition is the degree to which theoretical sociologists like Sellin and Sutherland avoided the confrontation with standards which could have been used in fully evaluating *the moral justifications* of legal codes. Even Sutherland, who did most to question the justification for the separation between civil and criminal codes, went to great pains to show that his interpretation of white-collar crime was in *accord* with established legal precedents. However, if ruling classes and powerful interest groups are able to manipulate legislators to their own advantage, isn't it possible that there are instances of socially injurious behavior which have no legal precedents? Consider further the chance that there are practices by men of power which are highly injurious to most of mankind and which are neither defined nor sanctioned by civil or criminal laws, such as, for example, genocide and economic exploitation. Isn't it apparent, if Sutherland had consistently explored the use of ethical categories like social injury, that he would have concluded that there are, on one hand, socially non-injurious acts which are defined as crimes and, on the other socially injurious acts which are nevertheless not defined as either civil or criminal violations?

It is in relation to these logical possibilities that the ideological function of legal sanctions (as a defining criterion) is fully exposed. If the *ethical* criteria of "social injury," "public wrong," or "anti-social behavior" are not explicated, then the *existent ethical standpoint of the State is taken as a given* when the criterion of sanctions by the State is also used in the definitions of crime. This is why the meanings of such categories as social injury are so critical for the definition of crime.

In light of this, it can be concluded that, in the controversy over the definition of crime, the only argument which transcended the State was ostensibly value-free,[26] while, in addition, the only argument which admitted moral criteria, considered these criteria applicable solely if they were embodied in the law. What explains the extreme selectivity which is manifest in the controversy over the definition of crime? Why hasn't any American sociologist proposed that these definitions of crime are *not* the only possible definitions? The answers to these questions and those raised at the conclusion of the previous section will be suggested in the form of a very terse review of the historical development of the *ideological* perspective which has unduly dampened the controversy over the legal definition of crime.

Ideological Aspects of the Controversy over the Definition of Crime

Ideological Influences on the Usage of Categories

It can be readily understood that, in the desire to examine and utilize apparently more precise categories, scholars might overlook the degree to which their own scientific behavior is determined by the same political conditions which gave rise to legal definitions in use. But this is insufficient for explaining why conventional political categories have succeeded in superseding all other ethical, as well as professional, criteria for defining the nature of crime. Nor can inertia supply the reason for the supremacy of conventional political standards. These political standards are more than an encroachment on the autonomy of science. They are also in contradiction to the truly scientific and humanistic mandate that it is not the professional's function to be a mere technician who complies, wittingly or unwittingly, with established authorities. According to this mandate every professional is morally responsible for his own actions: this responsibility can not be justifiably delegated to agents of the State.

Corporate Liberalism and Metatheoretical Categories. Are non-legal definitions of crime currently in use among sociologists? At one point in his argument, Sellin (1938: 8) declared that "Innumerable definitions of crime have been offered which if not read *in their context* would appear to go beyond the legal definition. Upon examination, however, almost all of them prove to be the legal norms clothed in sociological language" (our emphasis). This observation is as accurate and observable today[27] as it was in 1937. Less clear, however, is the degree to which highly formal and nominal definitions of crime have persisted even in cases where scholars have explicitly repudiated their use.

American sociology abounds in formal and nominalist categories which are metatheoretical in nature. It is often not realized that the most influential categories of this type have been generated only after scholars have reflected on the meanings of previous theoretical works and singled out properties or relationships which seem to have been used time and time again by different theorists. Therefore, although these properties or relationships are nominally defined, they are not to be considered arbitrary distinctions. Instead, they refer, indirectly, to the theories of human behavior which have claimed the attention of sociological interest for some time. Such categories as "conduct norms" or "normative conflict" are the outcomes of this process. For purposes of analysis they can be termed "metatheoretical categories" because they are derived by abstracting relationships designated by theories.[28]

The metatheoretical categories which maintain legalistic definitions of crime were generated during the formative years of sociology. Works which mark the beginning and end of this period were Lester Ward's *Dynamic Sociology* (1883) and William F. Ogburn's *Social Change* (1922). During this time, traditional liberal assumptions as to the nature of man and society were substantially altered by leading scholars, not only in sociology and criminology but in every other discipline and professional field. As a consequence, a new variant of the liberal ideology, corporate liberalism, came into being.[29] In sociology, the leading American scholars[30] involved in the modern reconstruction of liberalism included, besides the above mentioned, Albion Small, Frank Giddings, Edward A. Ross, W. I. Thomas, Robert E. Park, and Ernest W. Burgess, among others.

Particularly after the publication of a series of essays by Ross beginning in 1895,[31] scholars urged the study of every conceivable type of social relationship from within the framework of a liberal functionalist metatheory of *social control*. These essays accelerated an intellectual development which culminated in the systematic combination of corporate liberal concepts of social control with those derived from the classical liberal notion of the harmony of interests.[32] This combination was utilized in order to solve what sociologists call the "problem of social integration" or, synonymously, "the problem of *order*."[33]

In formulating solutions to the problem of integration, American and European scholars were spurred by the extraordinary social instabilities which accompanied the rise of monopoly capitalism. During the last quarter of the nineteenth century, the United States, for example, sporadically experienced sixteen years of depressions and recessions (Mitchell 1927). From the turn of the century until the First World War, the United States was still economically unstable (Kolko 1967); it was characterized by extensive immigration and rapid industrial change. There was no diminution of industrial violence (Adamic 1931), and the very foundations of American capitalism appeared to be threatened by the emergence of progressive movements, labor unions, and socialist parties (Weinstein 1968). Some, but not all members of these movements, were also militantly opposed to the new and aggressive foreign policies which were instituted by the American government (Preston 1963). These policies vigorously supported the penetration of economic markets overseas with every means possible including armed forces (Williams 1961).

American sociologists from Ward onwards utilized their theoretical ideas to criticize socialist doctrines, as well as the "effete minds" (i.e., intellectuals)[34] who opposed American imperialist wars. They also attacked the laissez-faire capitalist ("the Robber Barons") and the older laissez-faire liberal theorists like Herbert Spencer, because they opposed political regulation of the economy. The new liberal sociologists proposed that the State should actively rationalize and stabilize the economy. This proposal was substantiated by their new conceptions of man and society. These conceptions admitted the existence of "the perpetual clash of interest groups" but suggested ways of stabilizing and restraining this conflict. The expanded powers of the State, it was claimed, would enable it to perform an effective role in reconciling or regulating conflicts between "interest groups" within the framework of capitalism.

The American scholars also turned their attention toward ways of maintaining established institutions such as the family. In the process, they developed theories and metatheories focusing on solutions to the problem of integration from their new ideological point of view. In time, their efforts produced categories and generalizations which led directly to the modern liberal functionalist orientations called pluralism and structural-functionalism.

Space limitations preclude an adequate discussion of these general developments or consideration of the role they played in contributing to Sellin's interpretation of the concept of norms. It can be demonstrated, however, that his concept was derived from a very general functionalist orientation which implicitly assumed that certain "optimum" social relationships were functionally imperative to the associated life of man. These relationships were called "natural" or "normal" states. And the functional prerequisites for these states were utilized as criteria for evaluating all behavior which was considered inimical to optimum functioning (i.e., a gradually changing but stable order). In theory, these prerequisites were usually hypothesized as "norms"; and unnatural or *abnormal* conduct was perceived as a *normative* departure or deviation from "normative expectations."[35] Within this general perspective, normal societies were actually depicted as being repressive. They repressed and channeled the anarchic, egotistic tendencies allegedly inherent in the nature of man by the "judicious" application of rewards and sanctions.

Technocratic Doctrines.   Side by side with the development of basic corporate liberal orientations, the early American sociologists also professed and greatly elaborated the *technocratic doctrines* which were expressed in rudimentary form by Henri Saint-Simon.[36] These doctrines can be regarded as an independent system of ideas[37] but they were developed in conjunction with an intellectual tradition which can be called "liberal syndicalism."[38]

Basic to the definition of technology is the vision of a society managed not by common people but by experts or enlightened leaders who are highly informed by expert advisors.[39] Another hallmark of technocratic doctrine is the implicit use of the norms of established institutions as standards for identifying "abnormal," "pathological," or "deviant" behavior. A further indicator of the use of technocratic doctrines is the contention that sociologists are involved in a *value-free* or ideologically neutral enterprise in the very shadow of their simultaneous subscription to established norms.[40]

What was the state of criminology almost two decades after the formative period? At the time when Sellin challenged the legal definition of crime, sociology had long been rooted in corporate liberal theories of human relationships. In addition, crime was perceived as but one instance of the structural relationships within the larger and more general culture. Criminal personalities were seen as little more than simple homologues of these social relationships.[41] Solutions to the problem of integration also encompassed the concepts of criminal behavior. These stressed the creation and maintenance of normative consensus. (Conflict was to be minimized, reconciled, or regulated; consensus was to be maximized because of its role as a functional imperative to the maintenance of a stable and socially integrated order.) Conflict and disorganization! These key words signified the preconditions for crime. Consensus, harmony, and equilibrium! These terms referred to stability and order.

Value-Free Sociology

In light of these developments it is possible to understand the essence of Sellin's seemingly radical proposal, as well as his *complementary*, rather than contradictory, relation with Sutherland's legalistic position. Sellin proposed, in essence, that the organizing principles for examining and explaining the nature of criminal behavior be derived from the highly general propositions and categories which were being used by sociologists at the time. By proposing that the concept "conduct norm" be used instead of the legal definition, Sellin was simply advising sociologists that they would not get far with the highly descriptive contents of the legal definitions. If they wanted to explain crime, the notion of conduct norms was a key to unlocking a whole stockpile of axioms, mechanisms, and categories derived from the theories which corporate liberal scholars had found useful for solving the problem of integration.

Armed with this strategy, Sellin did *not* advocate the elimination of the legal definition. To the contrary, he (1938: 367) specifically suggested that this definition be used to indicate *criminal* departures from the conduct norms of "political groups." (These norms, he observed, were different from other norms because they are legally codified.) But Sellin also suggested that the scientific explanation of these departures would have to take into account theoretical concepts which emerged from the study of both legal *and* non-legal norms. He proposed further that, since the relation between the criminal and civil law is ambiguous from this larger point of view, the criminologist's "concern with *crime norms* and their violations may well be *broadened to include legal conduct norms* embodied in *the civil law*" (1938: 39). Thus, even though Sellin began his journey from a more abstract starting point, he arrived at the same destination as Sutherland.[42] This is not surprising, considering that both scholars were using similar metatheoretical assumptions in approaching the subject of criminal behavior.

At bottom, therefore, Sellin's argument reinforced rather than challenged the broader legalistic approach which had been developed by Sutherland. It did not challenge this approach because it was woven from the same corporate liberal and technocratic ideologies which had emerged among the founders of American sociology. These founders constructed a view of the world which was of service to the new corporate liberal state and implicitly justified the use criteria which favored the maintenance of established institutions. In the metatheory of social control, departures from norms of established institutions were "abnormal" and conducive to social instability. Normative sanctions, therefore, were considered an important mode of social integration. Individual behavior had to be controlled by these sanctions if the established institutions were to survive.

Guided by the metatheory of social control, many American criminologists functioned as technocratic "consultants" who spent their lives gathering information which would be of use to the men who managed existing institutions, whether they were aware of this or not. The profession of ideological neutrality on their part was by no means a guarantee of this neutrality. Instead, it was one of the great myths which prevented principled scholars from being aware of the ideological character of their basic theoretical assumptions.[43]

A Modern Humanistic Alternative

Because of space limitations, the final section of this paper will not attempt a definitive alternative to the legal definition. Instead there will be suggested, in desperate brevity, what is hoped will be useful points of departure for those interested in exploring new approaches to this problem. It is felt that this discussion will have served a useful purpose if it stimulates the development of a number of alternative approaches at this time,[44] when so many received doctrines are being called into question.[45]

Moral Criteria for Definitions of Crime

No scholar involved in the controversy about the definitions of crime has been able to avoid direct or indirect use of moral standards in a solution to this problem. In spite of this, the choices of defining criteria have been accompanied by a technocratic incapacity to confront the moral implications of this selection. It is not clear, for example, that the acceptance of procedural law as a defining criterion delegates personal responsibility to agents of the State. But this delegation is no less a moral act and therefore cannot avoid complicity in the actual definitions made by official agents. Just as moral is the explicit use of sanctions or the implicit use of other defining criteria,[46] derived from functional imperatives of established institutions or political economies. In light of this, the claim that value judgments have no place in the formulation of the definition of crime is without foundation.

An alternative solution to the definition of crime should openly face the moral issues presented by this definitional dilemma. Traditionally, these issues have been inadequately represented by such unanalyzed terms as "social injury," "anti-social act," or "public wrongs." But how does one confront the problem of explicating "social injury" or "public wrongs"? Is this done by reference to the functional imperatives of social institutions or by the historically determined rights of individuals? In our opinion, the latter is the only humanistic criterion which can be used for this purpose.

There has been an expansion of the concept of human rights throughout history. And political events have made it possible, at this time, to insist on the inclusion of standards clustered around modern egalitarian principles, as well as enduring standards such as the right to be secure in one's own person, the right to speak one's mind, and the right to assemble freely. We refer to these ideas as modern because they are to be distinguished from those fashioned in the eighteenth century when a rising middle class formulated a challenge to the economic prerogatives of feudal aristocracies. At that time, the functional imperatives of the patriarchal family, price-making market, and political state were reified, by recourse to natural law, as basic human needs. In this reified form, equality was primarily perceived as the immutable right to compete *equally* with others for a position in social, economic, and political spheres of life. In the context of our modern political and economic institutions, however, competitive equality has not had, as an empirical outcome, the furtherance of human equality. Instead, it has been used to justify inequalities between the sexes, classes, races, and nations.

Life in industrialized nations over the last two hundred years has clearly indicated that rhetoric regarding the equality of opportunities cannot preserve the spirit of the egalitarian credo. Nor can liberalism, the ideology which, above all others, has laid claim to the concept of equality of opportunity, be used in defense of egalitarianism. Liberalism is, at bottom, a highly elitist ideology. It has justified and helped perpetuate social inequality in the name of equality. It was in the name of free competition and laissez-faire liberalism, for example, that Western nations converted the people and natural resources in South America, Asia, and Africa into sources of cheap labor and raw materials during the nineteenth and twentieth centuries.[47] Because of the use of the concept of equality of opportunity by liberals, ostensibly egalitarian notions cannot be taken for granted. They must be subjected to careful scrutiny.

When the concept of equality of opportunity is analyzed, it is found that it does not refer to egalitarian principles at all. Instead it refers to principles of equity or fairness which should govern the ways in which social *inequality* is instituted in our society. In its most defensible form it stipulates that meritarian standards rather than lineage, race or other "natural" criteria should regulate the unequal distribution of the goods of life. But there is no society on the face of this earth which actually distributes the goods of life on the basis of differences in *natural* talents of individuals. The differences which actually determine the distribution of rewards are for the most part socially determined. As a consequence, even in democratic societies, the notion of equality of opportunity serves more as a justification for gross inequalities established on the basis of class, race, sex, ethnicity, and other grounds. Within the framework of liberalism, moreover, equality of opportunity is merely one among many standards which justifies an elitist morality. This morality can rightfully claim that each individual should be treated equally, but in practice, some preferred criterion is always inserted to guarantee that some men are treated more equally than others.[48]

In opposition to the ever increasing demand for equalitarianism, elitist social scientists have formulated theoretical justifications for social inequality.[49] We deny the ethical and empirical validity of these theoretical justifications! Irrespective of claims to the contrary (Warner 1949; Moore 1963), there is no universal moral rule or empirical property which is inherent to man or society which makes social inequality a functional necessity. Above all, there is no valid moral or empirical justification for the outstanding forms of social inequality in existence today including economic, racial, and sexual inequality. If the traditional egalitarian principle that *all* human beings are to be provided the opportunity for the free development of their potentialities is to be achieved in modern industrial societies, then persons must be regarded as more than objects who are to be "treated equally" by institutions of social control. All persons must be guaranteed the fundamental prerequisites for well-being, including food, shelter, clothing, medical services, challenging work, and recreational experiences, as well as security from predatory individuals or repressive and imperialistic social elites. These material requirements, basic services, and enjoyable relationships are not to be regarded as rewards or privileges.[50] They are rights!

In formulating a conception of human rights which can be useful to criminologists, it is important to recognize the political *limits* of the ethical doctrine of *equal intrinsic value* when applied to human beings. This doctrine asserts generally that all men are to be regarded not as means but as ends in themselves. This doctrine has been found useful by philosophers and other scholars in formulating a logically consistent defense of egalitarian principles which subordinates criteria based on social expedience and utilitarian logic, to those based on some kind of "ultimate," irreducible "natural" equality of men. However, although philosophers of ethics and legal scholars may require logically consistent and persuasive justifications for equality (and common sense may contend that men are born free and equal), the plain fact is that throughout all history, equality has been decisively defended, not on the basis of formal logic but on *political* grounds. Most of the inhabitants of this earth, furthermore, have never been born free and equal. The achievement of freedom and equality has been won at great cost to individuals and their families.

By delineating the naturally intrinsic qualities of men, philosophers have attempted to transcend the politically controversial issues posed by the abrogation of human rights. Their natural law principles, however, cannot be substituted for a substantive and historically relevant interpretation of human rights, which takes into account the political ideals men have, as well as the kinds of social institutions which can nullify or realize these ideals. It is not enough to provide good reasons for the achievement of broader human rights or to catalog these rights. Criminologists must be able to identify those forms of individuals' behavior and social institutions which should be engaged in order to defend human rights. To defend human rights, criminologists must be able to sufficiently identify the violations of these rights—by whom and against whom; how and why.

This reconstruction of the definition of crime will entail the problem of priorities regarding different rights. This problem may be uniquely posed in varying types of political economies. In the Soviet Union, for example, the right to those basic conditions which allow for the fullest possible democratic participation in political life, such as free speech and assembly, would be given high priority. Likewise, in the United States, the right to economic well-being for all men should be considered crucial. This priority will come into conflict with the prerogatives of governing social classes, economic strata, or political elites. But this must be expected by humanistic criminologists. Also to be expected is the opposition from the legal interpreters of crime. If the right to be secure in one's own person is to have greater value than social inequalities based on the ownership of property, for example, then one should be prepared to define the use of deadly force on the part of police officers as unjustifiable homicide when this force is used in defense of property. (This would be the case, for example, were a thief to be slain by an officer while refusing to halt when ordered to do so.) There is no doubt that significant portions of the existing criminal law would overlap with the definition of crime on the basis of human rights. But, on the other hand, it is also true that many forms of behavior including those now defined as crimes without victims or crimes of consumption would not be defined as crimes within this new perspective.

There Are Criminal Social Systems

Perhaps there are no statements more repugnant to traditional legal scholars than those which define social systems as criminal. But this repugnance reflects the antiquarian psychologistic and technocratic character of the legal tradition. This tradition is blind to the fact that extensive social planning makes it possible to evaluate, mitigate, or eliminate the *social* conditions which generate criminal behavior. It is no longer sufficient to justify the restriction of criminology to the study of those institutions which define, adjudicate, and sanction *individual* criminals. It has become evident that any group which attempts to control or prevent criminal behavior by the activity of the traditional institutions of criminal justice alone is incapable of accomplishing this end.

As a rule, criminal behavior *does* involve individual moral responsibility and the assessment of psychological relationships, such as the motivated character of the criminal act. However, the science of crime has gone beyond the centuries old notion that crime can be conceived as a function of the properties of atomistic individuals alone.[51] Social scientists today are intensely involved in scrutinizing social relationships which generate criminal behavior. This activity is reflected in the *real definitions* of crime which have been and are being developed by sociologists, economists, anthropologists, and political scientists.

The logical strictures on the definition of social systems or relationships as criminal are removed when it is realized that real definitions by social scientists establish a diachronic relationship between the notion of criminal rates, for example, and the *socially* necessary and sufficient conditions for these rates.

If crime is defined by scientists in terms of the *socially* necessary and sufficient conditions for its existence, what would be more logical than to call these social conditions criminal? After all, crime has been traditionally defined by legalists on the basis of nominalist definitions or descriptive definitions which refer to the ways in which agents of the State react to criminal behavior. To be sure, some legalists have used ethical terms such as "public wrongs" or "social injury" in earmarking criminal behavior. But isn't a real definition of crime vastly superior to a nominalist definition or a definition which does not even define crime but merely refers to how the State reacts to it? And isn't a scientist justified in making a logically implied, normative evaluation of what he considers to be the cause of crime? And given the acceptance of criminal institutions and social-economic relationships as real definers of crime, what more ultimate claim can social scientists use to justify their unique role as criminologists, than to use the term *crime* to identify social systems, which can be regulated or eliminated in order to control or prevent crime? What better term than *crime* can be used to express their *normative* judgments of the conditions which generate criminal behavior?

It can be argued that the term "criminogenic" be used to designate the *social conditions* which cause crime. But, this term obfuscates the main point being made here; namely, that the social conditions themselves must become the *object* of social policy and that it is not an individual or a loose collection of atomistic individuals which is to be controlled, but rather the social relationships between individuals which, give rise to criminal behavior. (Even if we put everybody involved in criminal behavior at any one time behind bars, there is no guarantee that a new generation of criminals would not emerge given the maintenance of social conditions which originally made these individuals criminal.) In this context, the term *crime* as a label for social systems becomes a warrant, not for con-trolling atomistic individuals, or preventing an atomistic act, but rather the regu-lation or elimination of social relationships, properties of social systems, or social systems taken as a whole.

Are Imperialistic War, Racism, Sexism, and Poverty Crimes?

Once human rights rather than legally operative definitions are used to ear-mark criminal behavior, then it is possible to ask whether there are violations of human rights which are more basic than others and to designate these rights as most relevant to the domain of criminology.[52] Basic rights are differentiated be-cause their fulfillment is absolutely essential to the realization of a great number of values. Although the lower boundary of this number is not specified here, the sense of what is meant can be ascertained by considering security to one's person as a basic right. Obviously a danger to one's health or life itself endangers all other claims: A dead man can hardly realize *any* of his human potentialities.

Similar assessments can be made of the right to racial, sexual, and economic equality. The abrogation of these rights certainly limits the individual's chance to fulfill himself in many spheres of life. These rights therefore are basic because there is so much at stake in their fulfillment. It can be stated, in light of the previous argument, that individuals who deny these rights to others are criminal. Likewise, social relationships and social systems which regularly cause the abro-gation of these rights are also criminal. If the terms imperialism racism, sexism, and poverty are abbreviated signs for theories of social relationships or social systems which cause the systematic abrogation of basic rights, then imperialism, racism, sexism, and poverty can be called crimes according to the logic of our argument.

It is totally irrelevant, in this light, to consider whether leaders of imperialist nations are war criminals by virtue of legal precedent or decisions by war tribu-nals.[53] Nor is it relevant to make note of the fact that property rights which underlie racist practices are guaranteed by law. It is likewise unimportant that sexual inequality in such professions as sociology is maintained by references to the weight of tradition. Neither can persistent unemployment be excused be-cause it is ostensibly beyond the control of the State. What is important is that hundreds of thousands of Indo-Chinese persons are being denied their right to live; millions of black people are subjected to inhuman conditions which, on the average, deny them ten years of life; the majority of the human beings of this planet are subjugated because of their sex; and an even greater number through-out the world are deprived of the commodities and services which are theirs by right. And no social system which systematically abrogates these rights is justifi-able.

Is there wonder why we have raised questions about the legalistic definitions of crime when the magnitude of "social injury" caused by imperialism, racism, sexism and poverty is compared to that wrought by individual acts which the State legally defines as crimes? Isn't it time to raise serious questions about the assumptions underlying the definition of the field of criminology when a man who steals a paltry sum can be called a criminal while agents of the State can, with impunity, legally reward men who destroy food so that price levels can be maintained while a sizable portion of the population suffers from malnutrition. Our nation is confronted with a grave moral crisis which is reflected above all in the technocratic "benign neglect" shown in the unwillingness to recognize the criminal character of great social injuries inflicted on heretofore powerless people, merely because these injuries are not defined in the legal codes.

Modern Libertarian Standards

The limits of this paper do not permit the detailing of operating standards[54] which might be useful for earmarking the kinds of behavior which should be of central interest to criminologists, but neither these standards, nor the notion of basic human rights itself, are more difficult to define than the operating standards and notions underlying legal conceptions of "social injury" or "public wrong." The solution to this problem is also no less political. Indeed, it is time to recognize that all of the above concepts are brought to light and operationalized by the political struggles of our time.

It is not claimed that a satisfactory solution to the problem of defining crime has been offered in this paper. What is sure is that the legalistic definitions cannot be justified as long as they make the activity of criminologists subservient to the State. It is suggested that an alternative solution can be developed which is based on some of the traditional notions of crime as well as notions organized around the concept of egalitarianism. In this process of redefining crime, criminologists will redefine themselves, no longer to be the defenders of order but rather the guardians of human rights. In reconstructing their standards, they should make man, not institutions, the measure of all things.

NOTES

The introduction to this essay is new to this volume. In the original article, the authors expressed their appreciation to Sheldon Messinger, Anthony Platt, Paul Takagi, and Joseph Weis for their advice and criticism. They thanked, in particular, Menachem Amir and Anatole Shaffer for their detailed suggestions that helped clarify the work. The original article first appeared in *Issues in Criminology* 5 (1970): 123–57; reprinted here with permission.

1. Criminological studies, therefore, provide knowledge which is diachronically or synchronically related to *legally* defined crimes and criminals.

2. Because of this, Sutherland's discussions on this topic attempted to demonstrate the connection between criminal and civil violations via analogy, historical parallels, and

certain similarities between civil and criminal procedures, etc. (e.g., He wrote, ". . . although many laws have been enacted for the regulation of occupations other than business, such as agriculture or plumbing, the procedures used in the enforcement of these other laws *are more nearly the same* as the conventional criminal procedures . . .") (1945: 139, our emphasis).

3. The term *agents* is used in the broad sense. It includes, for example, legislators, judiciary, and police because the definition and operative interpretation of crime are not restricted to lawmakers.

4. Sutherland [and Cressey] (1960: 19) stated:

However, for scientific purposes it is not necessary that every decision be made in court; the criminologist must only know that a certain class of acts is defined as crime and that a particular person has committed an act of this class. Just as there is justification for writing of "crimes known to the police" and "unsolved crimes," there is justification for writing of "unapprehended criminals" and "criminals at large."

5. Gresham Sykes' evaluation of Tappan's criticism of the use of ethical criteria is one example. Sykes (1956: 20) states, in regard to the attempts by sociologists to equate "criminal" with "anti-social," that

Paul Tappan, as a lawyer-sociologist, has carefully indicated the hazards surrounding this position: It invites subjective value judgments; it substitutes the rather vague category of anti-social behavior for the more precise category of crime; and what is perhaps more important, it is apt to make the social scientist forget that all social rules are "relative, impermanent, variable."

6. No better example can be given than Richard Quinney's meticulous definition of crime. Quinney (1970: 6–7) writes:

[C]onduct is not regarded as criminal unless three conditions are present: (1) the label of crime has been officially imposed on conduct (2) by *authorized persons and agencies* (3) of a *politically organized society*. Crime is, therefore, a legal category that is assigned to conduct by authorized agents of a politically organized society. The criminal is, it follows, a person who is assigned the status of criminal on the basis of the official judgment that his conduct constitutes a crime" [our emphasis].

7. For an insightful discussion of the relation between definitions of crime and scientific concepts, see H. Bianchi (1956: 90–111).

8. For the meanings of such terms as "operational," "analytic," "nominal," and "real" definitions as well as the "explication," see Carl G. Hempel (1952).

9. It should be noted in passing that Tappan's defense of the precision of the legal definition is inconsistent because he had been a foremost critic of the "Imprecision" of the legal codes defining criminal behavior among juveniles (Tappan 1947).

10. Our interpretation of the real definition is broader than Hempel's. He generally restricts real definitions to causal definitions.

11. Sellin's criticism of the legal definition, as we will note later, represents an unsuccessful and incomplete attempt to question this definition on the basis of the autonomy of science.

12. Michael and Adler (1932: 22) stated, "The most *precise* and least ambiguous definition of crime is that which defines it as behavior which is prohibited by the criminal

code" (our emphasis). Tappan also used the term precision in criticizing definitions of crime not grounded in the criminal law. In 1967, Leonard Savitz ([1967] 1970: 46–47) indicated that "If the defendant is not convicted, or the conviction is not upheld by appellate courts, he is not a criminal." Savitz added that

> It is disconcerting to note that often, even in serious research projects, the terms *crime* and *criminals* are used with considerable lack of *precision*. It seems to be often assumed that anyone who is arrested is necessarily a criminal. As these are basic concepts upon which the field of criminology is based, such casual indifference is somewhat, difficult to understand. (our emphasis)

13. These sensitizing concepts and hypothetical constructs appear vague because their meanings often vary depending upon the usage to which they are put by different theorists and researchers. Furthermore, these categories are often reformulated in light of additional knowledge. But this very property of impermanence, and the rich connotations which are characteristic of these ideas, make them useful to scientists interested in the discovery of heretofore unknown empirical relationships. The fact that there are a number of these definitions at any one time cannot be taken as a sign of the inability of scientists to formulate "precise" notions of criminal behavior.

14. If Tappan's insistence that scientists use the legal definition instead of their own causal definitions is pushed to its logical limit, then it means that no other definitions of crime are warranted. This insistence, for example, means that there should exist no competing causal definitions of crime in general or of any type of criminal behavior.

15. For example, Michael and Adler state (1932: 23), "However inadequate conviction of crime may be as a test of criminality, in no other way can criminality be established with sufficient certainty for either practical or scientific purposes. The criminologist is therefore quite justified in making the convict population the subject of his studies, as he does." This reference obviously utilizes the legal definition to operationally define criminals.

16. In recent years, in particular, criminologists engaged in delinquency research have begun to systematically reject the use of official data altogether as measures of the actual distribution of delinquency in a community. By constructing measures of delinquency other than those prescribed by criminal law, they have suggested that the official political procedures are invalid for scientific purposes (Cicourel 1968; Nye, Short, and Olsen 1958; Dentler and Monroe 1961; Empey and Erickson 1966; Gold 1966.)

17. As an illustration of this discrepancy between formal and substantive contents, compare the instructions on any self-report delinquency questionnaire with the substantive contents of the statutes defining these same offenses in the criminal law.

18. Although not sufficient, the behavior is obviously necessary for the existence of the social processes which lead to a definition of crime.

19. Even with the possibility that "labeling" theories of crime (Werthman 1969; Becker 1963; Kitsuse 1963) are proven valid for some types of crime, it is doubtful that most crimes will ever be explained on this basis. (This point will be expanded in our forthcoming book tentatively entitled *Ideology and Adolescence*.)

20. The determining relation between crime and the law has been noted by many criminologists, including, for example, H. Bianchi (1956: 97), and it is particularly apparent in the analysis of "white collar crime."

21. Again we note the irony in Tappan's remarks to the effect that his orientation is

an "objective" one, and that sociologists are engaged in some sort of immoral or subversive enterprise when they do not use the traditional legal definition of crime. It is now a matter of record that modern research in delinquency (which is not dependent on official statistics) has produced clear evidence of class and racial bias in the administration of the law. It is curious how morally appropriate these "immoral" sociologists can be.

22. From this empiricist point of view, the legal argument that criminal status is, by definition, necessarily determined by the criminal justice system leads to an empirically *unfalsifiable* corollary. It logically implies that *all* persons who actually violate a statute but are not adjudicated by these institutions are not criminals. (Such persons include, for example, those who have committed unsolved crimes.) This corollary, however, is scientifically unacceptable because its truth-value is determined solely on logical grounds. If a scientific definition is meant to signify relations in the real world, there must be some empirical criteria by which it can be ultimately evaluated. In order to utilize these criteria, the definition of criminal behavior itself must be formulated so that it can be empirically tested. This formulation, it is argued, cannot be made without operationally defining criminal behavior *independently* of legal sanctions or procedures which are commonly used to identify crime.

23. Turk (1969: 22) states:

> Thus, anyone who is defined officially as a violator . . . is criminal in the *generic* sense, whatever he may be called in accord with the terminologies and assumptions currently in vogue. That there are differences in the ways in which authorities perceive and process violators does not negate the fact that . . . our observations are of the *sanctioning process*. (our emphasis)

24. An outstanding example of the determining relationship between the law and crime includes the development of criminal syndicates involved in the illegal production and sale of alcoholic beverages during the prohibition year. Today a similar relationship exists with respect to narcotics.

25. The term "differential social organization" was also used to refer to this general theory of crime (Cressey, 1960).

26. The concept of "value-free" sociology has been under sharp attack in recent years. For references to this controversy, see John Horton (1966) and Alvin Gouldner (1968).

27. In 1968, for example, Irving L. Horowitz and Martin Liebowitz (1968: 282) offered this "radical" definition of deviancy: "Deviancy is a conflict between at least two parties: *superordinates* who make and *enforce* rules, and subordinates whose behavior violates these rules" (our emphasis). The authors indicate that their definition is based on a "conflict model." When the context of this definition is examined, it is found that in most cases, the authors refer to behavior defined by law involving prostitutes, homosexuals, drug addicts, illegal forms of civil disobedience, etc. The "superordinates" in this case are therefore agents of the State and the reference to rule enforcement involves State sanctions. Finally, when the principles underlying Horowitz and Liebowitz's "conflict model" are examined, they turn out to be old fashioned, pluralist principles regarding the nature of social conflict and conflict resolution.

28. The prefix, *meta*, in this case symbolizes a process of abstracting relationships contained in theories. (The outcome of this process is a collection of formal categories, axioms and mechanisms which may or may not be systematically related in a general

orientation or strategy of theory construction in specific types of inquiry.) The suffix, *theory*, indicates that the object of study is not the real world but theories of that world.

29. European scholars were also involved in this task, including Emile Durkheim and Sigmund Freud [(1930) 1957].

30. For discussions of the complex relations between the development of corporate liberalism and the social, political and economic changes during this period, see for example Williams (1961), Kolko (1963), and Weinstein (1968).

31. These essays appeared later in a single volume entitled *Social Control* (1901).

32. For an extended discussion of corporate liberal concepts of social control, see the forthcoming work, tentatively entitled. *Sociology: The Formative Years: 1883–1922* by the Schwendingers, Herman and Julia.

33. Scholars grapple with this problem when they are concerned with explaining the persistent features of social systems. How do social systems remain stable? What is at stake in achieving a stable social order in the midst of great conflicts or accelerated change? These are the kinds of questions which pose the problem of integration.

34. Long before Vice President Spiro Agnew's reference to "effete snobs," Ward ([1903] 1911: 240) stated that most "peace agitation is characterized by total blindness to all the broader cosmic factors and principles and this explains its complete impotence." Identifying individuals who agitate for peace as "effete minds," he noted that "it is the mark of the effete mind to exaggerate small things while ignoring great things" and reminiscent of contemporary references to "silent majorities," he added, "the crude instincts of the general public are far safer guides to the evaluation of war than "maudlin sentimentality and . . . certain minds which, from culture or advantage, gain the credit of constituting the cream of the most advanced intelligence."

35. Sellin (1938: 6) states, for example, "It would seem best, in order to avoid misunderstanding to speak . . . of normal and abnormal conduct, i.e., conduct in accord with or deviating from a conduct norm."

36. American sociologists have generally mistakenly attributed the origins of technocrat and positivism to Comte. Although Comte insisted on the originality of his conceptions, most of them were plagiarized from Saint-Simon. In addition, technocratic doctrines were developed further by the disciples of Saint-Simon, such as Bazard, Laurent and Engantin (who we called the Saint-Simonians); although as Georg Iggers (1958) points out, these doctrines were made subservient to theocratic standards and principles.

37. The independence of technocratic doctrines from corporate liberalism is testified by the fact that socialist scholars have also subscribed to them.

38. In the United States, corporate liberal syndicalists included Small and Weatherly. In Europe, De Greef, Tarde and Durkheim were numbered among the outstanding liberal syndicalists. It is important to note that this type of syndicalist thought is most responsible for the later development of modern pluralism. For a discussion of some of the salient characteristics of this form of syndicalist thought, see Williams's (1961: 356–60, 384–86) description of the development of "American syndicalism."

39. For a classic criticism of this approach, see Mills (1942) and Mills (1959: 84–99).

40. Although Ward insisted on the doctrine of a value-free social science as early as 1883 (and symbolized this in his distinction between "pure" and "applied" sociology in a two volume work in 1903), it was not until the early twenties that this doctrine took firm hold among the Americans. At that time, the scholarly academics opposing this doctrine

were chiefly represented by the "Christian sociologists." Their influence on the way in which professionals defined the field disappeared after President Wilson's administration.

41. In this view, the "abnormal" conditions which produced criminal behavior and criminals were, on the level of social relationships, culture *conflict* and social *disorganization*; on the level of personality relationships: personal *conflict* and personality *disorganization* (Blumer 1937).

42. The differences between Sellin and Sutherland disappear altogether when Sutherland considers the definition of the "nature of crime from a *social* point of view" (our emphasis). In the discussion of the "social" nature crime, Sutherland (1960: 14–15) uses three criteria to distinguish crime: (1) values of a political group, (2) isolation or culture conflict, and (3) sanctions. If the term "conduct norms" was substituted for "values" then this interpretation would be identical with Sellin's.

43. To a great extent, the ostensibly value-free character of criminology in the United States is derived from the fact that it developed historically under the aegis of sociology rather than law (as was the case in Europe). It is interesting to note in passing, however, that Tappan's argument supported a definition of crime which was actually posed by Michael and Adler, who edited a 1932 report by a committee under the auspices of the School of Law of Columbia University on the feasibility of an Institute of Criminology and Criminal Justice. Sutherland and Sellin were members of the committee's staff, and obviously objected to the narrowly stated legal definition of crime in the report. Their objections, emerging in 1937 and 1940, as noted, reflected a broader sociological approach to the statement.

44. There are scholars today who analyze legally defined relationships from a socially critical standpoint. It is not the purpose of this section to deny their humanitarian outlook. The logic of our previous argument, however, suggests that the humanistic content of their theories are not derived from their use of a value-free methodological perspective nor the use of a legal definition "in-itself." Instead, the humanistic content is derived from a concept of rights which tacitly regulates their scholarly activity. Because of this it is felt that a definition of crime which is squarely based on conceptions of human rights will make explicit what is now inchoate, inconsistent and implicit. The charge will be made that our alternative to the legal definition will "taint" the objective, scholarly character of criminology by bringing each scholar's political biases to the fore. The answer to this objection is that a scrupulous inspection of theories in the field will indicate that individual ideological biases have always existed although the mystique of a value-free methodology has obscured their inexorable influence.

45. One cannot ever estimate the degree to which even doctrinaire interpretations of the more humanitarian legal definitions of crime, which were originally extended as a result of the Second World War, are being rejected as a result of contemporary events. One example is the insistence of George Wald (Nobel Laureate in Physiology and Medicine) that the directors and managers of the Dow Chemical Corporation be held responsible for participating in a "crime against humanity" by their production of napalm. A similar case against Dow is made with regard to herbicides and defoliants (Wald 1970).

46. These other criteria usually define crime as a departure from "normal" states, which may be vaguely signified by such exceedingly formal terms as "the mores," "the group," "the political group," "superordinates," "the public," or "society."

47. The inequality inherent in the relation between the colonial and colonizer was,

and still is, among the most profound of human inequalities. Nevertheless, during the second half of the nineteenth and the beginning of this century, social Darwinism, propounded first and foremost by the liberal scholar, Herbert Spencer, was used to justify the subjugation of peoples of color on the grounds that they were genetically inferior; and the exploitation of domestic labor in the name of equality of competition between nations and equality of opportunity between individuals.

48. As Stanley I. Benn (1967: 68) has succinctly stated:

Although the elitist would allow that ordinary men have interests deserving some consideration, the interests of the super-man, super-class, or super-race would always be preferred. Some men, it might be said, are simply worth more than others, in the sense that any claim of theirs, whatever it might be and whatever its specific ground, would always take precedent. Such a morality would maintain that there was some criterion, some qualifying condition of race, sex, intellect, or personality, such that a person once recognized as satisfying it would automatically have prior claim in every field over others.

49. For a classic debate on this issue, see the discussion between Davis (1953), Moore (1963) and Tumin (1953a, 1953b).

50. The degree to which the fulfillment of basic human needs is equated with dollars in our society is revealed in the American Medical Association's persistent denial of the right of all persons to medical services. As John H. Knowles (1970: 74) states, ". . . a significant group of doctors has the attitude as stated by a past AMA president, that health is a privilege, not a right. I think that health is as much a right as the right to schooling or decent housing or food, and the people have begun to perceive it as a right."

51. The science of crime has gone beyond this even though the legalists may not have progressed this far. It is vital, however, that legalists be informed that social scientists are not merely interested in isolated criminal acts but in personality relationships, social relationships and systems of social relationships which generate a succession of criminal acts on the part of distinct individuals, on one hand, and socially distributed instances of criminal acts by many individuals, on the other hand. The psychiatrist or psychologist, for example, interested in the moral careers of individuals, has moved beyond the empirical issues which were traditionally addressed by legal scholars and which are still reflected in the way in which the criminal law is fashioned today.

52. The basic human rights, it should be reiterated, that are not being referred to here are those alleged rights which are intrinsic to the nature of man, or which are functionally imperative for social stability and order. A prime example of the reification of social imperatives is Garafolo's [1885] depletion of "natural crimes" on the basis of basic moral sentiments of *pity* (involving empathic feelings) and *probity* (involving the respect for rights of private property). These "basic moral sentiments" are functionally necessary for the maintenance of "modern societies." Garafolo's theory was in the *reform* Darwinist tradition initiated by early corporate liberals. This tradition was used to justify the expansion of the political power of the State in order to regulate the uncontrolled competitive processes represented by laissez-faire capitalism.

53. It is rather incredible to find sociologists publishing what appear to be poorly written legal briefs criticizing the war in Indo-China. We suggest that they spend their time explaining the imperialist nature of this war and leave the legal criticisms to lawyers who also recognize the unjust character of this war. Generally, sociologists have used legalistic

justifications where the status of the behavior in question is equivocally defined from the standpoint of the criminal law and in practice, are usually concerned with the analysis of business and political crimes. But certain assumptions underlie this legalistic mode of justifying the definition of behavior as criminal. For example, when to call genocide a crime is justified on the basis of legal precedents. It is assumed that agreements arising out of a contractual relationship, "freely" entered into by a group of nation states, provide the essential criterion for defining such a crime. As a result, the *procedural conventions* existing between these states are imposed as necessary conditions for deciding whether an indisputably grave injury to mankind has taken place in any specific case. Isn't this an absurd and arbitrary basis on which to identify a crime of such magnitude as genocide? This decision to use a procedural convention is an *ethical decision*. And the fact that contractual or other agreements are necessary to establish precedents for these conventions does not, by any means, make these agreements necessary for recognizing that genocide is a heinous crime or, on the other hand, that men are able to commit genocide without ever being charged with their crimes by the State.

The reliance on legal precedent elevates the importance of procedural standards in spite of the fact that in following this approach, one can just as easily contend (by tautological reference to these standards) that genocide did not exist before the Nuremberg trials; that the act of dropping one hundred thousand tons of bombs on a Vietnamese city is not sufficient proof of complicity in a war crime on the part of American military personnel; that the Biafran people were not victims of genocidal acts; and that political leaders of powerful imperialistic nations cannot be considered war criminals after ordering the devastation of smaller nations unless they are brought before an international tribunal and found guilty.

54. Such as infant mortality, length of life, quality of food diets, medical and recreational services, employment opportunities, etc.

REFERENCES

Adamic, Louis. 1931. *Dynamite: The Story of Class Violence in America.* New York: Harper & Row.

Becker, Howard. 1963. *Outsiders: Studies in the Sociology of Deviance.* New York: Free Press.

Benn, Stanley I. 1967. "Egalitarianism and the Equal Consideration of Interests." In *Equality,* ed. J. Roland Pennock and John Chapman. New York: Atherton, pp. 61–78.

Bianchi, H. 1956. *Position and Subject-Matter of Criminology: Inquiry Concerning Theoretical Criminology.* Amsterdam: North Holland.

Blumer, Herbert. 1937. "Social Disorganization and Individual Disorganization." *American Journal of Sociology* 42: 871–77.

Bonger, W. A. 1936. *An Introduction to Criminology.* London: Methuen.

Cressey, Donald R. 1960. "Epidemiology and Individual Conduct: A Case from Criminology." *Pacific Sociological Review* 3 (Fall): 47–58.

Cicourel, Aaron V. 1968. *The Social Organization of Juvenile Justice.* New York: Wiley.

Davis, Kingsley. 1953. "Reply to Tumin." *American Sociological Review* 18: 394–97.

Davis, Kingsley, and Wilbert E. Moore. 1945. "Some Principles of Stratification." *American Sociological Review* 10: 242–49.

Dentler, Robert, and Lawrence J. Monroe. 1961. "Early Adolescent Theft." *American Sociological Review* 26 (October): 733–43.

Dewey, John. 1938. *Logic: The Theory of Inquiry*. New York: Holt.

Durkheim, Emile. [1893] 1933. *The Division of Labor in Society*. Glencoe, Ill.: Free Press.

Empey, LaMar, and Maynard L. Erickson. 1966. "Hidden Delinquency and Social Status." *Social Forces* 44 (June): 546–54.

Freud, Sigmund. [1930] 1957. *Civilization and Its Discontents*. London: Hogarth.

Garofalo, Raffaele. 1885. *Criminology*. Boston: Little, Brown.

Glaser, Daniel. 1970. "Victim Survey Research: Theoretical Implications." In *Criminal Behavior and Social Systems*, ed. Anthony L. Guenther. Chicago: Rand McNally, pp. 136–48.

Gold, Martin. 1966. "Undetected Delinquent Behavior." *Journal of Research in Crime and Delinquency* 3 (January): 27–46.

Gouldner, Alvin W. 1962. "Anti Minotaur: The Myth of a Value-Free Sociology." *Social Problems* 9 (Winter): 199–213.

———. 1968. "The Sociologist as Partisan: Sociology and the Welfare State." *American Sociologist* 3 (May): 103–16.

Hempel, Carl G. 1952. "Fundamentals of Concept Formation in Empirical Science." In *International Encyclopedia of Unified Science*, vol. 2, no. 7. Chicago: University of Chicago Press.

Horowitz, Irving H., and Martin Liebowitz. 1968. "Social Deviance and Political Marginality: Toward a Redefinition of the Relation between Sociology and Politics." *Social Problems* 16 (Winter): 280–96.

Horton, John. 1966. "Order and Conflict Theories of Social Problems as Competing Ideologies." *American Journal of Sociology* 71: 701–13.

Iggers, Georg C. 1958. *The Doctrine of Saint-Simon: An Exposition: First Year, 1828–1829*. Trans. with notes and an introduction by Georg C. Iggers. Boston: Beacon.

Jenkins, R. L., and Lester Hewitt. 1944. "Types of Personality Structure Encountered in Child Guidance Clinics." *American Journal of Orthopsychiatry* (January): 84–94.

Kaplan, Abraham. 1964. *The Conduct of Inquiry*. San Francisco: Chandler.

Kitsuse, John I. 1963. "Societal Reactions to Deviant Behavior: Problems of Theory and Method." *Social Problems* 9 (Winter): 247–56.

Knowles, John. 1970. "U.S. Health: Do We Face a Catastrophe?" *Look Magazine* (2 June): 74, 78.

Kolko, Gabriel. 1963. *The Triumph of Conservatism*. New York: Free Press.

Lemert, Edwin M. 1951. *Social Pathology*. New York: McGraw-Hill.

Michael, Jerome, and Mortimer J. Adler. 1932. *An Institute of Criminology and of Criminal Justice: Report of a Survey Conducted for the Bureau of Social Hygiene under the Auspices of the School of Law of Columbia University*. New York: Bureau of Social Hygiene.

Mills, C. Wright. 1942. "The Professional Ideology of Social Pathologists." *American Journal of Sociology* 49 (September): 165–80.

———. 1959. *Sociological Imagination*. New York: Oxford University Press.

Mitchell, Wesley C. 1927. *Business Cycles*. New York: National Bureau of Economic Research.

Moore, Wilber. 1963. "But Some Are More Equal Than Others." *American Sociological Review* 28: 13–18.

Ogburn, William F. 1922. *Social Change*. New York: Viking.

Nye, F. Ivan, James F. Short, Jr., and V. J. Olsen. 1958. "Socio-Economic Status and Delinquent Behavior." *American Journal of Sociology* 23 (January): 318–29.

Preston, William, Jr. 1963. *Aliens and Dissenters*. Cambridge, Mass.: Harvard University Press.

Quinney, Richard. 1970. *The Problem of Crime*. New York: Dodd, Mead.

Ross, Howard A. [1895] 1901. *Social Control*. New York: MacMillan.

Savitz, Leonard. 1970. "Crime and the Criminal." In *Criminal Behavior and Social Systems*, ed. Anthony L. Guenther. Chicago: Rand McNally: 42–47. (Originally published in Leonard Savitz, *Dilemmas in Criminology*. New York: McGraw-Hill, 1967: 9–16.)

Schur, Edwin M. 1965. *Crime without Victims*. Englewood Cliffs, N.J.: Prentice Hall.

Sellin, Thorsten. 1938. *Culture Conflict and Crime*. Bulletin No. 41. New York: Social Science Research Council.

Sutherland, Edwin H. 1940. "White Collar Criminality." *American Sociological Review* 5: 1–12.

———. 1941. "Crime and Business." *Annals of the American Academy of Political and Social Science* 217: 112–18.

———. 1945. "Is 'White Collar Crime' Crime?" *American Sociological Review* 10: 132–39.

———. 1949. *White Collar Crime*. New York: Holt, Rinehart & Winston.

Sutherland, Edwin H., and Donald R. Cressey. 1960. *Criminology*. New York: Lippincott.

Sykes, Gresham M. 1961. *Crime and Society*. New York: Random House.

Tappan, Paul R. 1947. "Who Is the Criminal?" *American Sociological Review* 12: 96–102.

Tumin, Melvin. 1953a. "Reply to Kingsley Davis." *American Sociological Review* 18: 394–97, 672–73.

———. 1953b. "Some Principles of Stratification: A Critical Analysis." *American Sociological Review* 18: 387–93.

Turk, Austin T. 1969. *Criminality and the Legal Order*. Chicago: Rand McNally.

Wald, George. 1970. "Corporate Responsibility for War Crimes." *New York Review of Books* (2 July): 4–6.

Ward, Lester L. 1883. *Dynamic Sociology*. New York: Appleton.

———. [1903] 1911. *Pure Sociology*. New York: MacMillan.

———. 1906. *Applied Sociology*. New York: MacMillan.

Warner, W. Lloyd. 1949. *Democracy in Jonesville: A Study in Quality and Inequality*. New York: Harper.

Weinstein, James A. 1968. *The Corporate Ideal in the Liberal State: 1900–1918*. Boston: Beacon.

Werthman, Carl. 1969. "Delinquency and Moral Character." In *Delinquency, Crime and Social Process*, ed. Donald R. Cressey and David A. Ward. New York: Harper & Row, pp. 613–32.

Williams, William Appleman. 1961. *Contours of American History*. New York: World.

Part II

New Directions

6

Crime as Social Interaction

Leroy C. Gould, Gary Kleck, and Marc Gertz

One of the most popular semantic problems posed to first-year philosophy students is "Is there 'sound' when a tree falls in the forest and there is no person within earshot to hear it?" This problem is sometimes paired with another: "Is there 'sound' when a psychotic person 'hears' voices that no one else hears?" The answer, of course, is "It depends on the definition of 'sound.' " If the definition focuses on objects producing pressure waves in the air, then there is sound in the first example, but not in the second; if the definition focuses on human perception, then there is sound in the second, but not in the first.

Although people are free to choose whichever definition they want, the choice makes a difference. Defining sound as pressure waves in the air places emphasis on the physical properties of sound and is more likely to attract the attention of physicists than of psychologists. Defining sound as human perception places the study of sound primarily within the domain of psychology.

And so it is with the definition of "crime." Although criminologists are free to define crime however they like, their choice affects the aspects of crime they will study and the academic discipline that is best equipped to study it.

BACKGROUND

When criminology began, with the publication of the essay *On Crimes and Punishments* by Cesare Beccaria ([1764] 1963), the emphasis was the law and its enforcement (Jeffrey [1959] 1960). Some criminologists—for example, Gary Becker (1968) and Isaac Ehrlich (1981)—still think of crime this way. For the vast majority of criminologists, however, the concept "crime" refers not to the law but to the behavior of offenders. As Matza (1964: 3) described the situation:

> The most celebrated and thus the most explicit assumption of positive [scientific] criminology is the primacy of the criminal actor rather than the criminal law as the

major point of departure in the construction of etiological theories. The explanation of crime, according to the positive school, may be found in the motivational and behavioral systems of criminals. Among these systems, the law and its administration are deemed secondary or irrelevant. This quest for explanation in the character and background of offenders has characterized all modern criminology, irrespective of the particular causal factors espoused.

At the time Matza was writing these words, several criminologists were in the process of changing this focus. Wilkins (1964), for example, showed that the availability of automobiles was an important determinant of the volume of theft from automobiles. Biderman (1966) argued that prosperity, which creates increases in the amount of property, influences rates of property crime. Gould (1969, 1971) and Mansfield, Gould, and Namenwirth (1974) showed that rates of automobile theft and bank robbery are highly correlated with rates of automobile ownership and the amount of money available in banks to be stolen.

These studies, which shifted attention from offenders to victims and crime targets, first came to be known as "criminal opportunity theory" (Cook 1986: 2) and then as "routine activities theory" (Felson 1987). Other important works in this tradition include Boggs (1965), Luckenbill (1982), Ziegenhagen and Brosan (1985), Stark (1987), Kleck and Sayles (1990), and Kleck and DeLone (1991).

The purpose of this chapter is to suggest a conception of crime that includes elements from each of these criminological traditions. It is a conception that views crimes as interactions among three distinct elements: offenders, agents of social control, and crime targets. It is a conception that accommodates different theories of "crime." It suggests that the most productive criminological question is not "Why do certain people commit crimes?" but rather "Why do crimes occur?" Crimes occur, the argument goes, partly because people are motivated to commit them, partly because they are not deterred from committing them, and partly because there are opportunities for their commission.

CRIMINAL EVENTS

Albert Cohen (1985: 86) was among the first criminologists to make a distinction, theoretically, between crime as a social event and crime as the behavior of individual offenders:

> Even the most profound and lucid understanding of the actor's state of mind and of the motives and the history that led him to do what he did, however useful it may be for establishing guilt and doing justice, does not explain the occurrence of the criminal act. It may explain the actor's part in or contribution to the criminal act, which may be important to know, but it does not equal an explanation of the act. If we want to explain the criminal act, we must start with the appropriate question.

That question is not, "Why would somebody do something like this?" but rather "What made it happen?"

At the same time, Hirschi and Gottfredson (1987: 958) were working along similar lines:

> We have been developing a general theory of crime designed to account for the distribution of all forms of criminal behavior (Hirschi and Gottfredson, 1986 and 1987; Gottfredson and Hirschi, 1987). This emerging theory starts from a distinction between crimes as events and criminality as a characteristic of people. Whereas traditional positivistic theories begin by looking at offenders, we begin by looking at crime.

Crediting an earlier, unpublished, paper by Hirschi and Gottfredson, Wilson and Herrnstein (1985: 22–23) defined a "crime" in their book *Crime and Human Nature* as an "act committed in violation of a law that prohibits it and authorizes punishment for its commission." "Criminality," in contrast, "refers to stable differences across individuals in the propensity to commit criminal (or equivalent) acts" (1985: 23). There is a difference, in other words, between people's propensity to commit criminal acts (criminality) and the acts themselves (crimes). Indeed, Wilson and Herrnstein went on to say that their book was more "concerned with criminality than with crime" (1985: 23).

Like Cohen, Hirschi and Gottfredson, and Wilson and Herrnstein, we hold the point of view in this chapter that an important distinction must be made between criminal behavior and criminal events. Although the behavior of individual offenders is an important component of criminal events, it is, as Cohen (1985) suggests, only one of several important components. Also important are crime targets, victims, law enforcement officials, and other members of society.

CRIMINAL EPISODES

What is being argued here is that the unit of analysis of criminology needs to change. The unit of analysis should not be the individual offender. Neither, however, should it be the law or crime targets. Rather, the unit of analysis should be the criminal event itself. Indeed, the criminal event may even be too narrow a focus. *Criminal episode* might be a better term. In addition to the immediate, overt interaction among offenders, victims, law enforcement officials, and other members of society implied by the term *event,* the term *criminal episode* would include various overt and symbolic interactions among these actors that precede and follow the event itself. Casing several liquor stores before robbing one, for example, would represent an interaction between potential offenders and potential crime targets that preceded a robbery. Tracking robbers down, bringing them to trial, convicting them, and sentencing them to prison would involve interactions between offenders and law enforcement agents that follow a robbery. This broader context is important to criminology for it includes activities, both those that precede an event and those that follow, that can play an important role in whether an event occurs. If a potential robber concludes after casing several liquor stores, for example, that robbing a liquor store is not likely to result in very much money or is too risky, he or she may decide to rob another type of target—for example, a convenience store—or not to engage in robbery at all. A potential robber's estimate of risk, in turn, will depend on her or his expectation of what will happen during and after the robbery: "Does the manager keep a gun? Will he or she use it? Will I be seen leaving the store? How long will it take for the police to get there? Will I be captured? How much time does a person do for robbery?" Things that the potential offender anticipates might happen during and after the event, in other words, play a role in whether the event will occur.

The importance of interactions leading up to and following criminal events does not end with potential offenders. A liquor store owner, for example, will decide to keep (or not to keep) a gun on the premises, in part because he or she thinks it will or will not deter robberies, in part because of the risk a gun poses to customers and employees, in part because of the law, and in part because of the presumed effectiveness of the police and other criminal justice agencies in preventing robbery.

The actions of law enforcement officers, in turn, may be influenced by their conceptions about the robber, the victim, and the crime target. Whether the police will intervene while a robbery is in progress or wait until the robber leaves the store, for example, will depend in part on whether the police believe the robber, or the store clerk, is armed with a gun and whether either is likely to use it.

Criminal episodes, in other words, are complex social phenomena that take place over extended periods of time. They involve not only a criminal event but also social interactions that precede and follow the event itself. To understand why criminal events occur, then, it is necessary to understand the motivations and actions of offenders, victims, and official agents of social control, before, during, and after the event.

The Interactionist Approach

Thinking of crimes as social, rather than as individual, units of analysis implies not only that criminal episodes are multifaceted—involving the actions several people—it also implies that they are interactive. Indeed, the "interactive" component of criminal episodes may be their most important conceptual characteristic (see Cohen 1985). Criminal episodes contain many potential interactions. There are potential interactions between offenders and crime targets. There are potential interactions between offenders and agents of social control. There are potential interactions between agents of social control and crime targets. There are potential interactions among offenders, victims, law enforcement agents, and those who witness criminal events. There are also potential interactions among offenders themselves, when a criminal episode involves more than one offender, just as there may be interactions among more than one victim, more than one law enforcement agent, and more than one observer of a crime. These interactions may be overt, symbolic, or both (Mead 1934). That is, they may involve both the anticipated and the direct interplay among the various actors in the drama.

The cast of characters in a criminal episode may become quite large, and each character may play more than one role. Even the distinction between the offender and the victim sometimes does not become apparent until well into the episode (Wolfgang 1957; Luckenbill 1977). This is particularly true of crimes like assault or murder. Victims may play not only the role of crime target, as in crimes against persons; they also may play the roles of social control agent and witness. Similarly, police officers sometimes play the dual roles of observer and control agent.

All of these interactions, among many individuals playing several roles, are components of criminal episodes. To conceive of criminal episodes in ways that do not include all of these individuals and all of these interactions is to miss much that is important about crime. This complexity, however, is exactly what traditional criminological conceptions of crime—those that conceive of crimes as violations of law or as the actions of criminal offenders—overlook.

THE CONCEPT "CRIME" IN EVERYDAY LIFE

This complexity, although sometimes overlooked by criminologists, is not overlooked by ordinary people. Consider, for example, Gary Fineout's description of a criminal episode that appeared in the 26 April 1989, *Florida Flambeau:*

> The state attorney's office has subpoenaed 12 more members of the Pi Kappa fraternity of Florida State University in the ongoing investigation into the possible sexual battery of an 18-year-old female student found unconscious from intoxication in a fraternity house. A medical report found she had been "sexually violated by more than one person." A Pi Kappa Alpha fraternity member spoke to officials Monday while the other 11 will talk to a representative of the state attorney's office this afternoon. All 12 live on the third floor of the "Pike" house, which the victim said was the site of the alleged sexual assault. Also subpoenaed by the state attorney's office were four women, two of whom belong to the Delta Delta Delta sorority. One of the four is a member of the Alpha Delta Pi sorority. . . . FSU police spokesman Lt. Jack Handley would not comment directly on any of those subpoenaed. Handley said FSU police and the state attorney are continuing their investigation.
>
> "We spent a good part of today doing interviews," FSU police spokesman Lt. Jack Handley said. "We will be continuing tomorrow. We are obtaining new information

from those individuals. We hope to conclude this investigation in the near future." The latest subpoenas follow last week's grand jury investigation in which seven members of the fraternity and the fraternity adviser were summoned before the state grand jury. FSU officials, members of FSU police, and three female students went before the grand jury last week. . . .

The state grand jury released an interim report late Thursday claiming Pi Kappa Alpha members were "evasive" and "uncooperative" with investigating police and that "some evidence of witness intimidation existed." The grand jury is investigating the March 5 incident in which the woman was found abandoned in the hallway of the Theta Chi fraternity house with a "life-threatening" blood-alcohol level. Theta Chi was cleared of any wrongdoing in the incident but FSU police began an investigation in conjunction with the state attorney's office, which continues at this time.

The interim report said the woman testified that she met a Pi Kappa Alpha fraternity member whom she knew at the Late Night Library bottle club where she had been drinking beer and tequila. He invited her back to the third floor of the Pi Kappa Alpha house, she said. Her host then offered her a bottle of wine which she drank. At that point, she said, the fraternity member sexually assaulted her and she passed out.

The woman was found by FSU police at 5:30 a.m. on March 5 with bruises, scratches, and crude words and a fraternity symbol written on her thighs. Medical tests showed that she had been "sexually violated by more than one person."

One day after the grand jury released their report FSU officials suspended the fraternity pending a hearing to be held Wednesday at 2 p.m. But while the fate of the fraternity as a whole won't be decided until then, FSU police and the state attorney's office has been continuing its investigation. . . . The Pi Kappa Alpha fraternity will go before FSU officials in a hearing Wednesday. The charges specifically being directed at the fraternity are violations of two sections of the student code.

Those two sections read: "Obstructs or interferes with the reprimand, discipline, or apprehension of another person who is involved in the commission of an offense under this rule, Board of Regents rules, or Florida Statutes . . ." or "Intentionally acts to impair, interfere with or obstruct the orderly conduct, processes, and sanctions of the University."

This account was one in an ongoing series of articles that appeared in the *Florida Flambeau* and the *Tallahassee Democrat* describing a criminal episode that occurred in Tallahassee, Florida. Earlier articles described the criminal event that occurred in early March; later articles reported such developments as the expulsion of the Pi Kappa Alpha fraternity from the university and the arrest of several of its members and an out-of-town visitor on charges of sexual battery.

Crime Stories

The particular kind of episode described in these articles may not be common, but articles like these are. They are "crime stories." Such stories have several common characteristics.

First, they describe a single criminal episode. The sexual battery case described by the Tallahassee newspapers began on 5 March when a member of the Pi Kappa Alpha fraternity had illegal sexual contact with a woman whom he had invited to his fraternity house. It continued when some of his fraternity brothers also had illegal sexual contact with the women and then left her, unconscious, in another fraternity house.

Although the primary criminal event ended here, the criminal "episode" did not. Following the initial crime, the police were called and medical help was summoned. The police, the state attorney, and university authorities initiated investigations, both of the precipitating incident of sexual battery and of subsequent attempts by members of Pi Kappa Alpha fraternity to impede official investigations. Eventually a state grand jury was impaneled, people were arrested, trials were held, and at least one person went to prison.

The point is this: to the average citizen—to those who write crime stories for the newspaper as well as to those who read them—crimes are singular phenomena. They are not various violations of the law, as they might be to a legal scholar, nor are they a series of individual illegal acts committed by individual offenders, as they are to many criminologists. Rather, they are singular social episodes that happen in social time and space. As in the example cited here, individual criminal events can become chapters in longer criminal episodes involving protracted dealings with the criminal justice system and the community. Although their characterizations may change as new information or interpretations of events come to the fore, these episodes nevertheless retain a singularity over their entire life spans.

COMPONENTS OF CRIMINAL EPISODES

Criminal episodes may involve more than one violation of law (charge), more than one offender, more than one victim, and several law enforcement agencies. The sexual battery case described earlier began when the fraternity member offered alcoholic beverages to someone who already had been drinking and may well have had too much to drink. To offer alcohol to someone who is already drunk is a violation of law.

The case continued when the fraternity member had sex with the victim. Whether this sexual was an "assault," as the victim reported, is immaterial; having sex with someone who is too drunk to give informed consent is sexual battery according to Florida law. This, therefore, was the second violation of law. As additional fraternity brothers had sex with the victim, additional violations of law occurred and additional offenders entered the episode.

As the police and the university pursued the investigation, members of the Pi Kappa Alpha fraternity were uncooperative and tried to intimidate witnesses, which are violations of Florida law and university regulations. Indeed, as the episode continued to unfold, many agencies of social control became involved: the Tallahassee Police, the Florida State University Police, the state attorney, a grand jury, and a Florida State University hearing panel. Eventually, the court and the penal system were called on as well.

Overall, this one criminal episode (newspaper reporters would call it a "story;" the police and state attorney's office would call it a "case") included many violations of law, many offenders, several victims (including those who were "intimidated"), many witnesses, and several agencies of social control. In addition, it involved several newspaper reporters, writing several newspaper articles, read by thousands of Tallahassee residents.

The case illustrates the point that although criminal events usually occur at one rather well-defined time and place, they also usually have histories and ramifications that transcend the immediate events themselves. This means that a crime, in the broadest sense of the term, consists not only of an immediate illegal event (or events) but also of the forethought and human interactions that led up to the event and the considerable drama that often follows the event. In its fullest sense, then, a crime begins with planning and premeditation and ends with the administration of criminal justice (see Black 1989).

Interactions

Episodes of crime usually involve many elements. Most of these elements are persons or the things that persons do. More specifically, they are things that persons do to other persons. They are social interactions. Since criminal episodes involve human interaction, crimes (if crimes are defined as criminal episodes) are social phenomena, by definition. Although the actions of each individual actor in a criminal episode could be thought of, reasonably, as individual personal events, the episode itself is most reasonably thought of as a social phenomenon: a series of social interactions to which the actors, and others, give singular meaning.

Social interactions may be either overt or implicit (what sociologists would call "symbolic"). Overt interactions involve people acting in such a way that their actions affect the subsequent actions of other people. Having sex is an overt interaction. A symbolic interaction does not involve overt behavior; rather it involves "expectations." When one person alters his or her behavior because of what she or he thinks another person will do (or might do or should do), the two are engaging in "symbolic" interaction (Mead 1934). What the fraternity brother thought the woman in the bottle club would do, or "might do" or "had in mind," as he invited her to the fraternity house, in other words, probably played a role in what he and the other fraternity members did later.

Typification

There was no doubt in the mind of the newspaper reporter who wrote about the incident of sexual battery described previously that the incident was criminal. In other times or other places, it might not have been so categorized. Sex, per se, is not viewed as a crime by most people, and most residents of Tallahassee probably would not even consider sex between unmarried adults to be illegal, although some would consider it wrong.

What made this incident particularly noteworthy was the fact that more than one man had sex with the same woman on the same occasion and that the woman was too drunk to resist (or, indeed, even to say no). It was an incidence of rape according to Florida law. The event became a crime, however, not simply because it occurred but because members of the community in which it occurred viewed it as criminal. The incident became a rape, first, because the Florida legislature had defined these kinds of interactions as rape but also because the victim, the medical examiner, and the police depicted the event in such a way that it could not be construed as some lesser infraction, such as adultery or lascivious carriage, or as no infraction at all.

The newspaper article also went to some length to report that the offenders were members of a fraternity and that the victim was a sorority member. (Other articles noted that members of this particular fraternity had been in trouble with the law or with university authorities on other occasions.) This identified the principal actors in the drama as university students. Attempts by members of the fraternity to impede the investigation, as well as the university's appointment of a hearing panel, indicate how important the event was to the reputations of these organizations. Criminal episodes, then, depending on how they are depicted, may become matters of concern not only to offenders, victims, and agents of social control but to others in the community as well. How a crime is depicted, then, becomes an important component of the event itself.

CRIME, CRIMINALITY, AND CRIMINAL BEHAVIOR

As discussed earlier, classical criminologists referred to crimes as violations of law, whereas positivist criminologists used the term to describe certain forms of human behavior. The central contention of this chapter is that neither should be called a crime. Rather, each should be considered as a component of a crime. A violation of law, more commonly referred to as a charge or an offense, is a particular kind of interaction between a person and a crime target that is proscribed by law. Criminal behavior is the proscribed action on the part of the offender.

Victims and Targets of Crime

It is useful to distinguish between a crime target and a crime victim. The *target* of a crime is what an offender wants. The *victim* of a crime is the person, persons, or institutions that are harmed by the crime, because they either own the target, as in the case of burglary, or are the target, as in the case of sexual battery.

Not all crimes have a victim. Indeed, criminologists use the special category "victimless crimes" for these kinds of offenses (see Schur 1965).

It would appear, however, that all crimes have a target. The target of a drug crime is drugs. The target of assault is another person. The target of theft is money or property. The victim, in this latter case, is the owner of the crime target. In the case of drugs, there is no victim, per se.

Including a victim in the definition of a crime would be a mistake because it would imply, first, that the presence of a victim is inherent in the "nature" of crime and, second, that crimes are inherently "predatory." The fact that some societies have made things such as gambling and drug use illegal attests to the fact that neither the presence of a human victim nor predation are necessary prerequisite for societies to deem certain activities to be criminal.

Including a victim as part of the conception of crime also has the effect of obscuring the various, and quite different, roles that victims may play in criminal episodes. Not only is the victim the aggrieved party, as in theft or assault, but often he or she is the person who reports the crime to the police and sometimes also may act, independent of the police, as an agent of social control.

Agents of Social Control

Until the development of the modern state, responsibility for crime control rested primarily with the crime victim or the victim's kin. There were no police, no lawyers, no full-time judges, and no prisons. If a party were aggrieved, it was that party's responsibility to secure amends (see Kittrie 1971).

In modern societies, formal agencies of crime control—police, courts, prisons—perform many of these functions. This does not mean, of course, that victims play no role in controlling crime. Owners of property, for example, contribute significantly to whether their property is stolen by where they locate it and how well they guard it (Kleck 1988). Similarly, people increase or decrease the risk of being assaulted by where they go and what they do (Cohen, Kluegel, and Land 1981).

When discussing crime control in modern societies, it is necessary to differentiate between individual, private control, usually administered by the victim or the potential victim, and public control, administered by agencies of the state. Those who administer the former are often referred to as "informal agents of social control" and the latter as "formal agents of social control" (or as law enforcement agents or officers of the law). Given that Americans spend more money each year on private than on public protection (Cook 1986: 10–14), informal social control is probably more important than formal, state control.

STUDYING CRIME

From the point of view put forth in this chapter, a theory of criminal behavior is not the same thing as a theory of criminal episodes. Since criminal behavior is only one of several elements that make up criminal episodes, knowing why such behavior occurs is not the same thing as knowing why criminal episodes occur. Crimes, in other words, occur for several reasons, only some of which involve offenders.

Criminologists, therefore, should be very precise when they specify which aspects of criminal episodes their particular theory applies to. Is it a theory of law, criminality, criminal behavior, criminal events, or criminal episodes? Although a comprehensive theory of criminal episodes—that is, a comprehensive theory of crime—will include theories of law, criminal behavior, and criminality, it will also include theories of criminal opportunity and theories of social control.

This chapter does not propose such a comprehensive theory. Such a proposal, at this time, is surely premature; criminology does not yet know enough about each of the components of criminal episodes, let alone the interactions among the components, to develop a comprehensive theory of crime.

Nevertheless, the conception of crime outlined here may be a useful guide for studying crime. It should direct attention to questions not addressed by conventional criminological theories and raise doubts about some of the assumptions concerning the nature of crime and the nature of social control employed by policymakers. If the chapter does these two things, it will have accomplished its mission.

Prospects for Theoretical Integration

Conceptualizing "crime" as social episodes opens new avenues for investigation and provides a mechanism by which the several seemingly disparate (and sometimes quarreling) schools of criminology might be united. The conceptualization is quite consistent with labeling theory, critical criminology, economic theory, and opportunity theory; indeed, it grew in part from each of these traditions. The conceptualization is consistent also with the more traditional American positivist approach in that it acknowledges that the criminality of offenders is one component of criminal episodes.

To say that the conception of crimes as social episodes is consistent with each of these different criminological traditions, however, does not resolve the theoretical differences among them. It does not, for example, resolve the conflict between economic (or classical) theory, which assumes that differences in the propensity of individuals to commit crimes (criminality) is unimportant when it comes to explaining variations in crime rates, and traditional positivist criminology, which assumes that these differences can account for essentially all such variation. Rather, the conception leaves the question open.

Nevertheless, by acknowledging that crimes involve both the actions of offenders and the actions (or potential actions) of agents of social control, the conception implies that both of these factors probably have a causal role to play in crime. In the same way, by acknowledging that crimes also involve crime targets, the conception implies that characteristics of potential crime targets (how many there are, what they are worth, how well they are guarded, etc.) also play a causal role in crime. The conception implies, in other words, that variations in crime rates, across social time and social space, cannot be explained fully by knowing how inclined people are to commit crimes, how effective agents of social control are in deterring them, or how many opportunities there are to commit crimes; rather, variations in crime, which involve each of these factors (and perhaps others) will be explained well only if all are taken into account in a single model.

No school of criminology presently offers such a comprehensive model. Indeed, different schools of criminology still focus on different aspects of crime. Traditional American positivist criminologists, including Gottfredson and Hirschi, focus on offenders. Opportunity theorists focus on crime targets. Critical criminologists focus on the law. Economic theorists focus on applications of the law. Labeling theorists focus on the consequences of these applications. This does not mean that these different approaches to criminology are incompatible; it means only that they have been studying different aspects of crime. What now needs to be done is to integrate these various approaches.

Conceiving of crimes as social episodes is one means by which these different branches of criminology might be brought together. If crimes are thought to include the actions of rule makers, rule enforcers, offenders, and victims, then the work of criminologists who have been investigating these different aspects of crime all become legitimate parts of an integrated explanation of crime. If crimes are thought of more narrowly, as they have been in the past, there is no compelling reason that these different points of view should be combined.

REFERENCES

Becker, Gary. 1968. "Crime and Punishment: An Economic Approach." *Journal of Political Economy* 78:169–217.

Beccaria, Cesare. [1764] 1963. *Essay on Crimes and Punishments*. Indianapolis: Bobbs-Merrill.

Biderman, Albert D. 1966. "Social Indicators and Goals." In *Social Indicators*, ed. R. A. Bauer. Cambridge: MIT Press.

Black, Donald. 1989. *Sociological Justice*. New York: Oxford University Press.

Boggs, Sarah L. 1965. "Urban Crime Patterns." *American Sociological Review* 30: 899–908.

Cohen, Albert. 1985. "An Offense-Centered Approach to Criminological Theory." In *Victimology: International Action and Study of Victims*, ed. Zvonimir P. Separovic Zagreb, Yugoslavia: n.p. (Papers given at the Fifth International Symposium on Victimology.)

Cohen, Lawrence E., James R. Kluegel, and Kenneth Land. 1981. "Social Inequality and Predatory Criminal Victimization: An Exposition and Test of a Formal Theory." *American Sociological Review* 46: 505–24.

Cook, Philip J. 1986. "The Demand and Supply of Criminal Opportunities." In *Crime and Justice: An Annual Review of Research*, vol. 7, ed. Michael Tonry and Norval Morris. Chicago: University of Chicago Press.

Ehrlich, Isaac. 1981. "On the Usefulness of Controlling Individuals: An Economic Analysis of Rehabilitation, Incapacitation, and Deterrence." *American Economic Review* 71: 307–22.

Felson, Marcus. 1987. "Routine Activities and Crime Prevention in the Developing Metropolis." *Criminology* 25: 911–31.

Fineout, Gary. 1989. "Court Might Extradite Victim in Pike Rape Case." *Florida Flambeau*, 28 September, 1ff.

Gottfredson, Michael, and Travis Hirschi. 1988. "A Propensity–Event Theory of Crime." In *Advances in Criminological Theory*, vol. 1, ed. William S. Laufer and Freda Adler. New Brunswick, N.J.: Transaction.

———. 1990 *A General Theory of Crime*. Stanford, Calif.: Stanford University Press.

Gould, Leroy C. 1969. "Who Defines Delinquency: A Comparison of Self-Reported and Officially-Reported Indices of Delinquency for Three Racial Groups." *Social Problems* 16: 325–36.

———. 1971. "Crime and Its Impact in an Affluent Society." In *Crime and Justice in American Society*, ed. Jack Douglas. Indianapolis: Bobbs-Merrill.

Hirschi, Travis, and Michael Gottfredson. 1987. "Causes of White-Collar Crime." *Criminology* 25: 949–74.

———.1986. "The Distinction between Crime and Criminality." In *Critique and Explanation: Essays in Honor of Gwynn Nettler*, ed. Timothy F. Hartnagel and Robert Silverman. New Brunswick, N.J.: Transaction.

Jeffery, Clarence Ray. [1959] 1960. "The Historical Development of Criminology." In *Pioneers in Criminology*, ed. Hermann Mannheim. Montclair, N.J.: Patterson Smith.

Kittrie, Nicholas N. 1971. *The Right to be Different*. Baltimore: Johns Hopkins University Press.

Kleck, Gary. 1988. "Crime Control through the Private Use of Armed Force." *Social Problems* 35: 1–21.

Kleck, Gary, and Miriam DeLone. 1991. *Victim Resistance and Offender Weapon Effects in Robbery*. Tallahassee: Florida State University School of Criminology and Criminal Justice.

Kleck, Gary, and Susan Sayles. 1990. "Rape and Resistance." *Social Problems* 37: 149–62.

Luckenbill, David F. 1977. "Criminal Homicide as a Situated Transaction." *Social Problems* 25: 176–86.

———. 1982. "Compliance under Threat of Severe Punishment." *Social Forces* 60: 811–25.

Mansfield, Roger, Leroy C. Gould, and J. Zvi Namenwirth. 1974. "A Socioeconomic Model for the Prediction of Societal Rates of Property Theft." *Social Forces* 52: 462–72.

Matza, David. 1964. *Delinquency and Drift*. New York: Wiley.

Mead, George Herbert. 1934. *Mind, Self, and Society*. Chicago: University of Chicago Press.

Schur, Edwin. 1965. *Crimes without Victims*. Englewood Cliffs, N.J.: Prentice Hall.

Stark, Rodney. 1987. "Deviant Places: A Theory of the Ecology of Crime." *Criminology* 25: 893–909.

Wilkins, Leslie T. 1964. *Social Deviance*. London: Tavistock.

Wilson, James Q., and Richard J. Herrnstein. 1985. *Crime and Human Nature*. New York: Simon & Schuster.

Wolfgang, Marvin. 1957. "Victim-Precipitated Criminal Homicide." *Journal of Criminal Law, Criminology, and Police Science* 58: 317–24.

Ziegenhagen, Edward A., and Dolores Brosan. 1985. "Victim Responses to Robbery and Crime Control Policy." *Criminology* 23: 675–95.

7

Defining Crime in a Community Setting: Negotiation and Legitimation of Community Claims

Paul Schnorr

The definition of the social problem of crime within a community involves many claims and counterclaims by a variety of actors. These actors include community residents, community business owners, community organizations, police, and in some cases external institutional actors. The types of claims are influenced by the position of the actor, both as perceived by the actor and as other actors in the network of interaction perceive the actor. This chapter analyzes the negotiation of crime problems in an urban community area I will call Waltersville. This analysis will reveal that claims making about crime in the community is a complex process reflecting the class and status of the various actors involved. Claims making by lower-class community members reflects their position in an asymmetrical power structure favoring police definitions of crime problems. The analysis illustrates that the legitimation of citizen definitions of crime problems often depends on using institutional resources external to the community.

Crime, drug and alcohol abuse, poor education, environmental hazards, and so forth, have fluid status as "social problems." Growing, producing, selling, and using narcotic drugs only becomes criminal with the passage of specific laws regulating certain substances. Perceptions and regulation of alcohol production and use in American society has gone through phases of criminal status. The very definition of "legally drunk" continues to vary from state to state. The level of skills below which one is poorly educated changes as the economy and society evolve to demand more skills. And illegal dumping of hazardous chemical waste was once a common, accepted practice. In other words, social problems are more than objective conditions. Conditions or situations must be labeled as problematic *and* that definition must be accepted and enforced by legitimate authority before those conditions will be perceived as social problems. Furthermore, different individuals and groups have stakes in what conditions are defined as problematic. Hence, the definition of social problems is often a contested social process.

When introducing their model of the construction of social problems, Spector and Kitsuse (1987: 76–77) state:

> Our definition of social problems focuses on the process by which members of a society define a putative condition as a social problem. Thus, we define social problems as the activities of individuals or groups making assertions of grievances and claims with respect to some putative conditions. The emergence of a social problem is contingent upon the organization of activities asserting the need for eradicating, ameliorating, or otherwise changing some condition. The central problem for a theory of social problems is to account for the emergence, nature and maintenance of claims-making and responding activities.

This theoretical model concentrates on interactions involved in claims-making activity. Therefore, the definition of social problems may be identified in the negotiation of different subjective viewpoints of putative conditions. In reference to the definition of a crime problem, the claims made by groups of community residents reflect their perception of conditions they define as crime problems. The residents' interactions with police, who may have a quite different perception of the conditions in reference to crime, are the essential elements in the construction of the social problem of crime for that community. Therefore, the primary focus of the construction of the crime problem is not to identify objective conditions as crime problems but to concentrate on the assertions and counterassertions about putative criminal conditions in the community.

A second aspect of the claims-making model concerns the mechanisms of interaction employed by claimants.

> The fate of a claim may depend heavily on the channels through which it is pressed, the strategies used to achieve visibility of the imputed condition, and the auxiliary personnel who play a part in this process. Identifying the audience to which the complaint should be addressed is one important stage in the complaining process. If the groups complain to the wrong party they may get no results . . . or directions as to where they properly should go . . . long chains of referrals and buck-passing may occur with no organization willing to accept jurisdiction over the complaint. (Spector and Kitsuse 1987: 145)

Successful claims making is contingent on the channels through which interaction takes place. Claims making as an interaction is heavily dependent on a consensual agreement by both parties that a given mechanism of interaction is an appropriate channel for particular claims. Possibilities for a breakdown in this consensus are numerous. When channeling claims about putative crime problems, community residents often must use mechanisms constructed and controlled by a highly bureaucratic municipal, state, or federal government. If these channels are for narrow institutionally defined claims, the assertions of the claimant may be outside the bounds of acceptable claims. In this case the interaction will break down. For example, a call to 911 about a stripped, abandoned car may receive no response because the 911 number is designated as a channel to communicate emergency situations. Similarly, what appears to be a well-founded claim may go unrecognized or be ignored if complainant mechanisms are not treated as legitimate by respondent institutions or groups. For example, charges of police harassment emerging from a meeting of street gang leaders may be ignored because the police do not perceive the meeting of these individuals as a legitimate forum to discuss police behavior. Therefore, the study of the construction of social problems urges analyzing the mechanisms of interaction as well as the claims themselves.

A further complication in the construction of social problems is that often there is not simply dyadic interaction. Complex webs of interaction are involved in the construction of the social problem of crime in a community setting: community residents make claims about certain groups making it unsafe to walk the streets; community businesses make claims that different groups frighten away customers; external actors such as universities and citywide crime control agencies act as "moral entrepreneurs" (Becker 1963) claiming that community residents can live in a safer environment; and police make claims that they cannot stop people from being on the streets. The different personal and institutional interests of these actors will shape their claims and be reflected in the negotiations on crime problems.

The negotiation of the various actors in the definition of crime problems also reflects the actors' class and status. The police have the power to define how claims about crime problems are to be presented.[1] Individuals and groups may not understand the claims-making apparatus. Particularly, claims making by lower-class groups may be hampered by a lack of experience in dealing with complex bureaucratic systems. Also, deference of granted legitimacy in interaction is offered to actors presenting a demeanor deemed worthy of recognition by other parties (Goffman 1956). Lower-class individuals may not present themselves in ways taken seriously by avenues of potential redress.

Because the police often do not take seriously the claims of crime and disorder made by lower-class community residents, external actors can be very important in defining social problems within impoverished communities. The media, universities, and other interest groups can shape the assertions of community residents into forms that police recognize. Also, influence in allocation or control of monetary and nonmonetary resources by external actors may serve as a tool for legitimation of lower-class claimants. Furthermore, the possibility of exposés offering negative information on the response of police to community claims holds the potential of negative sanction for police. Likewise, the potential also exists for withdrawal of externally supplied capital resources to the police if the police are perceived by external actors as unresponsive to community claims. Therefore, police are sensitive to external actors, and external actors are important in the web of interaction defining community crime problems.

The claims-making model of the definition of social problems must be understood as embedded in a complex web of claimant interests. These interests are not just to claim that some putative condition is harmful but also to represent interests in negotiating a position of legitimacy so claims will be recognized. The positioning of actors to make legitimate claims is essential if claims are to be taken seriously. In short, what is at stake for police, community residents, and external actors is not just the definition of crime problems but also the status as legitimate claims makers about crime.

THE METHOD

The data for this chapter were gathered over five months in association with an experiment in crime mapping funded by the National Institute of Justice (NIJ). The data on community residents and businesspeople were gathered at four meetings set up by the Waltersville Community Organization (WCO). These meetings focused on issues of crime in the local community. A crime-mapping workshop conducted by the Metro Alliance for Neighborhood Safety (MANS) in conjunction with the NIJ project also provided data reflecting community perceptions of crime problems. I interviewed the executive director of WCO and the crime prevention coordinator at WCO and gathered field notes from observation of a block club meeting and CB patrol conducted by WCO.[2] Much of the data reflecting police perceptions of crime are from a MANS-initiated meeting with police commanders and detectives to discuss a particular crime problem in the Waltersville community. I also used other researchers' interviews with patrol officers and detectives to understand more clearly the perspective of local police workers in the Waltersville community.[3]

I am using an explicitly interactionist framework for understanding the social process of defining crime in Waltersville. This conceptualization of social problems as claims-making activity necessarily relies on interaction because "claims-making is always a form of interaction" (Spector and Kitsuse 1987: 78). I will concentrate on the interactions or verbal accounts of interactions of claims making among the various community actors. I will also discuss the mechanisms of interaction to understand the role they play in channeling claims.

The first section of the chapter discusses the actors involved in the claims-making activity in the Waltersville community. The second section of the chapter analyzes the nature of the claims and counterclaims made by various actors, claims about perceived conditions as well as claims to negotiate positions of legitimacy in relation to other actors. The third section of the chapter concentrates on the channels and mechanisms used by various actors as they attempt to define the problem of crime in the community. Finally, focus is on one particular case of claims about a "crime problem" presented to the police and responded to and perceived by some community resident and business claimants to have been resolved. I argue that the presence of university researchers controlling significant new technological resources influenced the behavior of police by providing information in a form that police found hard to dismiss. Furthermore, the police were sensitive to the researchers because these actors could significantly affect the perception of the police while influencing future allocation of resources to the police department.

THE ACTORS

The primary actors in the negotiation of crime problems in the Waltersville area were community residents, community businesspeople, WCO, police, and NIJ-sponsored institutions (Northwestern University, MANS, and the University of Illinois at Chicago). The actors had individual and institutional interests shaping their perception of situations. These interests emerged in their claims about crime problems in the community. What was defined as crime by one group was defined as a social problem, or no problem at all, by other actors. The embedded interests of each group in the negotiation process are essential to understanding the dynamics defining crime in Waltersville.

The most numerous actors were the community residents. Waltersville residents were racially mixed, but the transition from all white to an uneasy patchwork of blocked integration occurred very rapidly. Between 1966 and 1973, residential blocks changed over from all white to virtually all black at a rate of 37.5 per year (Taub, Taylor, and Dunham 1984). By the time of this study, 1988, this high transition rate had slowed, but many of the whites who remained were too poor to leave, and many of the African Americans moving into Waltersville did not have resources to move out of the community, either. At one block club meeting, a resident said, "Let's face it—this is the last of the last. Unless you win the lottery, this is where we are going to be. We have to make it work here. There is nowhere else to go." It may not be true that all the residents felt trapped in the community, but many residents' choices about whether or where to move were severely constrained by their lower-class status. Therefore, as the man speaking here put it, they had an interest "to make it work" in Waltersville.

What exactly does this mean, "to make it work"? In his study of black street-corner men, Liebow (1967) found that lower-class individuals value and aspire to what can be called traditional American values—a home, a family, a decent income, safety, and a future for their children. Stack (1974) also found that what middle-class observers see as disorder and instability in low-income communities reflects not different values but adaptive behavior in the face of structural barriers to opportunity and self-sufficiency. The executive director of WCO offered a similar portrait of the values and desires of Waltersville residents: "The people in this area are basically working poor . . . except for ethnicity [they] are about the same. They most want the same things: to keep their houses, to send their kids to school." The residents of Waltersville also held "middle-class values" about personal safety. They wanted Waltersville to be safe to walk the streets, and they wanted to come and go from their house without worrying about muggers, rapists, or even panhandlers. These expectations fueled resident's claims about crime in the Waltersville community.

The businesspeople in the Waltersville community also held what most would perceive as reasonable expectations in relation to running a business. Put simply, they wanted to operate without worrying about being held up, shoplifted from, or assaulted. Likewise, they felt that patrons should not be afraid to approach their business because customers think it dangerous to do so. The business conditions in Waltersville often did not live up to these expectations. For example, two business owners recounted this episode at a local convenience store:

> *Jim:* When I was in there [a local convenience store], there was a guy wrestlin' with one of the employees and another guy swinging around a broken bottle. Finally one of the other workers went and got a baseball bat and had to hit the guy.
>
> *Sue:* It's really hard to run a business when that kind of thing is going on . . . we are trying to cut down on the shopliftin' . . . we make people leave their shopping bags at the door . . . we only let five [people] in at a time at night. It used to be that winos would come in and drink our beer in the store.

The conditions in the convenience store may be extreme, but when we accompanied MANS and WCO workers in distributing crime report forms to businesses, six of the seven we visited immediately recounted a recent criminal incident. The businesspeople in Waltersville made their claims regarding crime problems based on their interest in wanting to operate without constant criminal interference.

The Waltersville Community Organization represented a more complex set of interests. First, the employees were residents of Waltersville who aspired to make the neighborhood better. In my interviews with several of the employees and my observation of the activities of WCO, there was evidence of a sincere desire to help the community of Waltersville in whatever way possible. It can be assumed that the employees of WCO, as residents, felt that a safer neighborhood is a better neighborhood. Therefore, the employees of WCO had a personal interest in making Waltersville safer.

Beyond their individual interests, the employees of WCO also represented the institutional interests of the community organization. A primary interest of most community organizations is survival; WCO was no different. This interest meant scrambling for resources and attempting to apply them so as to appear viable to funding agencies.[4] The perception of crime in Waltersville was necessary for WCO to have a legitimate reason to continue operations. As I will illustrate, WCO's interest in having the perception of crime kept alive in Waltersville was reflected in their claims-making activity.

External actors participating in the definition of Waltersville's crime problems represented some similar interests to those of WCO. On the one hand, academic researchers researching crime have a stake in defining crime in terms that lend them legitimacy and continued funding for future research. In other words, the academics working in Waltersville wanted to define crime as an issue within the realm of their disciplinary knowledge and as something they have a continuing responsibility to study. But on another level, the representatives of MANS, Northwestern, and the University of Illinois at Chicago were moral entrepreneurs (Becker 1963) who felt that somehow "improve[ing] the crime analysis capabilities of police and community organizations"[5] would make life better in the Waltersville community. Individuals representing these organizations were expressing humanitarian motives with an interest in reforming the crime situation in Waltersville through altered analysis techniques. These motives were formalized and institutionalized into a research agenda that included research "objectives." Regardless of the value position behind those "objectives," the researchers also had an interest in accomplishing those objectives to make future funding more likely.

The final actors in the definition of the crime problem in Waltersville were the police. The successful definition of social problems by the community depended on their claims being recognized and legitimated by parties capable of altering a perceived situation. Crime control in America is under the jurisdiction of the police. Therefore, community claims of crime problems were perceived (correctly or incorrectly) as problems to be addressed by the police. Which claims of community residents and the type and degree of response to those claims was a function of police perceptions of crime problems and police perceptions of their duties. Several factors played a role in how the police define their duties and consequently their responses to assertions of crime problems by the community.

The police are a long established agency for dealing with crime problems. "Agencies have their own idea of the work they are authorized to do and the clientele who can legitimately demand their services" (Spector and Kitsuse 1987: 83). Formally, as a public agency, the police are obligated to serve all clients. However, as Lipsky (1980) points out, public agencies exercise considerable discretion in client selection and treatment. Police departments have formal guidelines of institutional responsibility to guide some of the interactions between police and citizens. However, the individual discretion of commanders, officers, and dispatchers pervades police definitions of crime problems. Skolnick (1975: iii) summarizes well the nature of discretion in police work:

The legal order is popularly envisioned as the most formally normative of all social organizations because it contains a codified and carefully interpreted body of rules. But, in practice, it continues to be a highly discretionary order at every level, mediated by subtle, sometimes unarticulated, yet discernible norms held by actors in the system. Consequently, the administration of criminal justice in America is still best understood as an ironical phenomenon expressed in the contradiction between a context of formal written rules, interpretations, and practices mediated by subjective values, perceived organizational needs, and a continuing drama of human personalities and aspirations.

The "subjective values" and "perceived organizational needs" greatly influenced the claims making of police when interacting with citizens about crime in Waltersville.

CLAIMS-MAKING ACTIVITY

Two types of claims-making activity occurred in the Waltersville community: claims to define the problem of crime; and claims to negotiate positions of legitimacy in the eyes of other actors. Assertions of the first type—to define problems—were of little consequence if they were not perceived to be emanating from legitimate sources. Without perceived legitimacy, an actor's claims making was not part of an interaction but simply futile action on the part of the claimant. Analysis of claims making, therefore, requires attention to the context and intent of claims made by the actors to determine the claimant's goals.

Citizen Claims of Crime

Most of the data reflecting community claims of crime problems in Waltersville were collected at WCO-sponsored meetings that were called for the expressed purpose of discussing crime problems. Two of these meetings were attended by MANS personnel attempting to apply the NIJ mapping project to crime reporting in the Waltersville area. These meetings functioned as a forum for individuals to present claims about what they perceived as problems. Many of the assertions by citizens at these meetings were diffuse claims that certain groups in Waltersville were contributing to crime problems. Groups asserted to be causing trouble were as follows:

"People from Project Housing"

We got people movin' from ___ ___ . . . these—I call them kids—but they is eighteen and nineteen years old [and are] movin' in around here. They don't know how to do nothin' but be purse-snatchers.

"Drug Dealers"

One of the problems we have is that this area is very concentrated with drugs now. We have always had them, but it seems that people are getting busted in the south and they are renting apartments here and sending the kids out to deal for them.

"Ethnics"

[T]hose Spanish people, they sit out in front of their houses and drink beer all the time. In the winter they just throw bottles out of the house, but in the summer they will be out in front of the house drinking a case of beer every night and throwing the bottles on the lawn.

Residents made assertions that these people contributed to the social problem of crime in their neighborhood. Spector and Kitsuse (1987: 83) state, "The more vague the sense of dissatisfaction, the less able is the group to affix responsibility or propose remedies for its discontent." But in fact the sense of dissatisfaction was not vague. The "kids," "people getting busted in the south," and "Spanish people" were asserted to be committing crime. What *was* difficult was attributing *direct* responsibility in these statements of "fact." Stereotypical generalizations (founded or unfounded) offer a diffuse sense of responsibility. However, construction of claims that allowed police response was difficult with such general attribution of responsibility for these "crime problems."

Other claims by residents revolved around conditions they "knew" existed:

Drugs

There is more dope pushed on Wilson and 12th in a four block area than in all the rest of Waltersville. I know it, you know it, why don't they do something about it. . . . I know people who are buying their drugs in the same place now as they were six months ago . . . they all know where it's at—Harris Liquor.

Prostitution

There is a U-Haul trailer parked down the block where prostitutes are working.

Gangs

The garages in our neighborhood have been graffitied . . . and these people are calling themselves "The Kings."

These situations were asserted to exist and to be part of the crime problem. These more pointed claims could yield defined remedies. These claims, however, were made to WCO and MANS personnel and not to the police. There was assertion, but not interaction with the potential response institution of the police. The fate of these claims, therefore, was dependent on whether and/or how they were presented to the police.

An important aspect of the claims-making activity in the Waltersville community area was that "the community" was not homogeneous in its interests or its claims. An illustration of the different interests represented in the community concerns perceptions of an objective condition as a crime of different severity. A WCO worker, when commenting on the problem of shoplifting, did not severely condemn certain types of shoplifting: "Some of these people [shoplifters] have no money and they will be taking loaves of bread and stuff. That's not so bad. . . . If they steal a loaf of bread they [the businesses] aren't out that much." From the point of view of the business owners in the community, however, shoplifting was an acute crime problem. Though the following comment was made in jest, it illustrates some businesspeople's views: "I think we should do like in Iran, Saudi Arabia, and China. If someone is on drugs, they can shoot 'em in the street." Someone else chimed in, "I think we should shoot shoplifters, too." Different individuals within the same community have different interests. Consequently, the same objective situation may be viewed very differently by those different individuals.

Waltersville Community Organization Claims

Perhaps the diffuse nature of citizen claims about who was responsible for crime reflected the forums in which I heard them expressed. After all, a meeting about crime problems is when people will generalize, while, if somebody is breaking into your car, you will attempt to notice more particular features and report these to the police. Regardless of the forum, however, the citizens of Waltersville seemed to feel that crime was a constant problem. That feeling translated into ambiguous claims making also: people "are sending kids out to deal for them." When? Or, "they sit out in front of their houses and drink beer all the time." How often is "all the time"? While this type of claims making created problems for police response, the shared sense of constant threat diminished the sense of ambiguity of these claims for citizens. Furthermore, the shared belief and understanding of these claims allowed citizens to feel legitimate in their collective claims of crime. By asserting that there was "a lot" of crime and asserting that certain situations happen "all the time," they truly believed that the police were ignoring their responsibility. Citizens used these ambiguous claims—which, because of their ambiguity, were difficult to refute—to establish for themselves a subjective feeling of legitimacy for making their claims.

WCO, on the other hand, was consciously mobilizing around those diffuse and ambiguous claims to legitimize their operations. As an organization, WCO focused on crime because of the perceived "durability" of crime in Waltersville. The executive director of WCO made this clear:

> [T]here are other things, housing—it was a big thing and it is getting big again. Then there is education. People are always saying that the education can be better,

but there are private schools around and people can deal with it. But what do you do with crime? There are some people who don't ever go out anymore and the business strip shows it. People used to go for walks, but they don't do that anymore. They used to sit on the front porch, now they sit inside. . . . They used to go for a walk to get a beer or a sundae. Most people cite crime as the reason they don't do it anymore.

WCO needed an issue to organize around. The perception of crime in the community was expected to prevail, partially because of the ambiguous citizen claims that made police response difficult. Simply listening to the claims from citizens and then forwarding those claims to the police, as ambiguous as they may have been, legitimized WCO's continued operation in the eyes of citizens. Therefore, many of WCO's claims resembled those of citizens.

Police Claims of Crime

Police claims making about crime in Waltersville can best be understood through their response when confronted with the claims of the community residents and businesspeople. Within the heterogeneous Waltersville community there was no shortage of claims made to the police about situations perceived to be crime problems. Police responses (or lack of response) to citizen claims were essentially assertions by the police of their definition of crime problems. Several elements were evident in the response of police to citizen claims: the police perceptions of their power in defining crime problems, the formal bureaucratic nature of the police as an institution, and the view that police are individual "street-level bureaucrats" (Lipsky 1980) interacting with the public.

The position of the police as enforcers of the law gave them a position of power in defining crime problems in Waltersville. The police perceived themselves as legitimate in their definition of crime problems because they were commissioned to be professionals responding to codified definitions of criminal situations. Formally, police are commissioned to enforce the laws protecting citizens and maintain order in society. However, as Skolnick (1975) points out, enforcing the "law" and maintaining "order" are often incompatible. In questions of law and order, the police can legitimately respond to violations of law and still leave plenty of disorder, particularly if the situations perceived to cause the disorder are not in direct violation of law.

This perceived disorder, or incivility (Hunter 1978), is viewed by police as an illustration of social problems, but not crime problems. Claims made about crime problems often can be dismissed as other social problems by the police. For example, the following is a discussion of a crime "hotspot" among several high-level police officers in Waltersville:

> Smith: What it appears that we have here is a fear of crime which the people hanging out at these places inspires.

Olson: It's a perceived thing. If I walk into a 7-11 and there are six guys standing there playing video games, it makes me nervous. . . .

Jones: The people here are looking to the police to solve a social problem. I'm not sure it is ours to solve. All we can do is listen to their requests. If its reasonable, we can allocate resources; if not, we will have to say it does not represent that great a police problem. This is certainly not a gross police problem. Maybe they need to get in touch with other city agencies. It's a social problem which maybe the police can help with.

Given the guidelines of law, it is correct that the kids hanging out are not a police problem. However, citizens, particularly the workers at the 7-11, were making claims that these kids were part of the crime problem in Waltersville. Those kids were not, however, a part of the crime problems deemed by police to be within their jurisdiction. This is a situation of disorder not under the jurisdiction of law. If a police officer were to position himself inside the 7-11, the kids may be intimidated into leaving. But that approach would require manpower, and because the police were in a position to define situations constituting crime problems and allocate their resources to those situations, they did not want to include "kids hanging out" as a crime problem.

A second factor reflected in police's response to citizen claims of crime problems is the bureaucratic organization of police work. Police officers operate within a highly bureaucratic organization emphasizing managerial efficiency and ongoing operations (Skolnick 1975). Police work is measured through solved crimes, not prevented crimes—a reactive rather than a proactive stance. In the ideal world, detectives would know where crimes were going to occur, make themselves present at the scene, and thereby prevent all crime. This is not the way crime works, nor would those detectives go far in current police work. These detectives would be addressing crime problems, but not in a way measurable by standards of police work as currently organized. A situation defined by police as criminal is prerequisite to police action and potential organizational recognition of "work" done. Olson, the district commander in Waltersville explained this point of view:

Jim: Part of the problem which we heard from the people at 7-11 is the shoplifting and people hanging out. . . .

Olson: Shoplifting is a crime which we really don't handle. We aren't proactive. We don't arrest shoplifters; we get them after the fact. We don't patrol for them.

This evaluative system of the police work alters their response to community claims of situations defined as crime problems. Citizen claims of potentially criminal situations are not addressed because that is not the way police work is organized.

A third important factor reflected in the police responses to citizen claims of crime problems is that police are individual street-level bureaucrats. Regardless of the formally outlined police responsibility to serve all people equally, individual police must make compromises on formal agency goals (Lipsky 1980). Individual police officers have the discretion to impose their values when interpreting the law and defining what will be treated as a crime problem. This discretion means that, depending on where the same objective situation occurs, the police may choose to act or not act and therefore make similar behavior a "crime" or not. For example, police will often turn their head away from consumption of alcoholic beverages in parks during large festivals. Anyone who has attended a Grateful Dead concert knows that the police are not actively enforcing laws against using various controlled substances. These are situational acceptances of widespread behavior that police simply may not feel they can control. In other words, the police feel that given the people involved in the situation, certain behaviors that would otherwise be defined as "crime" are allowed. The standard of "order" in this case includes criminal behavior.

The police working in Waltersville appeared to believe that Waltersville was an area with a higher threshold of social disorder than many communities, because most of Waltersville residents were poor blacks and most of the police were whites living outside the neighborhood. In fact, the police blamed the victims of many crimes in Waltersville by asserting that "everybody" knows that if you are in Waltersville, you should take extra precautions or simply not be there. Lipsky (1980: 152) points out that blaming the victim is a way of absolving the police from blame by shifting responsibility for the claimants' problem. However, police blaming the victim may not necessarily be a conscious police indictment of the claimant. From the police's perspective, blaming the victim is often seen as simply giving advice for commonsense measures to prevent crime. For example, at a forum of police and community members, a police officer made the following statement:

> [Robberies] are typically crimes of opportunity—like smash and grabs. We need to educate the victims. We had one woman who called and said that she had been robbed at the same intersection three times. Well, she would pull up to the stop light with her purse on the front seat. . . . Now, the real question is why, after the first time, she didn't put it under the seat where it should have been.

Placing a purse out of sight is common sense if one perceives the presence of potential criminals. The "common sense" assumes that residents will label those in the community as criminals and perceive that citizens must protect themselves. However, community residents may not perceive their neighbors as criminals. It is questionable whether the police response would be the same if the complainant lived in a "good" part of town or a "safe" suburb.

Blaming the victim may be more extensive than the simple giving of advice illustrated above. Some individual police use the "triaging" that Lipsky (1980: 106) discusses in determination of where to allocate resources. In this case, the police "bureaucrat" may blame complainants for living in an area perceived to be so bad that the area does not warrant expected police service. The executive director of WCO gave the following account reflecting claims illustrating this triaging effect:

> They [the police] have to get to know the people in the neighborhood. Now, black or white, they talk to our women like trash, the kids are all treated like gang-bangers, the young girls are all tramps. For example, . . . my daughter . . . was running and four blacks grabbed her and beat her up . . . . When she was talking to the police to report it, they said that it wouldn't do any good to look for them because she would never recognize them anyway because she was white. . . .Then a sergeant from the detectives tells me, "it's your own fault. If you want to live with animals, we don't have to protect you." . . . One time I was mugged and this big policeman shows up here to talk to me and he says, "Was it a pork chop or a nigger?" . . . The police will say to people who have had trouble, "You live in this neighborhood—why? You should move out."

If this type of subjective perception from the police is pervasive, there could be serious implications for the effectiveness of claims-making activity by community members. Valid claims, even when defined as crime problems by police, may go without response if the police feel the complainant is responsible for the condition simply by being where he or she should not be.

MECHANISMS OF INTERACTION

The mechanisms—where and how claims are made—play an important role in the claims-making interaction revolving around defining social problems. Calling a drug hotline to report a stolen car probably will not result in the car being found—or even being listed as being stolen. Writing one's congressperson will probably not get a streetlight fixed. Knowledge about the channels established for claims making about crime problems is an important factor determining the success of different actors in defining crime problems. Moreover, as was the case in Waltersville, the perceived legitimacy of channels of communication by police, as well as citizens, influences the success of interactions. This section of the chapter will discuss the nature of various channels of claims making in Waltersville. Also, because mechanisms of interaction are dependent on perceived legitimacy for successful channeling of claims, I will discuss the activity of actors in negotiating legitimacy for mechanisms of interaction.

Many citizens of Waltersville perceive 911 to be the most direct channel to the police for claims about crime problems. The 911 number, however, is a mechanism controlled by the police. This position of control allows the police discretion in defining what claims may legitimately be channeled through 911. Consequently, many of the community's claims about crime problems were legitimately ignored given the outlined responsibilities of those receiving claims at 911. As an emergency line to the police, calls about abandoned cars, abandoned houses, poor or defective lighting, or loitering were not appropriate claims for 911. These were assertions of crime problems from citizens' perspectives, but they were not included in the institutional definition of claims requiring a response when channeled to the police through 911.

The police often ignored claims they defined as outside the jurisdiction of 911. But this created problems for citizens of Waltersville because they did not know where to go with their claims. City and state agencies potentially able to address situations outside of police jurisdiction control their own means of interaction. The complex, bureaucratic structure of public agencies usually results in a relatively narrow definition of responsibility. Knowing how to maneuver claims in the complex web of channels to public agencies is often difficult, even for well-educated people familiar with bureaucratic organizations. Many of the less-educated citizens of Waltersville probably found it very difficult to find an appropriate channel to communicate nonemergency situations.[6] It may be that citizens called 911 not just because they perceived a situation to be a crime problem but also because they knew they would get a voice on the other end of the line who would listen to their claim—even if there was no effective response.

Beyond the fact that the police ignored 911 calls not deemed as "emergencies," many Waltersville residents perceived problems with the promptness of response by the police to 911 calls, even when acknowledged as appropriate. One store owner commented, "Until 911 we had a direct line to the Seventh District. If there was a problem at the store and we called, they would be there in five minutes. Sometimes two or three cars. Now with 911 we are lucky to get a car in fifteen minutes."

Some Waltersville residents adapted to what they felt were slow responses to 911 by modifying their claims. When citizens learned that calls to 911 are queued and rated for exigency at the discretion of dispatchers, they made their claims sound more urgent. A business owner gave the following advice to other businesspeople at one meeting: "There are things to do to speed up 911. Tell them that they might have a gun. Tell them someone is in danger. Then they might come a little earlier than if you tell them that there is just a disturbance." These strategies for getting a response to what were perceived as legitimate claims may have been successful for some. Overall, however, the community's perception was that direct channels to the police were slow and ineffective.

The lethargic (or lack of) response to claims made through 911 caused a feedback effect for citizens. Dependence on what was perceived to be an unresponsive public institution led to feelings of powerlessness in making claims about crime in the neighborhood. One woman, when discussing the sluggish police response to what she thought was a legitimate claim, commented, "When you call the police like that and you don't get any response, it makes you feel like you don't control your own neighborhood." Lipsky (1980: 93) points out that often street-level bureaucracies use limited or lack of response as psychological sanctions to diminish client claims making. The lack of police response functions as feedback to complainants, discouraging future claims-making attempts to define crime differently from the police.

A second mechanism of interaction operating in Waltersville was WCO. On the one hand, while WCO probably would not list asserting the police definition of crime problems as one of its functions, this task was accomplished through its operations. WCO has an elaborate crime-recording system using police reports.[7] One of the uses for these reports was to combat rumors of crime in the community. The executive director described how this system worked:

> We really need the statistics because in a mixed area or a transitional community like ours, things will get blown way out of proportion. . . . When a block integrates, people fear crime coming in. . . . A few years ago I was asked to come up and speak in Elmwood when the first black family moved in. I heard of five rapes while I was there. I said that must really say something for our women. They must be so attractive that in one week that black man had gone out and raped five of them. Actually, when I checked the records, there were no rapes at all. By using police reports that reflected the police definition of criminal situations, WCO channeled police definitions of crime to the community. Citizens were being told that the simple presence of individuals or groups perceived to be responsible for crime problems was not a part of the police definition of crime.

It would be a mistake to say that WCO accepted these records as truly defining the crime problem in Waltersville. They also used them to check whether the police were responding to claims by citizens. That the police reports are not to be totally trusted was related by the director of WCO:

> You don't get some things on the sheets that you know are there. I was mugged out here, reported it to the police, and then when the report comes back, the incident isn't on the daily reports. They will say they are trying to keep from embarrassing you since they know you. But who knows how many incidents never make it to the reports?

Regardless of the verity of the police reports,[8] they did constitute a means for police to make claims defining crime problems. In WCO's operations, these police definitions of crime problems were channeled to the residents and businesspeople in Waltersville.

WCO also served as a channel for citizen claims to the police. It appears that this role, as a mechanism of interaction, was one of the important functions WCO fulfilled in the community. Community members often found themselves confused as to where to direct claims. In response to being told that people should not call 911 to report abandoned cars, one woman said, "We wouldn't know that. I wouldn't have known that if you didn't just tell me." Many Waltersville residents did not know how to channel their claims, especially when working with the highly bureaucratic structure of metropolitan public agencies. Therefore, it was no surprise that many of the community residents and businesspeople viewed WCO as an institution capable of channeling their claims.

The effectiveness of WCO in this role is questionable for several reasons. First, to summarize and clarify the myriad of often diffuse claims presented to WCO on the putative causes of crime was a difficult task. During my limited time at WCO, I heard different people speak about a reputed drug house on one corner, a store where drugs allegedly were sold on another corner, and kids on drugs robbing old women on their way from the bank on another street. All these putative conditions could be defined as part of a criminal drug problem in the community. The task of summarizing and forwarding a claim that involved all these aspects to the police for response, however, was difficult. Who are the victims? Who are the witnesses? When did the robberies occur? The cogent summarizing of crime problems (and scarce time and other resources for WCO personnel) was so formidable that many times WCO was unable to concentrate the diffuse claims into one the police would recognize. In effect, the channel of interaction was blocked.

A second factor stalling citizen claims entrusted to WCO was that WCO was limited in its channeling by potential response institutions. Assertions were made by community members that "Spanish people" were throwing garbage on the lawn or "kids don't know how to do anything but snatch purses." These claims were part of the community definition of crime problems that could not be forwarded to any institution with defined duties for dealing with them as "crime problems." Is it a crime to throw garbage on the lawn? What kids don't know how to do anything but snatch purses? These claims were asserted to WCO as a part of the residents' perception of crime problems, but WCO had nowhere to go with the claims.

The perceived legitimacy of WCO by the police was a third factor affecting the effectiveness of the organization's attempts to channel community claims of crime problems. If the police refused to view WCO as a source of legitimate claims of crime problems, interaction would be unsuccessful. In fact, because of the contested nature of the definition of crime in Waltersville, the police had an interest in leading community residents to question the legitimacy of WCO. The director of WCO related the following account of a meeting discussing crime around a hospital in Waltersville:

We had these maps and one of them wouldn't fit. We had north running in a different direction than up, and he [the district commander] made a big deal out of it. Through the whole meeting he kept making a big deal of the fact that north has to go up. He said. "Anyone intelligent knows that north goes up." Then there was another little error where what we had on one map didn't fit with something we had on the other and he picked that up right away. Pretty soon the people from

Sacred Heart started to agree. . . . He [the commander] really had it in for us that day.

WCO competed with the police as claims makers in defining crime in Waltersville. Therefore, by diminishing the legitimacy of WCO in the eyes of citizens, WCO had less of a base of power in relation to the police for asserting definitions of crime problems.

Despite problems, WCO could be an effective mechanism for claims-making activity. The owner of a funeral home in the community made the following claim to a WCO representative at a meeting:

> *Julie:* I know that people who park at the funeral home for funerals come in and complain that lots of things are happening to their cars.
> *Tim:* We will go out tomorrow . . . that's when Sam and Frank [foot patrolmen] are out. We'll go talk to them and have them watch that area when there are funerals.

Tim, an employee of WCO, told me that he has a good relationship with Sam and Frank. A claim made within the context of this personal relationship to the individuals responsible for neighborhood patrol is a more effective interaction than diffuse claims of vandalism made to 911. If nothing else, the claims were made directly to the police officers who could address the problem rather than being entrusted to a bureaucracy where the information may or may not trickle down to the street. In this case, WCO represented a channel for the funeral home owner that may have increased her chances for response to her claim.

The police also were aware that WCO was acting as a "watchdog" on their activities. Perhaps the most striking example of this role was the use of crime reports and mapping in claims-making activity. As I discussed earlier, WCO kept records of crime in the area. While these reports were tools for channeling police definitions of crime problems to the citizens, the reports also were legitimating tools for claims-making activities of WCO to police. Beyond written records, WCO also used pin mapping of incidents to analyze crime geographically. When asked whether the pin maps on the wall were effective in legitimating claims, the director of WCO responded, "I tell you it makes some of their eyes go ——. A few years ago [when he saw them], the superintendent almost had a heart attack. It shows a lot." The director also gave a specific example of how the mapping had been used to channel community claims of crime problems to the police.

> Last year people were calling on muggings. There were thirty-three to thirty-five muggings so we put pins on that map . . . we started to see a pattern. The police have different calls, different times, and didn't know what was going on at other times. . . . Finally, they [the police] started to work some only in that area.

WCO members took the reporting seriously and displayed the reports and maps prominently in their offices. The continuing record keeping and display of maps, even if the maps were several years old, indicated that WCO understood chan-neling community claims to the police as one of its responsibilities. Furthermore, the police occasionally changed their operations in response to information drawn from these maps.

A CASE STUDY: HAYDEN AND LYNN

During the five months I was collecting data, I had the opportunity to follow the development of claims made by the community into a recognized crime problem by the police. A particular intersection in Waltersville was claimed to be a "hots-pot" for crime. These claims were presented to the police, and the police re-sponded by deploying patrol cars at times asserted to be most problematic. While many aspects of this particular case may be typical (community claims of a prob-lem, initial police dismissal of the situation, and negotiation and positioning of these actors), a key feature of this particular case was the prominent role of aca-demic researchers and external activists in using new crime-mapping technol-ogy. In fact, the most instructive features of this case appear in the ways that its development deviated from the norm. In other words, innovation illustrates both what is possible as well as making more clear established practices.

How was the crime hotspot at Hayden and Lynn unusual? First, the claims about crime in Waltersville were not random complaints from residents and busi-ness people. Instead, MANS representatives solicited claims with the intention of formulating concrete geographic evidence of crime problems to be illustrated with the NIJ-funded computer mapping. A representative of MANS met with community residents and businesspeople, asking them what problems they thought existed in the community and where they perceived the problems to be the worst. Residents considered the intersection of Hayden and Lynn to be the worst trouble spot in Waltersville. Some of the claims made were vague:

> They [White Castle] let them sit out in the parking lot and they party all night. . . .
> They all come here. . . . all folks come here. Then they get lit up and fights start.
> Their Slim—you know what that is? That's what they call their women—are all
> sitting on the hoods of the cars and eatin' and drinkin' and smokin'. They got their
> little, no, those big radios playin' and they just sit out and party all night.

Other claims were more pointed: "I've been out watching the parking lot of the White Castle at night, and I've seen them passing dope for money from one car to another." An analysis of the information collected from the citizens was done by MANS and a report prepared for presentation to police. MANS was acting as a mechanism of interaction with the police much as WCO acts in forwarding citizen claims of crime problems to the police. A significant difference is that the resources utilized by MANS may have been greater in this case than those

employed by WCO as a channel for community claims.[9] Of particular significance was the use of computer-generated maps introduced during the NIJ mapping project. MANS analyzed the Hayden and Lynn intersection for types and
time of crimes. An elaborate computer-generated report was produced detailing
the complaints of residents, the nature of businesses on the corners, the geographic distribution of police-reported crimes, and the times of crimes.

The report was then presented to the police as a tool for legitimating community claims of crime. The initial response of the police during the meeting with
MANS representatives was skepticism at the existence of a situation within the
bounds of the police definition of crime problems.

> *Williams:* Commanders Jones, Olson, and myself [a police records officer] met and
> talked about this [intersection], and basically we don't see this as a problem. So what
> we have is a situation where we are perceiving this differently. . . . What we have
> got here is three robberies per night. That's not that terrible. It also doesn't look
> like a pattern. . . . I don't know what we can do about it. . . .
> *Olson:* As a policeman I don't see a problem.
> *Williams:* I don't see any problem, either.
> *Jones:* Crime concentrates where people concentrate. What we have is a busy com-
> mercial intersection, and as a consequence crime occurs.

In spite of the initial response by the police representatives, the district commander acknowledged the community perceptions of a crime problem. This asserted problem was perhaps outside the police definition of crime, but the patrol
commander began to acknowledge that some sort of police response was possible.

> *Williams:* Then they [the community] need to recognize that this isn't necessarily a
> police problem. It is a social problem.
> *Olson:* Everything you say is true, but we still have to respond to the perceived
> problem.

While these initial maps and report had not influenced the police officers to
define the situation as criminal, they considered offering a response. In other
words, community claims that would have been dismissed were translated into a
problem that the police would address.

To further make the case that the crime situation at Hayden and Lynn was, in
fact, a situation that the police should recognize as problematic, MANS analyzed
the three months of crime data. The activity on Hayden and Lynn was compared
to the reported criminal activity on a similar commercial intersection. This analysis revealed that indeed a higher proportion of neighborhood crime occurred on
this corner than the other. Moreover, MANS analyzed "disturbance calls"—calls
to report suspicious persons, loitering, or curfew violations—and found that the
majority of these calls came on weekends and during the early evening when
residents frequented the businesses on the corner. The situations prompting calls

for disturbances may not be criminal activity, but they contributed to residents' feelings of insecurity. The concrete, detailed report provided to substantiate the claims of the community offered hard evidence to support what otherwise could have been dismissed as unfounded citizen perceptions of problems.

In response to the community claims, the commander posted cars on the corner at times when the community had claimed the situation was the worst. There was evidence that some of the community perceived the problem solved. At a meeting of the businesspeople a month after the meeting with the police, a representative of a convenience store on the corner commented:

> I wanted to say about the police, whatever you folks said to the police it has really worked. The past four Sundays the police have been escorting people right down the block. . . . They have been around all the time since that last meeting, so whatever you said to them, they are doing something. . . . They even came in and searched all the people in the store. I couldn't believe it; we didn't know what was goin' on. But they really seem to be trying.

The crime maps were a tool to legitimate the claims of community residents about the crime problem at Hadyen and Lynn. Those maps, along with the effort of MANS, altered the police understandings of the problem of crime on that corner.

DISCUSSION AND CONCLUSION

The analysis of the claims-making interaction in the Waltersville community illustrates that the definition of crime involves many actors. In the complex web of claims and counterclaims of what are crime problems, it appears that the most important factor determining the outcome of interactions is the position from which claims are made. The fact that the police are a public agency with a monopoly on the enforcement of law and the maintenance of order in the community often made it difficult for residents to negotiate a position of power in the contest over defining crime problems. Likewise, because the police controlled a primary mechanism of communication, 911, they were in a position to exercise control over the interaction with the community citizens attempting to make claims.

Community members were dependent on the police for cooperation in their claims making. If citizens did not express their claims of crime problems to the police in a form the police recognized, no interaction occurred. Similarly, if the community residents or businesspeople attempted to engage the police through 911, they were subject to the judgments of a dispatcher to recognize their claim as legitimate within police jurisdiction.

Because of the asymmetrical power relations between police and citizens in the community, internal and external actors played an important role in mediating successful interaction between these groups. WCO was an internal actor that both legitimated police claims of crime problems to the citizens and attempted to channel unrecognized citizen claims of crime problems back to the police. The success of WCO as a mechanism of interaction was heavily dependent on their position of perceived legitimacy for both police and citizens. While WCO attempted to establish a position of legitimacy, the police had an interest in diminishing the legitimacy of WCO because that offered the police an advantageous position in negotiations.

In the Waltersville study, external actors played a great role in the interactions to define crime problems. On the one hand, MANS and academic researchers brought new resources of technology and manpower into the community to bolster community claims of crime problems. In fact, the whole process of claims making to define crime problems that I observed may have been distorted by the presence of external actors. The evidence that external actors influenced the negotiation process raises serious questions about "normal" claims making occurring in communities. Yet, the analysis reveals that the new tool of computerized crime mapping could serve as a powerful tool to put community claims into a form that police understand and respect.

Beyond the potential influence of mapping technology on the negotiation of crime problems, this study reveals various features about the negotiation of social problems. First, different actors and agencies have various interests—both individual and organizational—in defining given situations as problematic or nonproblematic. Social problems represent more than objective situations, but subjective evaluations of where and how the different actors will be affected by defining social situations in various ways. Community residents have a great stake in feeling safe in their community. Business owners depend on community residents' feelings of safety if they are to have regular business. Furthermore, business owners have a financial stake in receiving payment for their services rather than having their goods and services stolen. The police face more than personal safety issues; they also must operate within an organizational structure that defines what situations fall under their organizational responsibility. Each of these parties will attempt to assert their definitions of the social problem of crime to realize their interests.

Perceived and understood reality is not an objective situation but a constant ebb and flow of subjective evaluations and assertions about given situations. Within the complex webs of interaction over what is "real" and what is not, power, perceived legitimacy, and tools of negotiation play a significant role in whose definition of reality will prevail. The crime-mapping technology used in Waltersville did not create the situation that community residents asserted to be a crime problem, but it formalized "facts" about the situation so that it would be recognized by police. As society becomes more bureaucratized and based on rationalized evaluation of "hard facts," the less educated and those on the margins of formally organized institutions are increasingly hindered in making their definitions of social problems affect the behavior of the avenues of redress. The definition of crime problems in Waltersville indicates that communities' control over defining problems in their limited social space depends less on community norms than on the ability to channel their perceptions of community problems into formally organized claims accepted by rationalized institutions.

NOTES

1. Lipsky (1980) points out that when an agency's clients have no other options for service—as is the case with the police—the agency has disproportionate power in reference to clients because the agency has nothing to lose if the client is not satisfied. With nothing to lose, police have a great deal of freedom to dismiss citizen claims they do not want to manage.

2. One of the functions of WCO is the maintenance of block clubs in the Waltersville community. These block clubs had their origin in attempts to reduce racial tension during the racial transition that took place in Waltersville between 1960 and the present. Now they serve as bases for the organization of block watch programs for citizen crime prevention programs. The CB patrol of WCO is a function funded by a city gang control agency. Citizens ride around the community area and call in perceived criminal activity to WCO. WCO then contacts the police.

3. I thank Doug Thompson and John Walsh, also part of the NIJ research team, for sharing their data with me.

4. Albert Hunter and Suzanne Staggenborg (1988) discuss the importance of credibility and legitimacy of community organizations in the eyes of external institutions for continued funding. WCO was chosen as a participant in the NIJ project partially because of their longevity in Waltersville.

5. From the fourth quarterly progress report on "Mapping Crime in Its Community Setting" (unpublished progress report to NIJ, Fall 1987).

6. Part of the confusion of citizens about where to direct their claims may be tied to governmental reform and professionalization in large cities. While political machines had many negative features, one of the positive features for the uneducated citizens was that they knew their ward committee members or block captains. A loyal voter at least knew where to direct complaints and understood that loyalty or party work would lead to certain favors such as repaired street lights, increased police presence, or even the condemnation and razing of abandoned houses.

7. WCO surveyed the daily police reports and highlighted crime incidents in the Waltersville area. They transferred those crimes to a separate record for each block. These records were grouped by years, with large binders containing all the information on crime by period and block in the Waltersville area.

8. For a good discussion of manipulation of police reports to meet institutional goals, see Seidman and Couzens (1974).

9. During the time I was observing WCO, they had a computer on which to enter and analyze data but had nobody who was trained to operate the system. Therefore, WCO continued to use paper and pencil to transfer police records to their own crime records.

REFERENCES

Becker, Howard S. 1963. *Outsiders*. New York: Free Press.

Goffman, Erving. 1956. "The Nature of Deference and Demeanor." *American Anthropologist* 58 (June).

Hunter, Albert. 1978. "Symbols of Incivility: Social Disorder and Fear of Crime in the Neighborhoods." Presented at the 1978 meeting of the American Society of Criminology, Dallas, Texas.

Hunter, Albert, and Suzanne Staggenborg. 1988. "Local Communities and Organized Action." In *Community Organizations: Studies in Resource Mobilization and Exchange*, ed. Carl Milofsky. New York: Oxford University Press.

Liebow, Elliot. 1967. *Tally's Corner*. Boston: Little, Brown.

Lipsky, Michael. 1980. *Street-Level Bureaucracy*. New York: Russell Sage Foundation.

Seidman, D., and M. Couzens. 1974. "Getting the Crime Rate Down: Political Pressure and Crime Reporting." *Law and Society Review* 8: 475–93.

Skolnick, Jerome H. 1975. *Justice without Trial*. New York: Wiley.

Spector, Malcolm, and John Kitsuse. 1987. *Constructing Social Problems*. Hawthorne, N.Y.: Walter de Gruyter.

Taub, R., Taylor, D. G., and J. Dunham. 1984. *Paths of Neighborhood Change*. Chicago: University of Chicago Press.

8

The Media's Role in the Definition of Crime

Ray Surette and Charles Otto

What is considered a crime is historically both fixed and evolving. In this chapter, we will examine the question of how new crimes come into existence. Why is it, for example, that in certain periods of history consuming alcohol was a crime and in others it was not? We will argue that the media have played a powerful role in the crime definition process and today comprise the primary engine in the criminalization and decriminalization process.

Examine Figure 8.1, a simple representation of the conjunction of crimes and law-abiding behaviors. At the center are sets of behaviors that are nearly universally defined cross-culturally and cross-temporally as crimes. Throughout recorded history and across varying cultures, the unprovoked killing of a complete stranger has been considered a crime. Incest, theft, and rape are other acts that fall into this fixed definition of crime and receive broad social support for their continued criminalization. The social definition of these types of behaviors as crimes has been nearly constant, and only in special circumscribed situations are they decriminalized. Thus, governments sometimes decree that killing complete strangers is acceptable or even mandated such as during a war or execution.

The second ring of behaviors in Figure 8.1 are those that are currently defined as crimes but for which there is not deep and consistent support. These crime definitions vary across time and culture. For example, in the United States it is a criminal act to consume marijuana for nonmedical purposes. However, in other countries and cultures, the recreational use of marijuana is not a crime. Also, time is a factor. Marijuana use was legal in the United States until its criminalization in the 1930s. Along the same lines, recently in the United States driving while under the influence of alcohol has been made into a more serious crime with much harsher penalties.

The third ring of actions in Figure 8.1 are those that are considered deviant

Figure 8.1   Crime and Deviance Consensus Continuum

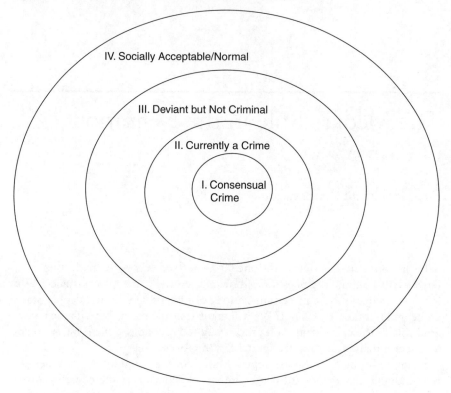

but not criminal. For example, it is seen as deviant to make a romantic gesture to your mother-in-law, but it is not a criminal act. Note that those actions that are considered deviant but not criminal also tend to vary over time and across cultures. In other words, sometimes actions are labeled as deviant but not as criminal; in other situations, times, or cultures, they are considered crimes.

Or the shift may be outward toward the forth ring, where once deviant behavior is seen as socially acceptable and normal. Reading this book is considered to be socially acceptable and normal; however, reading this book at a relative's funeral may not be considered criminal, although it would likely be considered deviant. However, reading it aloud in a library could be a criminal act depending on the laws of the state where the library was located. Again, activities that are usually considered normal may be classified as deviant in some settings or socially abnormal at some point in the future, or they may even be considered criminal in special circumstances or times.

The main point is that the behaviors move between the rings of figure 8.1. Behaviors in the second, third, and fourth groups migrate, and even the core

consensually perceived criminal behaviors are decriminalized in special circumstances. Our focus will be on the migration of behaviors among the outer rings
and the role that the contemporary mass media plays in the migration. This collective three set group of behaviors are variously defined as crimes, deviant but
noncriminal, or normal-acceptable behavior. The observation of this migration
has been cited as evidence of the relativism of crime—that whether a behavior
is considered a crime is relative. For every behavior, sometimes it is a crime;
sometimes it is not.

In contemporary America, the media will have the most impact on the definition and movement of the nonconsensual crimes. Admittedly, the media may
have very little influence on the classification of incest as a crime and would be
hard-pressed to cause its decriminalization. But the media do have a substantive
impact on the legalization, deviantization, and criminalization of the vast set of
behaviors that comprise figure 8.1's second, third, and fourth rings. One need
only to recall the history and social perception of varied recreational drugs to
sense the media's importance.

PRIOR APPROACHES TO CONCEPTUALIZING THE CRIME
DEFINITION PROCESS HAVE IGNORED THE MEDIA'S ROLE

Prior approaches to understanding the definition of the crime process have either
explicitly or implicitly acknowledged the evolution of these definitions but have
until recently ignored the media as having an important role in the definitional
process (Lanier and Henry 1998). Thus, the moral consensus view describes the
process as the reaction of a common public conscience causing moral outrage
and the defining of selected behaviors as serious offenses against society (Burgess
1950; Durkheim [1893] 1933; Roshier 1989). While generally viewed as stable
and independent of the need for formal criminal justice system recognition, the
ability of the common conscience to vary by culture and time is conceded.
Crime definitional changes, however, are expected to be slow and generational
in this perspective. The likelihood of rapid transformation (or migration) of a
behavior from one status to another is seen as low. In its defense, most of the
theoretical development in the moral consensus view precedes the late twentieth
century and the emergence of the current postmodern global mass media. Developed prior to a significant mass media, this perspective best applies to a pre–mass
media era.

In contrast to the moral consensus view, relativists and others here argued
for a more rapidly changing definition environment. In their competitive and
conflicting social environment, political power plays an essential role in the
crime definition process (Becker 1963; Chambliss and Seidman 1971; Quinney
1973; Tifft 1995). In this perspective, political power is crucial in rendering some
behavior criminal and in keeping other harmful behaviors invisible and non-

criminal. Here the media are seen as playing a role in the definition process, but they are secondary to political power and are perceived only as manipulated tools for those wielding political power. Those without power are perceived as effectively shut out from access to the media, and the media themselves are seen as substantially controlled by the powerful. Hence, significant broad-based media access, influence of media content by groups and individuals not of the political elite, or the media as independent actors in the crime definition process are not seriously considered in the moral consensus perspective.

However, in the 1960s, corresponding with the social impact of the first pervasive electronic mass medium, television, the concept of social competition was borrowed from the political power perspective and social constructionism emerged (Meyrowitz 1985). The social constructionist perspective saw the process of defining crime and other social realities as both competitive and free wielding. With social constructionism, for the first time access to the media and skill in utilizing media emerge as significant factors in the crime definition process (Barak 1994; Pfuhl and Henry 1993; Schur 1965, 1980; Surette 1998). The media are no longer seen as minor elements reflecting other long-term social processes, nor are they perceived solely as manipulated tools of political power or totally controlled by any single social group. They have become something more.

Constructionist improvements on the earlier somewhat unidimensional views of the crime definition process have produced a virtual geometry of crime definition models. Thus, one finds in the literature Young's (1997) "Square of Crime," Henry and Milvanovic's (1996) "Constitution of Crime," Hagan's (1985) "Pyramid of Crime," and Henry and Lanier's (1998) "Prism of Crime." Within this geometric development, initially the media were not explicitly incorporated. Their effects were first expressly included via the concept of visibility (Henry and Lanier 1998). Visibility is important because it raises the question of how the public becomes aware that social acts are socially harmful and therefore in need of criminalization (Henry and Lanier 1998: 619). The linkage via visibility between the media and crime definitions is seen as the comparative visibility of crimes reflecting the interests of the powerful rather than the inherent social harm of a behavior. The politically powerful are seen as capable of keeping some harmful behaviors invisible to the public by keeping them out of the media and simultaneously inordinately raising the visibility of other behaviors by having the media dwell on them. The politically powerful's interests are also seen as related to the mass media's commercial interests. In this view, the coalescing of the media, business, and politically powerful interests in turn contains and limits the definitional social construction of crime (Barak 1994; Surette 1996).

This initial and limited vision of the media role as serving only the interests of the economically and politically powerful has expanded within the social constructionist perspective. It now includes unanticipated effects from the plethora of entertainment images of crime and justice found in the popular culture and the news media sensationalization of "true crimes." Both popular culture and true crime sensationalization are seen as affecting the visibility of other possible social behaviors for criminalization (Henry and Lanier 1998: 619, citing Ermann and Lundman 1995; Poveda 1994). In its simplest conceptualization, the predatory crime that dominates popular culture and the true-crime genre simply crowds out other candidates from public consideration (Surette 1998).

As it has evolved, the most recent conceptual development of the definitional process of crime, Henry and Lanier's prism of crime explicitly includes the media as a crucial factor in the process. At one apex of the prism, "highly visible crimes" are recognized and emphasized by the media in both its news and entertainment content and at the other vector are "obscured crimes" that lack media attention but are not without social harm. For Henry and Lanier (1998: 623):

> The position of crimes in the prism varies over time. As vocal dominant groups and mass-mediated culture focus on different issues, so the public awareness of what counts as crime is formed and reformed. Acts are recognized as more or less visible, more or less serious, and more or less harmful. For example, the positions of domestic violence and sexual harassment have changed: Both recently have begun to move from the lower to the upper half of the prism. In contrast, other acts that formerly were located in the upper half, such as some religious offenses (e.g. working on Sunday), have become so common as to be hidden, are relatively harmless, and elicit neither public sentiment nor societal response.

The visual image is that of a lava lamp, with behaviors drifting upward and downward from criminal to noncriminal definitions and back again. It is our contention that the heat energy for this social crime definition lamp is largely provided by the media. Their attention provides the heat energy to raise behaviors to criminalization levels, and their lack of attention denies the necessary energy to nonconsensual crime behaviors to keep them in the upper half of the prism. Lacking the heat of media attention, these behaviors will drift down through declining visibility, benign sanctions, and eventual nonenforcement and decriminalization. As currently constituted, collectively the contemporary mass media are the thermal engine for the migration process. They are today so crucial that we argue that behavior cannot be criminalized without media attention and that intense media attention can result in the rapid movement of a behavior within the prism. Such rapid movements are indicative of an accelerated social construction process of crime definitions. To understand this criminalizing and legalizing media impact, it is first necessary to comprehend the social construction of reality process.

THE SOCIAL CONSTRUCTION OF REALITY PROCESS

Understanding the theoretical perspective known as the social construction of reality or social constructionism helps to better understand the impact of a pervasive mass media on crime definitions. Under this theoretical view, people create reality—the world they believe exists—based on their individual knowledge and from knowledge gained from social interactions with other people. This view is the opposite of the dominant Western tradition of logical empiricism, which views social knowledge as independent of social processes and grounded totally in events in the world. Knowledge of the world in logical empiricism is objective and uninfluenced by social processes. An objective social reality exists that is uninfluenced by social perceptions, and social perceptions can only distort one's perception of reality. Social knowledge reflects social facts that are, in turn, tied directly and objectively to social events that are (or should be) recorded identically by different observers.

Social constructionism differs in that it views knowledge as something that is created by humans, and this knowledge may or may not mirror an objective reality. This perspective does not question the physical reality of the world or the fact that social events actually occur but rather focuses on human relationships within the world and the way personal relationships affect how people perceive reality. Understanding of the world is sought by studying its shared meanings. Shared meanings are, in turn, the result of active, cooperative social enterprises. The degree to which a given constructed reality prevails is not directly dependent on its objective empirical validity but is instead strongly influenced by the shifting forces of social trends and interactions. The perspective recognizes the fact that social conditions become major social problems and then subside, without the physical situations they concern having undergone any significant change. Therefore, regarding the defining of crime, not only can social behaviors be criminalized or decriminalized independently of social conditions, but in social constructionism such occurrences are not unusual. It is expected that behaviors may be criminalized and decriminalized without the actual social level or conditions of those behaviors changing.

Within the social construction process the perceptions of conditions change as social knowledge about those conditions change. People acquire knowledge from four sources: personal experiences, significant others (peers, family, friends), other social groups and institutions (schools, unions, churches, government agencies), and the mass media. The first source, also termed *experienced reality,* is one's directly experienced world—all the events that have happened to you. Knowledge gained from experienced reality is relatively limited but has a powerful influence on one's constructed reality. Thus, personal victimization is the most powerful source for defining one's view of what constitutes a crime and how serious a crime is. Fortunately, even in a society fixated with crime like the United States, personal victimization remains comparatively uncommon. Serious victimization tends to concentrate in a high-risk group of citizens composed mostly of lower-income and minority persons (Koppel 1987).

The next three sources of knowledge are shared symbolically and collectively form one's symbolic reality. All the events you didn't witness but believe occurred, all the facts about the world you didn't personally collect but believe to be true, all the things you believe to exist but haven't seen, make up your symbolic reality. The difference between experienced and symbolic reality can be shown by a few questions: How many believe the moon exists? Why? Because you can see it directly—you have experienced-reality knowledge of its existence. How many believe the moon has an atmosphere? Why not? Because you've been told it has no air, you've read it has no air, and you've seen pictures of men in space suits on the moon. It is because so much of our social knowledge is gained symbolically that there is concern over its content and correctness, particularly its use of deception. Not surprisingly, the media are centrally involved in our symbolic reality knowledge formation. Regarding the definitional process of crime, it is from our symbolic reality that we obtain the vast majority of our crime-defining knowledge. In large, advanced, industrialized societies like the United States, the mass media dominate our symbolic reality, overwhelming the information we receive via conversations with significant others and our limited experienced reality. What we see as crimes tend to be described, delimited, and defined in the mass media.

The role of the media in the social construction of knowledge is diagrammed in figure 8.2, which presents the phases of social constructionism. In phase 1 we have the actual physical world we live in. In phase 2 is competition over how to define the physical world. This phase involves a number of theoretical concepts significant for social constructionism, including claims and claims makers, ownership, and linkage. Claims are the descriptions, typifications, and assertions regarding the extent and nature of phenomena in the physical world. These statements are promoted as facts about the world. For example, "Crime is out of control" is a claim about the factual physical condition of crime in society. "Cocaine is a dangerous drug whose use and sale must be criminalized" is a factual claim about what substances should be against the law.

Claims makers are the promoters, activists, professional experts, and spokespersons involved in forwarding specific claims about a phenomenon. They hope to have their claims accepted as the dominant social construction of reality. If the dominant social construction becomes "Crime is out of control," then those who have made that claim can consider themselves to have been successful. When the president states that the culture of violence in our schools must be addressed, he is forwarding a claim about the world that also incorporates a response to the claimed conditions of the world. New laws and policies directed against the "culture of school violence" would indicate the success of the president's construction of a new social problem.

In the United States, four frames compete in the media for domination of the crime definition process (Sasson 1995). The first frame, a faulty criminal justice system, holds that crime is a problem because of excessive due process procedures. The second frame, blocked social and economic opportunities, posits that crime is the result of individuals having opportunity unjustly withheld from

Figure 8.2   Phases of Social Construction

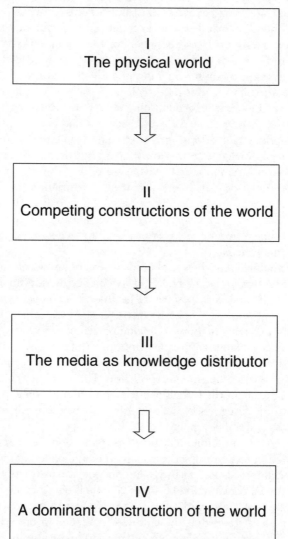

them. The third frame, social breakdown of family and community life, contends that crime is the result of the traditional family structure deteriorating. The fourth frame, an oppressive and racist criminal justice system, argues that crime is the result of an oppressive and racist society. Most crime and justice news stories fall into one of the four frames, and criminal justice policies tend to reflect one frame or another (Beckett and Sasson 2000).

Ownership is the identification of a particular phenomenon with a particular set of claims makers who come to own the issue in that they are sought out by the media for pronouncements regarding its nature and the reasonableness of competing social policies directed toward it. Some groups—by virtue of their superior power, finances, status, organization, technology, or access to the media—have greater resources to make their constructions appear legitimate, to make their version of reality stick, and to take effective ownership of an issue. The NRA, for example, is one of a group of claims makers that are vying for ownership of the gun access issue. While the NRA is striving to not have gun access further criminalized, other groups, such as Handgun Control, headed by Sarah Brady, work to have gun access further criminalized with the passage of the Brady Bill.

Lastly, linkage involves the typing or association of an issue with other issues. For example, drugs are often linked to other social problems such as crime. The linkage of one social phenomenon to another generally seen as more harmful raises the concern and importance of the linked issue. Thus, the social importance of drug abuse is heightened when drugs are linked to other social problems, and the same linkage makes other correlates of crime appear less significant. Hence, gun access is linked to school violence and makes both issues more pressing.

In the third phase, the media filter out the various claims and claims makers. This is where the media play their most powerful role. By giving some claims more credibility and coverage than other claims, the media make it hard for some claims makers to gain legitimacy and to affect the social construction of reality process. Claims makers who are not adept with the media are not able in most circumstances to get their claims and social constructions coverage. This effectively shuts them out of the social construction competition. For example, disorganized, poor, crime-ridden neighborhoods are frequently unable to get their community problems successfully constructed as serious criminal issues (Skogan and Maxfield 1981).

The final phase is the emergence of a dominant construction of the world. Since most of us have very little direct experience with crime and justice reality, the media play an important role in our conceptualization of crime and the reality construction that eventually wins the social construction competition. This dominant construction is the reality that most people accept as valid. For crime and justice, it will include those behaviors that have been accepted as criminal, deviant but noncriminal, and law-abiding. A social behavior will be perceived as a crime, or it will not.

For crimes and the definition of them, the social construction of reality process is therefore crucial, and the media are crucial for the process. The shared meanings of what social acts are considered normal, deviant, or criminal are socially constructed, constantly contested, and evolving. We believe that the mass media have emerged as both key players and crucial playing fields in the crime definition process. As claims makers, the media sometimes are directly involved in the construction competition, forwarding a specific new crime definition. When not involved as claims makers, the media provide the social arena in which other claims makers promote their constructions and compete in the reality-defining process. The next section discusses some examples of the application of the media-based social constructionism to crime definitions.

RECENT EXAMPLES OF MEDIA INFLUENCE ON THE CONSTRUCTION OF CRIME DEFINITIONS

Three Strikes and You're Out

Our first example demonstrates how various groups can use the media to affect the crime definition process—in this case, the "three strikes and you're out" legislation.[1] Serious crime was redefined in the process to include an explicitly quantitative element. The reaction to the initial idea of three strikes in the mid-1980s was not enthusiastic, and criminal justice professionals rejected the need for an expanded definition beyond the existing habitual offender laws. However, in 1988, Diane Ballasiotes was abducted and stabbed to death in Washington state by a convicted rapist who had been released from prison. In reaction to this crime, a group called "Friends of Diane" formed to seek harsher penalties for sex crimes. This group eventually joined forces with another Washington state policy group that was advocating for three-strikes legislation. Despite their combined efforts, however, through 1992 there was little legislative or criminal justice professional interest in three strikes in Washington state. The proposed legislation was perceived as similar to a habitual offender law already on the books, and a petition drive to get three strikes on a statewide ballot failed (Gest 1994).

It is important to note that Friends of Diane and the three strikes group did not have significant access to the media. In this sense, they were unable to forward a dominant construction of reality by being a claims maker that the media relied on to frame various crime stories. Although there was some media coverage, a receptive media environment was not in place.

In 1993, however, the three-strikes group (renamed the Washington Citizens for Justice) allied with the National Rifle Association and succeeded in getting the proposition on the November ballot. Despite some opposition from elements of the criminal justice community, 77 percent of Washingtonians approved the three-strikes law. As the Washington vote approached, a young girl in California, Polly Klass, was abducted and murdered, and a three-strikes campaign took off in California. Unlike in prior years, media coverage was extensive, and this time politicians and citizens across the nation and the political spectrum embraced three strikes (Surette 1996).

A number of social constructionist concepts clearly come to play in the three strikes saga. With the alliance of the NRA, Friends of Diane was able to become a much more powerful claims maker—the NRA was a group that the media would readily contact. Also, with the kidnapping and murder of Polly Klass, the three strikes stakeholders had a symbolic event that they were able to use to define the crime problem and influence policy. Symbolic events in the crime definition process are crucial because they ensure media access for claim makers, while providing dramatic evidence of the behavior that must be criminalized. In three strikes, the Polly Klass murder became the symbolic element that could absorb the media, focus heat and power, lifting the new crime-defining legislation in the social crime prism (Wilkie 1994).

Highway Violence

In our second example, we look at how the media define a new crime. The media do not usually take on this role as much as they act as a filter and playing field among various claims makers, but an example of a media-created crime definition can be seen in their treatment of highway shootings. Joel Best (1991) analyzed imagery concerning highway violence from several major newspapers and television stations. He found that, after an initial story dealing with highway violence appeared, the media began constructing a number of different types of highway incidents as indicative of a new social phenomenon of highway violence today known as "road rage." Best (1991: 332) summarized this situation by stating:

> In short, the media described freeway shootings as a growing problem, characterized by random violence and widespread fear. Without official statistics or public opinion polls bearing on the topic, reporters relied on interviews with their sources to support these claims. Thus, the eleven network news stories used thirty-eight clips from interviews: eleven with law enforcement officials promising to take action or advising caution; thirteen victims describing their experiences; ten person-in-the-street interviews revealing public concern; and four experts offering explanations.

Best further found that the media tried to explain and interpret the problem. The media would say, for example, that highway congestion coupled with the anonymity of the car could trigger these violent outrages in people. The media also offered competing frames for the problem of highway violence. Some interpreted it as a crime problem, suggesting that more law enforcement was the solution to the problem. Others saw it as a traffic problem. Freeway violence would be lessened if the roads were not so congested. Other frames were that freeway violence was a gun access problem or a lack-of-courtesy problem. Best concludes that in this case the media were the primary claims maker in the definition of road rage, taking on this role in part because the summer of 1987 was a slow news period. Needing a new crime, the news media went out and constructed one, in the process raising highway violence from a low-visibility event to a high-visibility "new" crime phenomenon.

Predatory Criminality and Serial Killers

An example of the media constructing a crime issue without constructing a new crime is provided by the historic role that predatory criminality plays in the U.S. media. The media in both its entertainment and its news components have defined predatory criminality by strangers as the dominant and most pressing crime problem in the nation (Surette 1995). The history of the media reveals that the image of the predator criminal has dominated news and entertainment for at least the last one hundred years. The repeated message is that predatory individuals who are basically different from the rest of us perpetrate crime and that criminality stems from individual problems. Media criminals have become more animalistic, irrational, and predatory and their crimes more violent, senseless, and sensational. Because of the media's efforts, the crimes that dominate the public consciousness and policy debates are not the common crimes but the rarest ones. The mass media have raised the visibility of the predator criminal from a minor character to a common, ever-present image. The public is led by the media to see violence and predation between strangers as a way of life (Scheingold 1984). Serious crime has been defined to symbolize the uncertainties of modern life, that criminals are evil, abnormal people (Cavender and Bond-Maupin 1993).

The genesis of the "serial killer" as a significant new type of crime in the 1980s epitomizes the news and entertainment media definition of predatory criminality as the most serious U.S. crime problem. Philip Jenkins (1988) reported that although there was some evidence of a small increase in the number of active serial killers, in total, serial killers account for no more than three hundred to four hundred victims a year, or 2 to 3 percent of all U.S. homicides. Media coverage of serial murderers and the success of fictional books and films about serial killers, however, have resulted in serial killers being redefined and accepted as the dominant homicide problem in the United States and symbolic of a society being overwhelmed by rampant violent predatory criminality (Kappeler, Blumberg, and Potter 1993; Surette 1995).

The effects of this dominant-constructed definition of serious criminality were crucial for subsequent criminal justice policies and legislation, especially the shift toward individual-focused retributive polices during the 1970s and 1980s (Beckett and Sasson 2000; Doppelt and Manikas 1990; Surette 1992). Criminal justice policy was transformed into a war being fought by semihuman monsters against society (Jenkins 1988). The resultant media-induced "serial killer panic" of the 1980s was embraced because media sensationalism and media manipulation by government agencies resulted in a societal quest against an "evil predator criminal foe." As a result, public resources and law enforcement efforts were heavily diverted to address the newly defined social menace (Jenkins 1988). The media-promulgated definition and image of predator crime has also helped to make the United States one of the most punitive countries on the planet (Beckett and Sasson 2000). In the final analysis, the media project the horrendous crime as the norm and maintain the predator criminal at the top of the crime definition prism (Elias 1986).

The Criminalization of Driving under the Influence

A final example of how the media influences the crime definition process in terms of raising the perception of a crime's seriousness can be seen with drinking and driving. Driving under the influence was something that has been legally defined as a crime for a long time. However, until recently it was an act that most closely fit into the second ring of behaviors. It was a deed that was defined as a crime, but there was not broad, consistent support for its criminalization, and, not surprisingly, enforcement was lax and haphazard.

Rick Inmon (1999) examined the media's construction of DUI and found that prior to the 1980s, it was constructed primarily as a rehabilitation problem. News accounts told of how lawmakers wanted to lessen the penalties for DUI. During this period, lawmakers rationalized that the current penalties were too harsh and that the imposition of stiff penalties such as license revocation would interfere with the offender's abilities to care for their families. Inmon also found that, during this time, the media used nonpejorative words such as *errant* to describe the actions of those convicted of DUI.

Craig Reinarman (1988) has also concluded that groups like MADD (Mothers against Drunk Driving) have impacted the dominant social construction of the drunk driver. Previously, drunk drivers were seen as troubled individuals. Socially reconstructed, currently they are seen as individuals who cause trouble. MADD could not have done this without waging successful media campaigns that, in turn, affected how crime is defined.

At the beginning of the eighties, therefore, DUI came to be constructed as a much more serious crime. The drunk driver was now characterized as a "killer drunk" and one of society's worst problems. There was clearly a shift in the media's depiction of drinking and driving and subsequently how society viewed drinking and driving. No longer was it viewed as an individual problem. Now, it was constructed as a menace to society, and support grew for much stricter DUI laws and nondiscretionary enforcement. DUI has shifted in figure 8.1 from the outside edge of ring 2 (criminal but no broad support) to close to ring 1 (consensually criminal). It became and is now an act that most people view as a serious crime.

CONCLUSION

We have argued that the media play a central role in the crime definition process because of the social construction of reality process. Most people do not have any substantial experiential reality to rely on when it comes to defining crime, so they rely on the media. The examples show that the media usually filter information from various claims makers, as they did with the three strikes legislation; they sometimes become the primary claims maker, as they did with the highway violence issue; they also raise rare criminal acts to disordinate public visibility and concern, as they did with serial murder; and they increase the seriousness with which a crime is perceived. The media can also have the opposite crime-defining effects. They can decriminalize behavior by ignoring or trivializing its prevalence and effects; they can block access to the public by crime constructing claims makers; they can keep significant and harmful social and harmful conditions invisible; and they can, by lack of attention, fail to validate and acknowledge truly new crime forms.

What is it that makes the difference between whether something becomes part of the dominant social construction? The answer is complex. Regarding the media, they cannot be simply tagged as manipulating mechanisms that force criminal justice policies and crime definitions down the public's throat. Nor can they be dismissed as objective neutral bystanders in the public policy arena. The reality is that the media play an indispensable but not independent role in the crime definition.

In the large, the media will not have much influence on our core set of crime beliefs. The media have its greatest impact on the crime definition process for those behaviors that are not fixed across time and culture. The limited set of anecdotal case studies suggests that they most easily influence the criminalizing of acts that were once considered deviant or socially acceptable. Because media attention provides visibility-raising energy, the media appear more effective and quicker at criminalizing than decriminalizing behaviors. Because of inertia in the criminal justice system, the removal of media attention needs a longer time period to cool off a behavior, allowing it to sink in visibility, than media attention needs to impart buoyancy to a behavior. Media-criminalizing attention can be achieved in a short time, while the cooling effects of nonattention appear to take longer. This likely explains a deficiency of decriminalization examples in the research literature. Rare, they remain largely undocumented and unstudied.

Speculating on the future, we forecast that as the media technologically develop and we become a mediated global society in the next millennium, the media's role in the crime-defining process will increase. The media-generated rapid escalation of behaviors into the criminalized sphere will be common. The ultimate concern is that reasoned public debate of the merits of defining some behaviors as crimes and others as not crimes will be replaced by a media-based, audience-share standard. Instead of addressing its most harmful behaviors as crimes, society will repeatedly chase a series of media-defined crime specters.

NOTE

1. A television commentator coined the slogan "three strikes, you're out" to denote a policy in which anyone who had been convicted of two serious crimes would subsequently face life without parole if convicted of a third nonmisdemeanor (Surette 1996, citing Gest 1994).

REFERENCES

Barak, G., ed. 1994. *Media, Process and the Social Construction of Crime: Studies in News-making Criminology.* New York: Garland.

Becker, H. S. 1963. *Outsiders: Studies in the Sociology of Deviance.* New York: Free Press.

Beckett, K., and T. Sasson. 2000. *The Politics of Injustice: Crime and Punishment in America.* Thousand Oaks, Calif.: Pine Forge.

Best, J. 1991. "Road Warriors on Hair-Trigger Highways: Cultural Resources and the Media's Construction of the 1987 Freeway Shootings Problem." *Sociological Inquiry* 61: 327–45.

Burgess, E. 1950. "Comment to Hartung." *American Journal of Sociology* 56: 25–34.

Cavender, G., and L. Bond-Maupin 1993. "Fear and Loathing on Reality Television." *Sociological Inquiry* 3: 305–17.

Chambliss, W., and R. Seidman. 1982. *Law, Order and Power.* 2d ed. Reading, Mass.: Addison-Wesley.

Dopplet, J., and P. Manikas. 1990. "Mass Media and Criminal Justice Decision Making." In *The Media and Criminal Justice Policy,* ed. R. Surette. Springfield, Ill.: Thomas, pp. 129–42.

Durkheim, E. [1893] 1933. *The Division of Labor in Society.* New York: Free Press.

Elias, R. 1986. *The Politics of Victimization.* New York: Oxford University Press.

Ermann, D., and R. Lundman, eds. 1995. *Corporate and Government Deviance.* New York: Oxford University Press.

Gest, T. 1994. "Reaching for a New Fix to an Old Problem." *U.S. News and World Report* (7 February): 9.

Hagan, J. 1985. *Modern Criminology.* New York: McGraw-Hill.

Henry, S., and M. Lanier. 1998. "The Prism of Crime: Arguments for an Integrated Definition of Crime." *Justice Quarterly* 15: 609–27.

Henry, S., and D. Milovanovic. 1996. *Constitutive Criminology.* London: Sage.

Inmon, R. 1999. "Drunk Driving Constructed in the United States." Unpublished manuscript, University of Central Florida.

Jenkins, P. 1988. "Myth and Murder: The Serial Murder Panic of 1983–1985." *Criminal Justice Research Bulletin* 3: 1–7.

Kappeler, V., M. Blumberg, and G. Potter. 1993. *The Mythology of Crime and Criminal Justice.* Prospect Heights, Ill.: Waveland.

Koppel, H. 1987. *Lifetime Likelihood of Victimization*. Bureau of Justice Statistics Technical Report, U.S. Department of Justice. Washington, D.C.: U.S. Government Printing Office.

Lanier, M., and S. Henry. 1998. *Essential Criminology*. Boulder, Colo.: Westview.

Meyrowitz, J. 1985. *No Sense of Place*. New York: Oxford University Press.

Pfuhl, E. H., and S. Henry. 1993. *The Deviance Process*. 3d ed. Hawthorn, N.Y.: Aldine de Gruyter.

Poveda, T. G. 1994. *Rethinking White Collar Crime*. Westport, Conn.: Praeger.

Quinney, R. 1973. *Critique of the Legal Order*. Boston: Little, Brown.

Reinarman, C. 1988. "The Social Construction of an Alcohol Problem: The Case of Mothers against Drunk Drivers and Social Control in the 1980s." *Theory and Society* 17: 91–120.

Roshier, B. 1989. *Controlling Crime: The Classical Perspective in Criminology*. Philadelphia: Open University Press.

Sasson, T. 1995. *Crime Talk*. Hawthorne, N.Y.: Aldine de Gruyter.

Scheingold, S. 1984. *The Politics of Law and Order*. White Plains, N.Y.: Longman.

Schur, E. M. 1976. *Crimes without Victims: Deviant Behavior and Public Policy*. Englewood Cliffs, N.J.: Prentice-Hall.

———. 1980. *The Politics of Deviance: Stigma Contests and the Uses of Power*. Englewood Cliffs, N.J.: Prentice Hall.

Skogan, W., and M. Maxfield. 1981. *Coping with Crime: Individual and Neighborhood Reactions*. Newbury Park, Calif.: Sage.

Surette, R. 1992. *Media, Crime, and Criminal Justice: Images and Realities*. Pacific Grove, Calif.: Brooks/Cole.

———. 1998. *Media, Crime, and Criminal Justice: Images and Realities*. 2d ed. Pacific Grove, Calif.: Brooks/Cole.

———. 1996. "News from Nowhere, Policy to Follow: Media and the Social Construction of Three Strikes and You're Out." In *Three Strikes and You're Out*, ed. D. Shichor and D. Sechrest. Thousand Oaks, Calif.: Sage, pp. 177–202.

———. 1995. "Predator Criminals as Media Icons." In *Media, Process, and the Social Construction of Crime: Studies in Newsmaking Criminology*, ed. G. Barak. New York: Garland, pp. 131–58.

Tifft, L. L. 1995. "Social Harm Definitions of Crime." *Critical Criminologist* 7: 9–13.

Wilkie, D. 1994. "Polly's Slaying Now Just Politics." *San Diego Union-Tribune*, 21 October, A1, A25.

Young, J. 1997. "Left Realism: The Basics." In *Thinking Critically about Crime*, ed. B. D. MacLean and D. Milovanovic. Vancouver, Canada: Collective, pp. 28–36.

9

Racing Crime: Definitions and Dilemmas

Katheryn K. Russell

Each spring, I teach an undergraduate course, "Race, Crime, and Justice." The course is designed to address a range of issues related to race and the operation of the U.S. criminal justice system. Topics address the relationship between crime and race from a variety of perspectives, including historical, political, and contemporary. Most students who take the course are college juniors. Class size ranges between forty and sixty students. A typical class is composed of mostly black and white students, with a small number of Hispanic and Asian students. Two exercises used in this course shed light on how definitions and images of crime are intricately linked with race.

On the first day of class, students take a "Race and Crime Literacy Quiz" (see figure 9.1). They are tested on a range of topics, including arrest and incarceration rates by race. For example, they are asked, "What percentage of arrestees are white?" Student responses, which are largely informed by media portrayals, are frequently wrong. Many are surprised to learn that whites comprise two-thirds of the people who are arrested each year (Bureau of Justice Statistics 1999). Likewise, many students are unaware that black women, not black men, are the fastest-growing race/gender group within the criminal justice system (Mauer and Huling 1995: 5). A 1995 study by the Sentencing Project found the following rates of increase: black women, 78 percent; white women, 40 percent; black men, 31 percent; Hispanic men and women, 18 percent; and white men, 8 percent (Mauer and Huling 1995). The quiz also asks students to define "racial disproportionality" and "racial discrimination."

Midway into the semester, as part of our discussion of media representations, students are asked about racial stereotypes. For the groups listed here, students were asked how each is represented by the mainstream press. What follows is a summary of the typical student responses.

Young Native American female: Proud, submissive, creative, spiritual
Young Native American male: Earthly, hunter, leader, alcoholic

Young white female: Quiet, arrogant, stuck-up, spoiled
Young white male: Carefree, rich, egocentric, spoiled
Young Hispanic female: Hot, argumentative, outspoken, controlling
Young Hispanic male: Strong, arrogant
Young Asian female: Shy, exotic, quiet, obedient
Young Asian male: Intelligent, artistic, hard-working, martial artist
Young black female: Loud, strong, outspoken, stubborn, proud
Young black male: Athletic, considerate, strong, proud, highly sexual, mili-
   tant, absentee father, criminal

Two things are striking about the student responses. First, of the ten race/gen-
der groups, "young black male" is the only given a label of "criminal." In some
classes, "young Hispanic males" are also given a deviant label (e.g., "car thief").
Over the years, however, my students have consistently stereotyped young black
men as criminal. Second, the responses reflect age-old, presumably long-ago retired, stereotypes. In fact, had a similar exercise been conducted thirty years ago,
it would likely have produced similar results. This exercise underscores the persis-
tence of stereotypes, even in the face of evidence to the contrary.

Together, these classroom discussions effectively demonstrate how the media
inform our perspectives on crime. As important, these images often take shape
without the benefit of accurate information. Sadly, my students are not alone.

Figure 9.1   Race and Crime Literacy Quiz

1. How many people are in U.S. prisons and jails? What percentage is
   white? Black?
2. How many people were arrested in 1998? What percentage was white?
   Black? Asian American? American Indian? Hispanic?
3. What percentage of homicide cases are interracial (offender and victim
   are different race)?
4. What percent of the U.S. population is Hispanic? Black? Native American? Asian American? White?
5. What does it mean to say that a racial group is "disproportionately under-
   represented" in crime statistics?
6. What does it mean to say that the criminal justice system operates in a
   "racially discriminatory" manner?
7. How many people are currently on death row? What percentage is white?
   Black? Hispanic? Asian American? Native American?
8. Which one of these groups is the fastest growing within the criminal justice system: Asian American men, Asian American women, black
   women, black men, Hispanic men, Hispanic women, Native American
   men, Native American women, white men, white women?

Their responses echo national poll data. Most Americans—white, Hispanic, Asian, Native American, and black—fear minority males, particularly young black males. This runs contrary to clear evidence that indicates that more than 75 percent of all crime involves an offender and victim of the same race.[1]

These two classroom exercises and their results provide an introduction to the issue of how racial images affect definitions of crime. This chapter explores this question by focusing on three topics. First, there is an examination of how some *racial groups* are invisible in discussions of crime and how this impacts those racial groups with hypervisibility. Second, I explore how some *crimes* and offenses are invisible in discussions of crime. Third, the harm caused by these empirical and social oversights—to the discipline of criminology and society at large—is described. The chapter concludes with five recommendations for redressing the current racial equation: crime = black crime.

IMPACT ON THE STUDY OF CRIME

Invisibility of Some Racial Groups

Most overt associations made between crime and race—by criminologists, the media, and the public—typically refer to blacks or Hispanics. This reality is evidenced by labels such as "black-on-black" crime and "black crime." These racial labels and others (e.g., "Hispanic gang") are so common, they have become household terms. The omnipotence of studies and news reports on black offending, however, obscures the criminal involvement of other racial groups.

Two examples illustrate this point. First, the skewed focus on black offending has left little room for investigating other minority groups, such as Native Americans and Asian Americans. The oversight of Native Americans is particularly problematic given that they have the highest rate of victimization of any racial group. A recent Justice Department study found that Native Americans are victims of violent crime at a rate of 124 per 1,000 (Bureau of Justice Statistics 1999). This rate is twice as high as the rate for blacks. As startling, most crimes committed against Native Americans involve offenders who are not Native Americans (70 percent). This reality runs contrary to a general rule of criminology: that crime is an intraracial phenomenon.

In addition to Native Americans, Asian Americans are also slighted in analyses of crime and race. There is relatively little academic study and public discussion of Asian American involvement in the criminal justice system. The invisibility of Native Americans and Asian Americans is largely the result of the predominant black/white paradigm in criminal justice research. An example of this is how Native Americans and Asians are typically classified for official data. Many measures of race are divided into three categories: "Black," "White," and the catchall "Other." The latter is an undefinable group with no common racial lineage. Using "Other" as a racial category collapses distinctly separate racial groups—Hispanics, Native Americans, and Asian Americans—into one category.

Second, whites represent another group whose involvement in the criminal justice system is mostly overlooked. As noted earlier, a review of arrest data indicates that the majority of people arrested each year—68 percent—are white (U.S. Department of Justice 1999). The white arrest figures for arson are the highest, at 74 percent (U.S. Department of Justice 1999: 228). Furthermore, whites comprise approximately 40 percent of the prison population (Bureau of Justice Statistics 1999). The "whiteout" in criminal justice research on crime and race appears to be directly tied to a focus on racial disparity. That is, the media and academic inquiry emphasize blacks and Hispanics—who are disproportionately overrepresented in criminal activity (e.g., Russell, Pfeifer, and Jones 2000).

The vice-grip hold that black and Hispanic offending has on the public and academic mind make it difficult, if not impossible, to discuss other racial groups. No doubt, much of the focus on blacks and Hispanics is the result of disproportionate offending. However, it is necessary to reject the contemporary equation "crime = black crime." For some groups, particularly those that comprise a small part of the population (e.g., Native Americans and Asian Americans), this overshadowing may increase their levels of distrust about the criminal justice system.

Invisibility of Some Crimes and Offenses

Directly linked to the fact that the public and academic arenas focus on the criminal involvement of particular racial groups is the mainstream focus on street crime. Specifically, there is an emphasis on index offenses, in particular murder, burglary, robbery, assault, and rape. A look at local evening news programming as well as the leading criminology journals underscores this point. The spotlight on black and Hispanic street crime supports race-based theories of deviance, such as subculture of violence theories (e.g., Wolfgang and Ferracuti 1967). Also, this focus intimates that there is something about blackness—something genetic—that explains deviance. Furthermore, the skewed emphasis on the index crimes of some racial groups creates a climate in which theories of racial supremacy flourish. The popularity of *The Bell Curve* (Herrnstein and Murray 1994) is perhaps the best example of this.

Several concerns are raised by the contemporary link between blackness and criminality. First, the overemphasis on black and Hispanic offending make it harder to "see" offenses committed *against* these same groups. Racial hoaxes are one example of this problem.[2] Over the years, there have been dozens of instances in which someone white has falsely accused someone black of a crime. The Susan Smith and Charles Smith cases are well-known hoax incidents. There are, however, more than sixty-five documented racial hoax cases (Russell 1998: 69).

Though hoax incidents appear to be a relatively rare phenomenon, their impact is broad.[3] Beyond the economic impact of hoaxes, which includes wasted police resources deployed to search for imaginary criminals, there are social costs as well. Racial hoaxes, particularly those that receive widespread publicity, have the effect of reinforcing negative stereotypes about crime and race. Specifically, that young black men are public enemy number one. The term *criminal black man* accurately describes this mythlike race/gender image of deviance. More important, for children hoaxes *create* negative associations between blackness and criminality. Additionally, racial hoaxes deepen racial fears and increase distrust between racial groups, and, for minorities in particular, they may increase levels of distrust in the justice system. The fact that most racial hoax offenders are never punished (e.g., charged with filing a false police report) renders their harm against minorities legally invisible.

"Driving While Black" or "Driving While Brown" (DWB) offer another example of how offenses against blacks and Hispanics have been overlooked (Russell 1998: 33; Yardley 1999). For years, blacks have complained that they have been victims of racial targeting by police. Specifically, they state that black men are frequently pulled over, questioned, harassed, and assaulted by police, on the basis of their skin color (Russell 1999; Harris 1998). Black men, famous and unknown alike, have detailed the range of DWB incidents. These include being stopped by police because they where driving a luxury car, an old car, or a rented car; driving too fast or too slow; driving in a white neighborhood or in a low-income, high–drug traffic neighborhood (e.g., Russell 1998: 33). The fact that racial targeting has acquired its own acronym, DWB, indicates the degree to which the practice has become routinized.

Until recently, the catalog of DWB anecdotes have been dismissed either as false or as a logical consequence of disproportionate minority offending. The fact that blacks have a disproportionately high rate of criminal offending has been used to justify unfair police practices. The fact that most of the criminals featured on the evening news are black only underscores the reality of disproportionate offending. It sends a clear message: Innocent or guilty, black men are reasonable criminal suspects.[4]

Three years ago, federal legislation was introduced that would have required police to record data from each traffic stop. The proposed law would have mandated that officers gather information on the race and gender of the driver, nature of the stop, and whether a citation was issued (*Traffic Stops Statistics Act* 1997). The legislation, which was ultimately defeated, faced heated objections, primarily from the law enforcement community. The response to the proposed law illustrates a classic catch-22 situation. The breadth of the harm and injury that blacks and Hispanics complained of cannot be addressed until it is empirically verified. Ironically, several highly publicized incidents involving police who knowingly falsified traffic stop data have placed DWB back onto the national agenda (New Jersey Department of Law and Public Safety 1999). The problem of racial hoaxes and DWB demonstrate that one consequence of defining crime as "a black thing" may cause us to overlook ways in which definitions of crime shut out racial minorities. This situation can only increase the levels of black and Hispanic mistrust of the criminal justice system.

A second concern raised by the link between blackness and criminality is that it mutes the role that race plays in other types of criminal offending. By using street crime as the touchstone for what constitutes "real crime," it becomes possible to overlook the incidence, prevalence, and social costs of other types of offenses. An example of this is white-collar crime. Studies indicate that white-collar crime exacts a heavy toll on society, both economically and in terms of cost to human life (e.g., Delgado 1994; Mokhiber 2000). Also noteworthy, race is rarely associated with or used as an explanatory variable to understand white-collar crime (Harris 1991). In effect, white-collar crime is racially invisible.

A third outcome is that the existing equation "crime = black crime" supports a viewpoint that black offending represents the greatest social threat. In turn, this perception has been used to justify various draconian crime measures. The federal crack law is the best example of this phenomenon. Under this statute, a person who is convicted of possessing five grams of crack cocaine faces a mandatory five-year sentence. Conversely, for someone to be sentenced to the same prison term for powder cocaine possession, they would have to be convicted of possessing *five hundred* grams of powder cocaine.

A review of the history of this law clearly establishes that the driving force behind it was the fear of black crime (e.g., *U.S. v. Clary* 1994). The U.S. Congress's decision to impose a 100:1 sentencing disparity was not based on any medical evidence that crack cocaine is one hundred times more potent than powder cocaine (its derivative). Nor was it based on empirical evidence that crack cocaine users are one hundred times more dangerous than powder cocaine users. Legislators were heavily persuaded by widespread and voluminous media reports indicating that crack, a largely urban phenomenon, was rapidly spreading to suburban enclaves. The fear of crack infiltration was so great, Congress dispensed with its standard, lengthy deliberative process: the proposed legislation became law within six weeks. In the mid-1980s, when the bill was under consideration, almost all of the media images of crack users and sellers were of black inner-city dwellers (e.g., *U.S. v. Clary* 1994: 783). This racial representation is both odd and ironic considering that the majority of people who use crack cocaine are white. Studies conclusively establish that whites make up approximately *two-thirds* of all people who use crack cocaine (e.g., U.S. Department of Health and Human Services 1997: 37).

Given the legislative history of the federal crack law, it is not surprising that blacks bear the brunt of those charged and convicted under the law. In fact, blacks comprise close to 90 percent of those sentenced under the harsh mandatory law. Hispanics constitute about 7 percent of those convicted under the statute (U.S. Sentencing Commission 1995: xi). Also, many state laws impose harsher sanctions for crack possession (Mauer and Huling 1995: 11), which has also resulted in racially disparate rates of incarceration. For example, in 1992 blacks and Hispanics accounted for 90 percent of the state prison population serving time for drug possession (Mauer and Huling 1995: 13).

In addition to the federal crack law, there has been an increase in the number of "get-tough" laws. These include "three strike" and mandatory minimum laws. As well, there has been an increase in the number of people sentenced under them. The Sentencing Project estimates that during the 1990s, the risk that a drug arrest would lead to incarceration increased by *400 percent* (Mauer and Huling 1995: 10). This reality has had a dramatic impact on black and Hispanic incarceration. This is starkly illustrated by the predicted incarceration rates by race. In fact, the lifetime likelihood that a person will go to prison is directly tied to race. For blacks it is 16.2 percent; Hispanics, 9.4 percent; and whites, 2.5 percent (Bureau of Justice Statistics 1997).

The Harm of Continuing Business as Usual

The prior discussion demonstrates the wide-ranging negative consequences of contemporary, mainstream definitions of crime. Beyond the fact that it means certain racial groups receive heightened scrutiny while others escape it all together, racialized definitions of crime encourage minority skepticism and mistrust of the justice system. The racial fallout from the O. J. Simpson criminal case is an acute reminder of this reality.

The current "crime = black crime" equation has numerous social consequences. First, it encourages blacks and Hispanics to distrust the criminal justice system. It provides fuel for the belief, held by many blacks, that "justice" means "just us." For example, Justice Department surveys consistently demonstrate that minorities have much less confidence in the criminal justice system than whites (e.g., Bureau of Justice Statistics 1999: 104).

In addition to buttressing a general cynicism toward the criminal justice system, the skewed emphasis on black crime has encouraged a range of problematic "self-help" responses. One of the more controversial responses has been a call for race-based jury nullification. Specifically, Paul Butler (1995) has argued that the exponentially increasing black incarceration rate—in large part driven by racial fear—has led to the over-incarceration of blacks. This has culminated in policies that treat nonviolent, first-time offenders the same as hardened criminals. To stem the ever-heightening tide of black prisoners, Butler boldly concludes that black jurors should acquit nonviolent black offenders, regardless of the evidence. To date, a national, empirical study of the prevalence of jury nullification has not been conducted. However, it is widely speculated that black jurors, particularly in urban areas, are sympathetic to nullification (e.g., Parloff 1997; Rosen 1997).

CONCLUSION: STEPS TOWARD CHANGE

This chapter outlines the ways in which our definitions of crime are intricately linked to race. The fear of black crime in particular has fueled several criminal justice system "reforms." These include an expanded list of crimes, enhanced penalties for offenses perceived as "black" crimes, and an increased likelihood of incarceration for existing offenses. Furthermore, this fear has enabled society to shield from view those crimes and other harms committed *against* blacks and Hispanics (e.g., racial hoaxes, racial targeting). Related to this, society's emphasis on black crime has obscured the crime committed by whites—"white crime." Likewise, crime and justice issues of other minority groups, such as Native Americans, are frequently overlooked. Moreover, the overemphasis on black offending can only increase the already high level of mistrust that blacks have in the criminal justice system. Additionally, the focus on black crime is at the expense of examining other types of offending, including white-collar crime.

As students of criminology and criminal justice, we should be concerned about the long-term negative consequences of associating crime with blackness. To this end, the following recommendations are offered:

- Studies and courses on "race and crime" should be expanded to include *all* racial groups, including whites.
- Studies and courses on crime and race should be expanded to include white-collar crime.
- Race/crime labels should either be used for all racial groups or not used at all. For example, if "black crime" is used, "white crime" should also be used.
- Greater attention should be given to "ethnicity" in discussions of the relationship between crime and race.
- Inaccurate media images should be challenged in the classroom.

These suggestions are offered as one step toward addressing the skewed emphasis on crime and race.

NOTES

1. This is not true for Native Americans and Asian Americans, who are most likely to be victimized by offenders of another race. See, for example, *American Indians and Crime* (Greenfeld and Smith 1999) at p. 7.

2. A racial hoax is defined as follows: "When someone fabricates a crime and blames it on another person because of his race OR when an actual crime has been committed and the perpetrators falsely blame someone because of his race" (Russell 1998: 70).

3. To date, no official data are available on racial hoaxes.

4. The DWB phenomenon has been primarily linked to black men. There are, however, instances in which black women are victimized by racial profiling. A March 2000

report by the U.S. Government Accounting Office indicates that black women are nine times more likely to be subjected to strip searches by U.S. Customs than white women. This is particularly striking considering that black women "were less than half as likely to be found carrying contraband as White women" (2).

REFERENCES

Bureau of Justice Statistics. 1997. *Lifetime Likelihood of Going to State or Federal Prison*. Washington, D.C.: U.S. Department of Justice.

————. 1999. *Sourcebook of Criminal Justice Statistics, 1998*. Washington, D.C.: U.S. Department of Justice.

Butler, Paul. 1995. "Racially Based Jury Nullification: Black Power in the Criminal Justice System." *Yale Law Journal* 105: 677–724.

Delgado, Richard. 1994. "Rodrigo's Eighth Chronicle: Black Crime, White Fears—On the Social Construction of Threat." *Virginia Law Review*, 80: 503–48.

Greenfeld, Lawrence A., and Steven K. Smith. 1999. *American Indians and Crime*. Washington, D.C.: U.S. Department of Justice.

Harris, Anthony. 1991. "Race, Class, and Crime." In *Criminology: A Contemporary Handbook*, ed. Joseph Sheley. Belmont, Calif.: Wadsworth, pp. 95–119.

Harris, David. 1998. "Car Wars: The Fourth Amendment's Death on the Highway." *George Washington Law Review* 66: 556–90.

Herrnstein, Richard, and Charles Murray. 1994. *The Bell Curve: Intelligence and Class Structure in American Life*. New York: Free Press.

Kappeler, Victor, Mark Blumberg, and Gary Potter. 1993. *The Mythology of Crime and Criminal Justice*. Prospect Heights, Ill.: Waveland.

Mauer, Marc, and Tracy Huling. 1995. *Young Black Americans and the Criminal Justice System: Five Years Later*. Washington, D.C.: The Sentencing Project.

Mokhiber, Russell. 2000. *Corporate Crime Reporter* <www.corporatepredators.org/top100.html>.

New Jersey Department of Law and Public Safety. 1999. *Interim Report of the State Police Review Team Regarding Allegations of Racial Profiling* <www.state.nj.us/lps>.

Parloff, Roger. 1997. "Race and Juries: If It Ain't Broke." *American Lawyer* (June): 5.

Rosen, Jeffrey. 1997. "One Angry Woman." *New Yorker* (24 February).

Russell, Katheryn. 1998. *The Color of Crime: Racial Hoaxes, White Fear, Black Protectionism, Police Harassment, and Other Macroaggressions*. New York: New York University Press.

————. 1999. " 'Driving While Black': Corollary Phenomena and Collateral Consequences." *Boston College Law Review* 40: 717–30.

Russell, Katheryn, Pfeifer, Heather, and Judith Jones. 2000. *Race and Crime: An Annotated Bibliography*. Norwich, Conn.: Greenwood.

Traffic Stops Statistics Study Act. 1997. H.R. 118, 105th Congress, H.R. Rep. No. 105–435 (1998).

U.S. v. Clary, 846 F. Supp. 768 1994.

U.S. Department of Health and Human Services. 1997. *National Household Survey on*

Drug Abuse: Population Estimates 1996. Rockville, Md.: U.S. Department of Health and Human Services.

U.S. Department of Justice. 1999. *Crime in the United States, 1998: Uniform Crime Reports*. Washington, D.C.: U.S. Department of Justice.

U.S. Government Accounting Office. 2000. *Better Targeting of Airline Passengers for Personal Searches Could Produce Better Results*. Washington, D.C.: U.S. Government Accounting Office.

U.S. Sentencing Commission. 1995. *Cocaine and Federal Sentencing Policy*. Washington, D.C.: Government Printing Office.

Wolfgang, Marvin, and Franco Ferracuti. 1967. *The Subculture of Violence: Towards Integrated Theory in Criminology*. London: Tavistock.

Yardley, Jim. 1999. "Some Texans Tiring of Stops by Border Patrol." *New York Times*, 26 January 2000, 1.

10

Constitutive Definition of Crime: Power as Harm

Dragan Milovanovic and Stuart Henry

As a response to the inadequacy of definitions that have been presented over the last thirty years (see the articles by Tappan [1947] and the critique by Schwendinger and Schwendinger [1970] reprinted in this volume), we have developed a constitutive definition of crime (Henry and Milovanovic 1991, 1993, 1994, 1996; see also Barak and Henry 1999). Admittedly, the critical versions of the earlier consensus definitions of crime conceived of harm as social injury. This view opened up the idea that victims of harm are found beyond those defined by law. They thus alerted us to the limits of relying on the concept of "individual" as the sole recipient of harm; harm can also be directed at groups and social categories and can be experienced as pain because of one's identification with such groups, rather than because harm was directed at any particular individual (e.g., hate crimes).[1] These critics also allowed us to see that harm was created by those in dominant positions of power and authority and even by social systems. But, in our view, these critical approaches also have their limits. By identifying specific individual or collective entities as abusers of others, such approaches are deficient in establishing the commonality that underlies all forms of harm: the exercise of power over others. We set out to examine whether all expressions of power are harmful or whether there is a particular set of conditions pertaining to the expression of power that constitutes its use as harmful.

RECONCEPTUALIZING HARM

When constructing notions of harm, we must keep in mind that two factors are relevant: the concept of "other" and the quality of the behavior that is found harmful. Schwendinger and Schwendinger (1970) indicated that the concept of socially injurious behavior should be extended beyond a focus on "other" as harm creator, to include social systems and social relationships that inflict injury. Indeed, in our view, the concept of other can range from more general collective categories (e.g., society, community, public, consumer, humanity, etc.), to more specific powerful collective groups (e.g., the state, agencies, organizations, etc.), to relatively powerless collective groups (e.g., employee, gender, sexual preference, etc.), to the much-celebrated category of "the individual." However, we believe that it is important to recognize that these are socially constructed subject categories and refer not only to the "other as offender" but also to the "subject as victim." So, while the more powerful collective offender can victimize the less powerful, as in the state victimizing women, the less powerful can also victimize the more powerful, as in employees victimizing organizations. The problem with conventional definitions of crime, particularly as reflected in law, is that they tend to overemphasize and overcriminalize actions of the kind where the less powerful victimize the more powerful. Furthermore, the law underemphasizes actions of the kind where the more powerful victimizes the less powerful. Insofar as it does this, the law constitutes a second level of crimes of the powerful. We will return to the issue of law as crime later, but for now this issue is relevant to the quality of behavior deemed harmful as a factor in defining crime, which we consider next.

Previous attempts at defining crime by traditional modernist theorists have tried to classify the various instances of these specific behaviors (e.g., harms against the person, harms against property, etc.). In the process these attempts miss the important issue of who recognizes these behaviors as harms and that as "crimes" these actions are discursive constructions that vary historically and contextually. This flaw was exposed by labeling theorists and later by conflict theorists, both of whom point out that dominant groups impose their definitions and standards on others. Richard Quinney's (1970: 15–16) early conflict assumptions marked a pivotal change in the critical perception of crime. He saw this as "a definition of human conduct created by authorized agents in a politically organized society [that describes] behaviors that conflict with the interests of the segments of society that have the power to shape public policy."

Building on Quinney's argument, our contribution suggests, more generally, that harmful behavior is framed in terms of two dimensions: reduction and repression. Moreover, these dimensions affect a particular position or standing. Both reduction and repression are an expression of existing power differentials and existent hierarchical relations. Harms of reduction "occur when an offended party experiences a loss of some quality relative to their present standing" (Henry and Milovanovic 1996: 103). Human subjects are constituted by a complex multiplicity of historically changing aspects, contemporarily distinguished as differences. Harms may thus find configurations around such complexes as economics (property, class), race and ethnicity (hate crime, petit apartheid, racism), gender (sexism), politics (corruption, power), social position (prestige, status, inequities), human rights (to self-realization), psychological state (well-being, security), self-actualization, biological integrity, morality, ethics, and so forth. Harms of reduction occur when a person is reduced on one or more of these different dimensions, each of which itself is socially constituted and therefore subject to change over time, as well as culturally. Thus, in a contemporary Western industrial society that values private property ownership, the economic dimension of harms of reduction would include: stolen property; the biological dimension would include bodily injury; and the social dimension might include forms of hate crime, as well as more invisible forms such as petit apartheid, in which a person of color is disrespected in particular encounters prior to formal police processing (see, e.g., Georges-Abeyie 1990; Russell 1998). In contrast, in a collective culture such as Native American Indian society, these aspects would be differently configured such that personal acquisition of property would be a harm of reduction against the land, bodily injury may be a harm of reduction against the ancestors, and so on.

The common feature in this analysis is that something is taken away from an existing constituted entity through the exercise of power, leaving it less than it was before the change. Whether this is a harm or simply a change depends critically on whether the entity suffering the change perceives it as a loss. This, in turn, depends on whether the person or entity is fully free to object to the exercise of power responsible for imposing the reduction, whether they are free to resist it, and whether their resistance is able to prevent the reduction occurring. This is crucial, since we are not suggesting that unless the status quo is maintained, a crime will have occurred. Rather, we are suggesting that change must be coproduced through a process of conscious active participation by all of those affected by it, such that those affected are able to define their own future, and particularly their own level of risk, and not have this imposed by others.

Harms of repression "occur when an offended party experiences a limit or restriction preventing them from achieving a desired position or standing" (Henry and Milovanovic 1996: 103). For example, because of the adverse effects inflicted by the intersectional positioning of race, gender, and class, a person or group may be unable to achieve a desired standing or position. Particularly illustrative here is Crenshaw's (1991: 114–16) tripartite analysis. This indicates that intersections can occur at various levels: (1) "structural intersectionality," by which she means the existence of "overlapping structures of subordination"; (2) "political intersectionality," referring to "the different ways in which political and discursive practices relating to race and gender interrelate, often erasing women of color"; and (3) "representational intersectionality," which indicates "the way that race and gender images, readily available in our culture, converge to create unique and specific narratives deemed appropriate for women of color." In short, crimes of reduction and crimes of repression are harms because they diminish a person's or group's position, or they deny them the opportunity to attain a position they desire, a position that does not deny another from attaining her or his or their own position. This last point is a crucial caveat to our argument, since without it one person or collective group could dominate another, as has happened historically, on the grounds that the dominated group stood in the way of the dominating groups' progress, development, civilization, and the like. Thus, we argue that satisfying positions of desire cannot occur at another's expense.

HARMS OF REDUCTION: THE CASE OF RACISM AND PETIT APARTHEID

Let us provide an example of a more invisible form of a harm of reduction. Ever since the U.S. Supreme Court decision *Brown v. Board of Education* in 1954, racism has received more formal, legal attention. In the earlier interpretations of the Court decision, "conditions" contributing to racism were underscored. Later, a backlash brought a new interpretation: one needed not only to make a *prima facie* case but also to prove "intent," a huge task indeed. Effectively, "conditions" were no longer targets for change, but sought were the "bad apples." In other words, larger issues that crystallize harms of reductions and repression are effectively dismissed. Later, critical race theory began to look at racial disparities in the criminal justice system with various outcomes (see MacLean and Milovanovic 1990). Recently, more invisible forms of racism are being studied. Thus, along a visibility continuum, there exists, at one end, more official police "profiling," then at a middle level of visibility, DWB ("Driving While Black"), to, at the other end, a more hidden form that has been identified as "petit apartheid." The latter form of racism, which we describe later, is perhaps the most invisible within the criminal justice system, but it is the basis for our definition of harms of reduction.

Georges-Abeyie (1990: 12) has offered the following notion of petit apartheid, which includes

[t]he everyday insults, rough or brutal treatment, and unnecessary stops, questions, and searches of blacks; the lack of civility faced by black suspects/arrestees: the quality, clarity, and objectivity of the judges' instructions to the jury when a black arrestee is on trial; the acceptance of lesser standards of evidence in cases that result in the conviction of black arrestees, as well as numerous other punitively discretionary acts by law enforcement and correctional officers as well as jurists.

Well within our definition of harm and its implication for new efforts for change, Georges-Abeyie's (1990: 32) call is for a grounded theory: "Such a grounded theoretical approach might also note the significance of 'Petit Apartheid' victimization (i.e., indignities) that go unreported, and thus undocumented, yet nonetheless indelibly impact upon community/police relations and expectations."

The term *microaggression* (Davis, cited by Russell 1998: 138) is also compatible with the notion of petit apartheid: these are racial assaults that are "subtle, stunning, often automatic and non-verbal exchanges which are 'put downs' of Blacks by [whites]" (Davis, cited by Russell 1998: 138). Russell (1998: 138–39) provides some examples:

A White person who will not make direct eye contact with a Black person while speaking to him, a White person who enters a business office and assumes that the Black person she sees is a secretary or a janitor, a cab driver who refuses to pick up a Black passenger, a White person who refuses to give directions to someone Black, and a White sales clerk who offers assistance to a White patron in line behind a Black patron.

We are reminded of a recent example at one of our campuses. An African American full-time faculty member was taking his own old computer out of his office and putting it in the trunk of his car. The campus police appeared promptly and subjected him to much interrogation and disrespect. A short time later, the campus police helped a white person loading his car on the same campus but later found out that the merchandise that was loaded was identified as stolen property. Or consider the case of the "enlightened" professor teaching a class of largely white criminal justice students, containing one or two black students. In asking the students in the class for their different views on bias in the criminal justice system, the professor drew out a diversity of ideas. But when the same professor turned to the one or two black students to address issues of racism in criminal justice from an African American perspective, as if these students could speak for all blacks, it suggested that African Americans have only one voice, not a diversity of different ideas and views. These black students were thus denied, reduced from what they might otherwise have been, feeling less than their white classmates who were respected for their individual differences. Thus, they were reduced both as a group and as individuals.

CONSTITUTIVE DEFINITION

To summarize our analysis so far, we argue that crime, as traditionally conceived, is a discursively constituted category with historical specificities. As such, "crime" is a composite category that often conflates some differences that are grounded in the social reality of meaningful relationships, while constructing others that are abstract and related to the contrived reality of legality. It is a conglomeration of harms of reduction and repression into a singular category, such as "property crimes" or "crimes against the person." It is the celebration of homogeneity over heterogeneity. This is not to say that these harms are of no consequence. Only naïve critics of earlier forms of nihilistic versions of postmodern analysis adhere to this view (Schwartz and Friedrichs 1994). However, it has no place in an affirmative postmodern analysis. What we emphasize instead is that people in relations of harm are subject to relations of inequality, whether it is in the instant as a momentary occurrence (many conventional crimes take this form) or continuously (as in the case of many crimes of the powerful, such as hate crime, corporate crime, and gender or racial discrimination). Through these relations of power they are reduced from a position they had (harms of reduction) or prevented from what they potentially could become (harms of repression). People, as discursively constituted subjects, find themselves on occasions in positions of disrespect. Thus, for us, harm can be defined as "the expression of some agency's energy to make a difference to others and it is the exclusion of those others who in the instant are rendered powerless to maintain or express their humanity" (Henry and Milovanovic 1996: 116).

By "agency" we mean those who invest energy in denying others through harms of reduction or repression. As defined earlier, these agents could be human beings, social identities (women, men), various groups, political parties, social and cultural institutions, agents of social control, the legal apparatus, the state, and so forth. In a more abstract way, we also include our notion of constitutive interrelational sets (COREL sets) as historical configurations of coupled iterative loops that vary in their effects in time, place, and manner (Henry and Milovanovic 1996). As we have seen earlier, one manifestation can be translated into the offerings of critical race theory of intersectional analysis; that is, race, gender, and class often intersect with consequential harms that are greater than the sum of their parts (Crenshaw 1991, 1992; see also Milovanovic and Schwartz 1999). In other words, we include the person, as is celebrated by the legalistic definition of crime, as well as various social relations and social systems, as incorporated in the Schwendinger and Schwendinger (1970) definition of social injurious behavior.

In short, then, harms, or "crimes," are expressions of the exercise by one or more agency of power over others, who in the instant of that expression, whether momentary or sustained over time, are rendered powerless to make a difference. Crime is thus a denial of the other's humanity. In the instance of its expression, the victim, therefore, is rendered a nonperson, a less complete human being, incapable of making a difference: "[C]rimes are nothing less than moments in the expression of power, such that those who are subjected to them are denied their own contribution to the encounter and often to future encounters, they are denied their worth. Crime is the power to deny others their ability to make a difference" (Henry and Milovanovic 1996: 116). Having defined the exercise of power as the harm that is crime, does this render the power of law crime? We will return to the discussion we introduced earlier.

ON THE POVERTY AND POWER OF LAW

Perusal of existing law indicates that it covers only a partial list of harms. Our definition begins in the context of pain inflicted, whether by way of harms of reduction or harms of repression. It includes a greater spectrum of socially injurious behaviors, extending from historically more invisible forms such as in family relations and forms of petit apartheid on the one end, to governmental crimes inflicted in the name of the state's self-interest. For example, in the ongoing Balkan conflicts, it would call for the UN War Crimes Tribunal to focus not only on individual cases of "war crimes" but on state crimes and crimes by collective entities and their leaders, including actions committed in the name of suppressing violence.[2] Other examples of applying our definition of crime are homelessness as an induced harm, hierarchical social relations, neglect of health and safety considerations, workplace harms, and violence against intimates.

Some leftist scholars and activists are not immune from the critique that they have a myopic view of harm as crime. Indeed, crimes according to our constitutive definition would includes the forms of "hate" or "revenge" politics that Drucilla Cornell (1991) says overzealous leftists inflict on identified/constructed investors in harm. This includes "exorcism" (Milovanovic 1991), whereby an overzealous activist attempts to construct the evil in the other and then attacks his or her own construction. Our constitutive definition also includes the praxis of "reversal of hierarchies" insomuch as hierarchies and domination are still sustained. It would include, also, the harms produced by more complex COREL sets, which, in their effects, systematically deny segments of the population their ability to self-actualize. Neglecting "conditions," for example, in the onset of institutional racism, and merely treating the effects in law abdicate critical inquiry in the interplay of constitutive interrelational dynamics that sustain subordination. Our definition includes those who benefit from the formality of contract law because of power inequities, as Max Weber, Emile Durkheim, and Karl Marx demonstrated many years ago. Crucially, it includes the fetishism of law, whereby abstractions such as the juridic subject and the equal protection clause of the U.S. Fourteenth Amendment subsume differences under a homogeneous principle, undermining individual difference. In a sense, Marx's conception of social justice, "from each according to his [her] abilities, to each according to his [her] needs," offers one beginning break from the repressive formalism of law and individual forms of criminal justice; here both abilities and needs are assumed to be inherently heterogeneous qualities.

In short, our definition is capable of application to historically changing forms of harms of reduction or repression. These are again discursively constructed categories of induced differences, born of the investment in power over others without the other having the ability to contribute to their own standing or desires. Insomuch as they are able to contribute, we find that various existent discourses will offer only limited capabilities for fuller expression or symbolization. We will also find that concretely inflicted injuries and their verbalizations will often, in a hierarchically organized society, be translated into more cleansed categories of law. Doing so further denies the local knowledges of disenfranchised, marginalized, disempowered, and brutalized peoples (see, e.g., Butler's [1997: 52–65] analysis of the legal apparatus's ability to reformulate "hate speech" into an issue of

First Amendment protections in a case of a burning cross placed on an African American family's front yard; Facchini and Grossman 1999). This point is painfully apparent with the disappearance of any analysis of "conditions" in court decisions in racism issues. In this process, hegemonic understandings of "reality," responsibility, crime, and appropriate responses will often be reified. Thus the violence of language would also be included within our schema (see Freire 1985; McLaren 1994; Aronowitz and Giroux 1991; Giroux 1992)—in other words, what Bourdieu (1977) has referred to as "symbolic violence"—a form of harm that takes place with the inadvertent complicity of the one being harmed.

In our view, therefore, law as it exists "creates" crime, the manifestation of which provides support, energy, and sustenance to existent legal classificatory schemas. Here tautology is the constitutive dynamic in the unilateral construction of "social reality." Thus, "we need to define crime and its harm in terms of specific, but historically contingent, victim categories, but *to be aware of the changing nature of the emerging social constructions whose relations of power are relations of harm*" (Henry and Milovanovic 1996: 119). This underscores the idea that "to change social construction of harm it is necessary to change the social forms and their implied power relations so that harm is not carried under the guise of law, in the expression of power over others" (1996: 118). That is, we recognize law as not only denying various forms of harms, but also as the agency that legitimizes the very power relations that continue to inflict harm on others. As such, law constitutes a second order of harm production through the exercise of its power to maintain the existence of existing harmful relations of power. In these cases law is crime.

THE CASE OF POWER AND PUNISHMENT

Our offering of a constitutive definition of crime as the harm of power requires further research along a number of dimensions. What of the case, the reader may ask, of legally convicting an assaultive offender and punishing him or her? Surely the punishment is a form of reduction and repression? A number of responses are possible. Clearly, since punishment is by definition a form of deprivation, it is a harm operating on two dimensions. It is a crime of reduction, which can occur on multiple dimensions depending on the form of punishment, and a harm of repression. Its impact typically spans beyond the individual to affect families and whole social groups. Punishment adds harm; it does not reduce it. At the outset, historians have indicated how well-intentioned activists have courageously made visible more hidden harms, especially of more powerful groups, and have been instrumental in developing a more punitive response to newly defined harms. Liberal observers often celebrate the case that now "true" equality of punishment has prevailed, and social justice reigns. But with further scrutiny, one realizes very quickly that in the name of an equivalence principle, the overall amount of harms inflicted has increased, not decreased. Thus, the equivalence principle is a flawed ideal. The call here is for the development of a social justice ethics that produces in its concrete consequence the gradual reduction of overall harm in society. We do not need an equivalence principle (perhaps a residue of the commodity fetishism principle and its further development by Pashukanis in the homologous legal fetish form that celebrates abstract sameness) but a difference principle (Laclau and Mouffe 1985). We can only begin to make some suggestions. This is surely a challenge for future critical thought in social justice principles.

Clearly being confined to the logic of a dominant order, accepting the hierarchy as a given, predisposes certain more restrictive reductive and repressive responses to the harmful expressions of power by others (i.e., more police, more prisons, more surveillance, more punishment). We need not be so confined. We offer two alternative visions. The "reformist remedial policy" (Henry and Milovanovic 1996) within criminal justice sees society as fundamentally pathological but recognizes that certain change in institutional and organizational adjustments can reduce the conditions constituting the harm that is crime. See, for example, T. R. Young's (1992, 1997a, 1997b) chaos-informed approach in which he suggests that identifying key social parameters and how iteration may proceed in nonlinear fashion may provide us with clues as to rearrangement of these key parameters.[3] In contrast, "the radical accusatory approach" assumes that the whole society contributes to the actions of human beings in some complex way and hence is also proportionally responsible, good or bad (see also Griffith 1970).[4]

In our constitutive analysis, we argue that there are various levels of responses to harm, extending from a focus on the agent, on the social-relational, and on the cultural and structural. Since we adhere to the notion of COREL sets indicating the interconnectedness of all aspects of society and following chaos theory, that even slight resonances can produce often disproportionate effects, good and bad, then responses to harms, too, must creatively work on all levels. Therefore, our view of the human subject is such that we find her or him at the center of an inner porous circle (see figure 10.1), surrounded by a porous circle representing social-relational networks encompassed by other porous circles representing structural and cultural institutions. These are interconnected: causality is reciprocal; feedback loops and iterative practices produce the unexpected; and, therefore, simply abstractly identifying an "individual" as a culprit overlooks strong conditioning forces stemming from several interrelated and intersecting levels. Critical race theory has already, as we have seen, offered intersectional analysis indicating how gender, race, and class intersecting may produce forms of harm greater than the sum of the parts. A social justice policy must formulate initiatives in which all levels are implicated with any harm inflicted.

In this formulation, we focus not only on what traditionally has been termed the microlevel but simultaneously on the macrolevel of analysis. Each "level" therefore contains within it the other levels; however, there are no stable levels in a constitutive view, and the use of the conceptualization is only a temporary ideal-type since it can quickly congeal into a reified structure. Therefore, in our schema, any harm forthcoming must indeed be responded to in terms of variable-sum game dynamics where responsibility is distributed across the various "levels" (see figure 10.1). This is already implied in mediation, conflict resolution, and reconciliation programs, although much theoretical work has not caught up with these innovations. Also, we again underscore that, from our perspective examples of agency are not restricted to individuals as excessive investors in harm but include other cultural, social, and institutional entities and arrangements.

Figure 10.1   Heuristic Model of the Context of Crime

Source: Anthony E. Bottoms and Paul Wiles. 1992. Explanations of Crime and Place. In David J. Evans, Nicholas R. Fyfe, and David T. Herbert, eds. *Crime, Policing and Place: Essays in Environmental Criminology*. London: Routledge, 29.

Elsewhere (Henry and Milovanovic 1996), we have argued for responses that attempt to reduce the overall amount of harm inflicted: a response of social judo whereby power is turned against itself (instances of petit apartheid, e.g., can be creatively challenged by reversing the process in first making it more visible and then turning it against itself); forms of mediation and reconciliation programs that overcome current criticisms, especially concerning the baggage of the desirability of consensus and of a mediation discourse that is restrictive in expressions of difference (see Schehr and Milovanovic 1999); the development of forms of narrative therapy for "repeat" or the most difficult offenders; and the development of replacement discourses whereby differences are allowed expression in a more diversely constituted discourse.

Pavarini's (1994: 56) Marxist view is that the definition of what counts as deviance and as social control is seen as decisively influenced both by those who have "the power to define" and also to those who have the possibility to "resist these definitions." Pavarini (1994: 57) goes on to say that "the more resistance is offered and opposed to the activity of control the more 'freedom' to define their own conduct is given to deviants, and vice versa." Similarly, Ewick and Silbey (1998: 209–13) have suggested the concept of "inversions." By this they mean that as a strategy of resistance, hierarchies of authority can be deliberately ignored, and with this the consequential "relays of respect, deference, and duty that are attached." As they tell it, "[b]ecause power and authority so often go without saying, ignoring these structural differences is disruptive precisely because it forces power to articulate itself, to reassert itself. By demanding power to own up to itself, it calls power's bluff" (210). In other words, their suggestion is well within our thesis of undermining the excessive investors of harm their own energy for renewal. Said differently, for Ewick and Silbey (211), "asymmetrical lines of authority are reversed; in each instance, a person forces someone occupying a position of greater authority to make explicit the prerogatives of that status and to demand rather than simply expect deference. In this sense, resistant acts impose costs, they require power to use additional resources of social interaction." In our view, this is consistent with the notion of undermining excessive investors; it saps them of their urge to impose difference. Another example that Ewick and Silbey provide is to refuse to defer or acknowledge bureaucratic lines of authority. They provide the example of leapfrogging over normal bureaucratic lines of authority. Here they show a person going right to the top of General Electric to take care of a problem that technicians were not able to. This, as they tell it, is also a form of reempowerment (see Henry and Milovanovic 1999 for further examples of the exercise of resistance through replacement discourse).

CONCLUSION

One of the most important challenges for critical criminological scholarship is in the revision of definitions of power as harm and in providing insights into the possible operationalization of these definitions. This is no small task. Our work over the last ten years in developing a constitutive definition of harm has led us to provide a provisional reconceptualization. Many other questions remain. For example, a special challenge is posed with cultural practices that induce reduction or repression, such as worldwide practices of female circumcision. Another challenge is with excessive investors of past repressive regimes or practices (i.e., South Africa, Northern Ireland, Central America, and the Balkans). These pose questions about appropriate responses informed by methods not increasing the overall amount of violence. UN War Crimes Tribunals are especially challenged to respond in ways that do not increase overall violence. The Truth and Reconciliation Commission of South Africa (and modeled in other areas) has been one recent attempt in coming to terms with past injustices, an approach still awaiting critical theoretical analysis as to the question of whether "justice" was being served (see http://www.wits.ac.za/csvr/). But how also to deal, for example, with U.S. governmental crimes: the systematic eradication of the American Indian, ongoing black genocide, the internment of Japanese-Americans in World War II? We make no pretenses that we have answered them all. We only wish to begin, or continue, various other critical analyses that have attempted to provide a new beginning in defining the harm of power and the power of harm more adequately.

NOTES

1. Nietzsche, in *On the Genealogy of Morals*, much earlier offered a critique of arbitrary connections between the "doer" and the "deed." For him the "individual" appears as a consequence of the call for accountability. The fictional individual is born within the requirements of attributing blame and thus for a discourse of moral accountability (see also Butler 1997: 45–46). In the Lacanian psychoanalytic semiotic version, the human subject is provided relative stability at the intersections of imaginary and symbolic determinants (see, e.g., his exposition in the topological construction of Schema R and in his Borromean knots; Milovanovic 1997). These are ultimately political economic determinants producing nodal points, temporary stability points from which a subject may speak (Laclau and Mouffe 1985).

2. Examples include the U.S. and NATO bombing attacks in 1999 on a hospital, a bus, a train, a convoy of farm tractors, TV and radio stations, power plants, the Chinese embassy—calling them, in most cases, "collateral damage." A recent *Chicago Tribune* article (30 December 1999, 24) notes that an internal, secretive report conducted by the UN War Crimes Tribunal is looking into the actions of the United States and NATO in the Kosovo war. The chief prosecutor is reviewing the document, for possible formal action, but according to the *Chicago Tribune*, "The tribunal can charge only individuals with crimes, not states, institutions or organizations." See also Dragan Milovanovic, "Violence, Historical Lessons, and Hegemony in the Balkans," 19 April 1999, http://sun.soci.niu.edu/critcrim/hot/dragkoso.html; and "War Crimes and Selective Prosecution," 30 December 1999, http://sun.soci.niu.edu/critcrim/hot/dragkos2.html.

3. Consider T. R. Young's (1997a: 95) two proposals on, respectively, social control and social policy: "to identify the key parameters, which drive the system into ever more uncertainty," and "to determine which setting of those key parameters is acceptable to the whole society."

4. This was already implied by Griffith's (1970) "family model" as an alternative to a "crime control" or a "due process" model in criminal justice.

REFERENCES

Aronowitz, Stanley, and Henry Giroux. 1991. *Postmodern Education*. Minneapolis: University of Minnesota Press.

Barak, Gregg, and Stuart Henry. 1999. "An Integrative-Constitutive Theory of Crime, Law, and Social Justice." In *Social Justice/Criminal Justice*, ed. Bruce Arrigo. Belmont, Calif.: Wadsworth.

Bourdieu, P. 1977. *Outline of a Theory of Practice*. Cambridge: Cambridge University Press.

Butler, Judith. 1997. *Excitable Speech: A Politics of the Performative*. New York: Routledge.

Cornell, Drucilla. 1991. *Beyond Accommodation: Ethical Feminism, Deconstruction and the Law*. New York: Routledge.

Crenshaw, Kimberle. 1991. "Beyond Racism and Misogyny: Black Feminism and 2 Live Crew." In *Words That Wound: Critical Race Theory, Assaultive Speech, and the First Amendment*, ed. Mari Matsuda, Charles Lawrence, Richard Delgado, and Kimberle Crenshaw. Boulder, Colo.: Westview.

———.1992. "Whose Story Is It Anyway? Feminist and Antiracist Appropriations of Anita Hill." In *Race-ing Justice, En-Gender(ing) Power*, ed. T. Morrison. New York: Pantheon.

Ewick, Patricia, and Susan Silbey. 1998. *The Common Place of Law: Stories from Everyday Life*. Chicago: Chicago University Press.

Facchini, Mark, and Peter Grossman. 1999. "Metaphor and Metonymy: An Analysis of *R.A.V. v. City of St. Paul, Minnesota*." *International Journal for the Semiotics of Law* 12, no. 2: 215–21.

Freire, Paulo. 1985. *The Politics of Education*. South Hadley, Mass.: Bergin & Garvey.

Georges-Abeyie, D. 1990. "Criminal Justice Processing of Non-Whites." In *Racism, Empiricism and Criminal Justice*, ed. Brian MacLean and Dragan Milovanovic. Vancouver, Canada: Collective.

Giroux, Henry. 1992. *Border Crossings*. New York: Routledge.

Griffith, John. 1970. "Ideology in Criminal Procedure or a Third 'Model' of the Criminal Process." *Yale Law Journal* 79: 359–417.

Henry, Stuart, and Dragan Milovanovic. 1991. "Constitutive Criminology." *Criminology* 29, no. 2: 293–316.

———. 1993. "Back to Basics: A Postmodern Re-Definition of Crime." *Critical Criminologist* 5, nos. 2/3: 1–2, 6, 12.

———. 1994. "The Constitution of Constitutive Criminology: A Postmodern Approach to Criminological Theory." In *The Futures of Criminology*, ed. David Nelken. London: Sage.

———. 1996. *Constitutive Criminology*. London: Sage.

———. 1999. *Constitutive Criminology at Work: Applications to Crime and Justice*. Albany: State University of New York Press.

Laclau, Ernesto, and Chantel Mouffe. 1985. *Hegemony and Socialist Strategy*. New York: Verso.

McLaren, Peter. 1994. "Multiculturalism and the Postmodern Critique: Toward a Pedagogy of Resistance and Transformation." In *Between Borders: Pedagogy and the Politics of Cultural Studies*, ed. H. Giroux and P. McLaren. New York: Routledge.

MacLean, Brian, and Dragan Milovanovic, eds. 1990. *Racism, Empiricism and Criminal Justice*. Vancouver, Canada: Collective.

Milovanovic, Dragan. 1991. "Schmarxism, Exorcism and Transpraxis." *Critical Criminologist* 3, no. 4: 5–6, 11–12.

———. 1997. *Postmodern Criminology*. New York: Garland.

Milovanovic, Dragan, and Martin Schwartz, eds. 1999. *Race, Gender, and Class in Criminology*. New York: Garland.

Pavarini, M. 1994. "Is Criminology Worth Saving?" In *The Futures of Criminology*, ed. D. Nelken. London: Sage.

Russell, Katheryn. 1998. *The Color of Crime: Racial Hoaxes, White Fear, Black Protectionism, Police Harassment, and Other Macroaggressions*. New York: New York University Press.

Quinney, Richard. 1970. *The Social Reality of Crime*. Boston: Little, Brown.

Schehr, Robert, and Dragan Milovanovic. 1999. "Conflict, Mediation and the Postmodern: Chaos, Catastrophe, and Psychoanalytic Semiotics." *Social Justice* 26, no. 1: 208–32.

Schwartz, Martin, and David Friedrichs. 1994. "Postmodern Thought and Criminological Discontent: New Metaphors for Understanding Violence." *Criminology* 32, no. 2: 221–46.

Schwendinger, Herman, and Julia Schwendinger. 1970. "Defenders of Order or Guardians of Human Rights?" *Issues in Criminology* 5: 123–57.

Tappan, Paul W. 1947. "Who Is the Criminal?" *American Sociological Review* 12: 96–102.

Young, T. R. 1992. "Chaos Theory and Human Agency." *Humanity and Society* 16, no. 4: 441–60.

———. 1997a. "The ABCs of Crime: Attractors, Bifurcations, and Chaotic Dynamics." In *Chaos, Criminology and Social Justice*, ed. Dragan Milovanovic. Westport, Conn.: Praeger, pp. 77–96.

———. 1997b. "Challenges: For a Postmodern Criminology." In *Chaos, Criminology and Social Justice*, ed. Dragan Milovanovic. Westport, Conn.: Praeger, pp. 29–51.

11

A Needs-Based, Social Harms Definition of Crime

Larry L. Tifft and Dennis C. Sullivan

One of the reasons that the question "What is crime?" deserves serious attention from everyone, criminologist or not, is that the response, if given honestly, tells us who we are, whether we can trust others and be trusted, and how interested we are in living a personal, as opposed to a power- or market-based way of life. In a certain sense, each distinct response to the what-is-crime question reveals differing core assumptions about social life and our beliefs about the root sources of pain and suffering. These responses also tell us of the extent to which we choose to become involved in taking up others' burdens in times of crisis or in ordinary times. Crime, then, is a reflection of what is larger and deeper in social life, of imagining a world without crime, of discovering what is possible in human existence (Quinney 1995: 147). How we think about crime indicates how we assess how social life is currently organized and how it might be better organized.

Maybe the best way to find out what a person believes about social harm, crime, and suffering is to follow that person around for a week and observe how he or she interacts with others. Pursuing the meaning of crime in this manner is, of course, risky business, for we are suggesting that we ourselves become engaged in an archeology of self, and, as well, lay out the discrepancies between what we say and write, how we live our daily lives, and how we believe social life ought to be organized in our families, workplaces, and communities. When we have begun to lay out what we believe are the bases for understanding each other in times of good and ill, we have begun to delve into our nature as human beings and the possibilities we have to live in greater accord with our core values. We have begun to ask what are the possible responses and what are our personal responses when faced with pain and suffering. In addition, we will have begun to ask what we can do to organize our lives differently to not be compelled to respond to harm by creating further harm.

Once we begin to think in terms of possibilities, we find ourselves in the realm of rethinking our relationships with each other and in the communities we have intentionally created or to which we have acquiesced. We have begun to ask ourselves about the desirability of the patterns of interaction within which we find ourselves. Are freedom, well-being, and participation, as well as the opportunities for developing one's potentialities acceptably, justly distributed in our families, at school, and in our places of work? Are the compensatory benefits we receive for work done, the distributions of opportunities for creating a positive sense of self, and our responses to failures, both personal and those of others, just? As you can see, these questions take us into the realms of human need and social justice. So, in the following paragraphs we share with you our vision of how life might be lived based on needs-based social justice and how harms might be defined and responded to in such life contexts.

A NEEDS-BASED CONCEPTION OF SOCIAL JUSTICE

All conceptions of social justice in one way or another are intertwined with the distributions of benefits and burdens throughout a society. The substantive and procedural rules for these distributions are derived from the major social arrangements (Miller 1976: 32). Social justice controversies always have to do with how intangible and tangible benefits and burdens are defined, distributed, and responded to. That is, how are the opportunities to create a positive sense of self, to participate in everyday decisions, and to meet one's basic needs distributed? As well, how are the distributions of respect, dignity, participation in meaningful work, access to health and medical care, and collective wealth distributed in our society generally and in all of our primary institutions: the family, the school, and the workplace (Tifft 1999, 2000)?

Differing conceptions of social justice have functioned as ideological supports for those with power to ensure their privileged access to the distributions. They have, as well, served to encourage those who are aggrieved and oppressed in their struggles against arrangements of institutional power and privilege. The opportunities each of us has to obtain a modicum of well-being in our daily lives and to receive positive support in responding to situations in which we find ourselves in pain or suffering derive from how social life is organized. The key to living in a just and relatively peaceful society is found in the continuous creation of social environments wherein people's needs are taken seriously such that they have little need, and little reason or desire, to act in socially injurious ways (Michalowski 1985; Sullivan 1980; Tifft 1979; 1994–95; 2000; Tifft and Sullivan 1980, 1998a: Ferrell 1999).

Peter Maurin, cofounder of the Catholic Worker Movement, used to say, "We seek a society in which it is easier for people to be good." When we concern ourselves with issues of crime, then, what comes to mind immediately is how are the distributions presently organized and how might we organize life differently so that we might better meet everyone's needs, make it easier for us all to be good, and enjoy ourselves among others. Indeed, as stated at the outset, our sense of social justice derives from the way we think of ourselves and one another, how we communicate and make decisions with one another, and how we imagine ourselves as responsive to and responsible for one another. To understand fully the diversity of criminological perspectives, the proponents of each different conceptualization of crime, harm, and social justice need to articulate fully and clearly what they hold most dear to themselves. They need to speculate how they imagine social life most desirably organized and how they see themselves in relation to others in the future. They also need to reveal how they live now— what social patterns of interaction and what core values they are attempting to foster in their daily lives and how they are dealing with their everyday struggle to create (or avoid) intimate relationships at home, day care, school, and work and how they respond to themselves and others when some harm is created in relationships in which they are involved.

NEEDS-BASED JUSTICE

The challenge facing anyone who seeks to realize a needs-based conception of justice is how to create social processes in which those involved can respond to the continuously changing needs of each person in a way so that each simultaneously feels an equality of well-being (Kropotkin 1924; Piercy 1976; Miller 1976; de Haan 1992; Tifft and Sullivan 1980; Sullivan and Tifft 1998a; Tifft et al. 1997; Sullivan et al. 1999; Heller 1987; Young 1990). Within the framework of equal well-being, the aim is not to distribute collective resources in equal quantities but, rather, in proportions according to each person's choice, need, and desire, but of course always taking into account the collective resources available.

To examine and illustrate needs-based social justice, we have selected family interaction patterns and processes, because, for most of us, family life is our most intimate and significant social sphere. When family members interact with one another according to a needs-based sense of justice, parents respond to, support, show their love for, and are with each child in the family in quite different ways (Tifft 1998; Sullivan et al. 1999). In such a family, each child experiences justice, for each child feels equally, though differently, acknowledged and respected. Each child is responded to in accord with the child's unique needs and essence. Each child feels indispensable and inexchangeable (Frankl 1973: 70–71). In this familial context each child understands through being with, listening, and participating in the family's decisions how it is that his or her siblings experience an equal level of well-being by having their different unique needs fulfilled (Tifft et al. 1997; Tifft 1998). In these families, there is no sense of having been cheated because someone else received more of something or something different. The children in such families develop a keen sense of moral intelligence and early on in life seek to extend this intelligence to others (Coles 1997).

Couples with children who organize family life according to a needs-based ethic tend to relinquish the "good provider" and "good caretaker" roles that have commonly led many coupled persons to live parallel lives in separate spheres (Bernard 1986; Schwartz 1994). Basing their relationships on love/companionship, equality, needs meeting, and giving each person's life plan equal consideration, these couples tend to create what Schwartz (1994) calls "peer marriages." In these partnerships (Le Guin 1975), many coupled persons experience a deep, rich, and intimate friendship through a mutual commitment to responsiveness and responsibility and a mutual provision of real conversation and warmth.

When we look at how family life is lived in these families, we see that the partners collaborate with one another to share an undertaking of family work ("household tasks"), a responsibility for making family decisions, and a created set of arrangements designed to attempt to ensure equal access to family resources (i.e., family TV, family money) (Tifft 1993, 1999, 2000). In families with children or, perhaps, an elderly parent, partners also share what others refer to as "the task of child care" (or elder care) or "the chore of taking care of the children." But, contrastingly, these partners see that these activities are simply "being with" the children (or Mom or Dad). Being with a child or an elderly parent is neither a self-sacrificing task nor a burdensome chore. Even when such relationships are riddled with pain, they can be a source of strength and greater self-authenticity.

Clearly, in our current society, few children experience family life organized as we have described, but this does not diminish the need children have to be cocreators of the family dynamic. To be a full participant is to be loved and trusted, to experience a world larger than self. To develop one's unique human potentialities, one must not be interacted with as a nonhuman object or as a subordinate of an interaction dynamic that generates inequality or stratification (Sullivan and Tifft 1998a, 1998b).

When a conflict, perceived injustice, harm, or dispute arises among the members of a family, patterns of interaction must be initiated that enable all to get to the root issues. If two children are quarreling, a conversation must ensue that elicits each child's feelings, thoughts, sentiments, realities, and understandings of the problem. Each child must have voice; otherwise, the genesis or root of the "trouble" will not be discovered and addressed. Furthermore, if the incidence of the troubling feelings or behaviors is to be decreased, different, mutually created patterns of interaction that better meet everyone's needs must be invented and initiated. Following the logic of this fluid, ever-changing problem-solving dynamic, we must, in all the spheres of our lives, engage in the search for interaction processes that are structurally preventative of harms and restorative of human dignity and equality when harms, disputes, or injustices occur (Sullivan and Tifft 1998a). That is, we need to respond collectively to harms and suffering in a manner that demonstrates that we do not find the harming actions acceptable, yet we acknowledge that we are collectively responsible for altering our patterns of interaction so as to prevent these harms from reoccurring. Rather than a committing to fossilized ways of doing things, we need to create processes that are restorative of our essential commitment to meeting each person's needs and to an equality of well-being, at home, school, and work (Tifft 1979; Ferrell 1999). One principle of needs-based justice, then, is that we are individually and collectively responsible for creating responsive social arrangements that meet needs; in addition, we are individually and collectively responsible for responding to harms and injustices by creating new arrangements that are preventive of non-need-meeting situations (Gil 1998, 1999; Kozol 1996; Tifft et al. 1997; Sullivan, Tifft, and Cordella 1998).

Returning to our family life illustration, Coles and others have convincingly argued that the sense of justice experienced in the family resides at the core of our moral development (Coles 1997; Brazelton 1982, 1992) and that the sense of morality that is developed is the quality by which each person reveals his or her essential being to others (Pieper 1996). If this is the case, we need to create familial environments in which we enable everyone to open their hearts to others. This will be achieved when each person experiences a real sense of participation and can feel their real voice emerging. Once we begin to feel our true self emerge, we begin to develop a greater sense of our own dignity as a person and that of others (Pepinsky 1991). Through this experience, we develop character, self-discipline, and an enthusiasm for life that we want to share with others (Tifft et al. 1997).

POWER

It is not easy for people in our society to grasp the essence of needs-based justice because the benefit/burden–reward/punishment systems of this society and the conceptions underlying them—whether in the family, school, or workplace—reward people when they pursue their own needs at the expense of others, when they create deficits for others in the pursuit of their own "well-being." To put needs-based justice into practice requires us to abandon the principal currency of relations in our currently organized society, power.

To understand the nature of the pain and suffering we "cause" one another and to work to alleviate it, we must understand the workings of power, for power resides at the base of all forms of violence, social harm, "crime," and punishment (Sullivan 1980: 123–36; Tifft and Sullivan 1980; Henry and Milovanovic 1993, 1996: chap. 5; Sullivan and Tifft 1998a; Sullivan et al. 1999). By making power a primary concern of our examination, we are not limited to examining only those acts that are defined by law as violent or criminal (Kennedy 1970; Schwendinger and Schwendinger 1970; Reiman 1998; Henry and Milovanovic 1993, 1996; Tifft 1994–95; Sullivan and Tifft 1998a). Nor are we limited to examining acts that any other set of people declare as worthy of the designation "crime" (Pepinsky 1991; Simpson 1994; Hagan 1977, 1985; Lanier and Henry 1999: 13–35). Included in our needs-based definition crime, is any power-based act that harms another (Tifft 1979, 1994–95; Pfohl 1994; Henry and Milovanovic 1993). While this set of acts includes those defined by law as crime, it also includes those violent actions that are claimed by some to be benevolent, managerially effective, and justified as being done in the name of justice (Miller 1996).

By focusing on power, we can begin to question the assumptions on which most perspectives on crime and punishment are based, for we are enabled to examine human interaction in each and every sphere of social life. For us it is axiomatic, therefore, that there is an integral link between power and justice, and social harms and our collective responses to these harms. It, too, is axiomatic that there can be no peace without justice and no justice through power- or violence-based action, regardless of the rationale offered for such violence (Prejean 1993; Sullivan and Tifft 1998a).

We feel confident asserting that the exercise of power is a form of violence because power-based patterns of interaction politically deny others who they are and economically charge them for what they need. They exclude, exact a price, or place others in debt (Sullivan and Sullivan 1998). With respect to responding to a harm done, power-based responses impose a counterloss or counterharm on the person designated as responsible for the harm. In our current power-based criminal justice system, it is argued that equalization ("justice") can only be achieved through the equalization of loss, through the creation of equal illbeing—that is, that a harm requires the administration of an equalizing harm, even though this equal or greater harm (for deterrence) contributes an additional harm to our social life (Sullivan and Tifft 1998c). What a contradiction!

It should not surprise anyone that the possibility of achieving "justice" through meeting the needs of, or fostering the personal healing of, either the victim/survivor or the harm doer is thwarted by responses grounded in power because such processes shut people down, deconstruct them (Denzin 1984; Scarry 1985; Tifft 1993) and produce a nonpresence—a nonresponsiveness. We can all think of examples of how those subjected to the violence of power are forced to sacrifice their true self, their voice, their energies, to pay for the satisfaction of the power wielder and the set of social arrangements or distributions for which the power wielder acts as a representative. A power wielder might be a stranger but might, as well, be a parent, teacher, physician, employer, corporate decision maker, or agent of state (Tifft 1993; Chomsky 1994: 203–340). In the processes of the equalization of ill-being, the collective response given by, for example, a criminal court judge serves up a counterharm to the offender, ignores the needs of the survivor, neglects the need all of us have for the prevention of such harms, and, most important, affirms the legitimacy of the structurally violent distributions or hierarchies implicated by the offending harm.

In contrast, needs-based community responses to harms attend to the needs of harm doers, survivors, witnesses, and members of the community directly and indirectly affected by the harm. Differing and conflicting needs that exist are neither dismissed nor sacrificed in the interest of some standardized formula or guideline. They are reconciled. Needs-based justice is restorative as is illustrated in family conferencing, community sentencing circles, and other participatory responses to social harm (Sullivan and Tifft 1998b). But such restoration can be created or achieved only when all involved are given the opportunity to collaborate in the justice-making process to fashion a reconciliation of differences that meets the needs of each as defined by each. It should be reiterated that restorative, needs-based justice does not simply mean responding to harms so as to meet everyone's needs; it means, as well, acting together to create new patterns of interaction (distributions) so as to take into account the needs of all from the outset, that is, structurally (Sullivan and Tifft 1998b; Gil 1998, 1999). In this sense, proponents of needs-based restorative justice take issue not only with how interpersonal harms are legally responded to in our current social order—that is, via a demonstration of superior power or vengeful, deficit-creating, harm-delivering actions. We take issue, however, with the hierarchical, power-based social arrangements—the distributions—that are symbolically restored and relegitimated. Furthermore, we object to these arrangements, since by definition these arrangements deny the possibility of the satisfaction of the needs of all (Sullivan and Tifft 1998a) and therefore constitute violent social harms. In short, needs-based arrangements differ radically from those that underlie social arrangements that are hierarchically ordered, based in power exercise, and structured to meet the needs of some at the expense of others.

Once we begin to define our relationships with others in power-based, hierarchical terms, in terms of superior/inferior or worthy/unworthy, we are forced to watch each other with a wary eye. Surveillance becomes an essential accompaniment of feeling the need to scheme and strategize against "them"—to keep "them" in their place, to contain "them" via social control policies designed to limit their expression, especially their demand for full participation in the creation of their personhoods and life activities.

Within these power-based patterns of interaction, when there is participation, it is defined by those higher up in the stratification system in terms of allowing those situated lower down to follow what is prescribed for them by their superiors (Mumford 1967). As alluded to earlier, the rationale for adhering to such disciplining measures derives from a morbid need for satisfaction logic that asserts that it is possible for us to achieve true self-enjoyment through strategies that distance us not only from others but also from ourselves and the world around us. Yet, transcendently we know that surveilling and controlling others, watching and being watched, are activities that allow us no self-enjoyment or even connection with ourselves. Such processes alienate and remove us further from (com)union with others. Thus, the potentiality of true self-joy is diminished.

Power and Self

When we relate with others through power, violence is directed not only toward others but toward ourselves as well. Power-based existence requires us to designate certain parts of ourselves as valuable and worthy of attention (presentable, deserving, marketable) and to marginalize the rest. Power-based existence is an entrapment in self-repression, social harm.

By denying participation to some parts of our self, we make it more difficult for us to be good, we deny ourselves the chance for true self-enjoyment because such enjoyment is possible only as we approach wholeness, as we become the self we truly are and are becoming (Kierkegaard 1941; Rogers 1961, 1980). Since repression on the inside always translates into repression on the outside, our engagement in self-marginalizing and hierarchizing actions appears in numerous ways in our feelings, thoughts, and interaction patterns with others. When power manifests itself in our intrapersonal relations, it is every bit as violent a social harm as the violent street crimes we are victimized by, read about, and see on TV every day. For by denying the voice and precluding the participation of other parts of self, power deconstructs human beingness (Sullivan and Tifft 1998a). Whether power-based actions take place in the family, the school, the workplace, or on the street, a person's life is reduced to acquiescence or obedience to power—to "not being." To survive economically, emotionally, spiritually, and even physically in such arrangements, many of us engage in a process of identity editing, of self-falsification (Tifft et al. 1997). The individualized sense of personal character that emerges from the currency of power is composed of self-protective, survivalist "character armor" designed to minimize emotional and psychological self-loss that must be paid in such relations. The self that emerges in power relations, from the detection of faults, failings, and errors and from a regimented training, is a battered self struggling to formulate, articulate, and voice its thoughts, ideas, and needs, struggling to be taken seriously by self and others, struggling to transcend, to be, struggling to express how it feels about the world in which it lives and how it might respond to this world in ways that do not reconstitute power dynamics (Tifft et al. 1997).

Character means responding to the world without controlling others and not allowing oneself to be controlled by others (Wieck 1975). It means the practice of living according to one's own lights, the practice of Satyagraha (Bose 1965) and not cooperating with what seems wrong (Quinney 1995: 154). In this light, if we wish children, for example, to develop moral character and self-discipline (i.e., a sense of self that is autonomous yet inseparable from the feelings, ideas, and needs of others), children must value the social world in which they live (Tifft et al. 1997). Children must experience membership in a community that is just, a community in which everyone joins together in creating the patterns of interaction and in defining and responding to the problems that arise in our shared life (Tifft et al. 1997). This perhaps, explains why so many people hate to go to work, school, or home, because the possibility of living a life of authenticity is virtually nonexistent. Imagine the energy it requires to survive, to endure, eight-plus hours a day not being yourself. Indeed, many of us do not have to imagine it because we live it! In these conditions, there is little hope of getting to the core of ourselves to discover and create who we are and how we are connected with others. Under such circumstances, trust of, and commitment to, others is denied a foundation, for we remain forever fearful that the dimensions of our self that we have repressed and keep hidden from view will collide with the hidden dimensions of others whom we control or who control us.

What is most insidious about this process of taking our lives to "have a life," to obtain the "cost of living," is that those of us who accommodate to these processes ultimately develop a self that negotiates the world without a real voice—as dummies worked from behind by ventriloquists of power. As those in positions of power define the hybridized forms of person that emerge as belonging to a whole other category of being, they provide themselves with justification for a further surveillance and disciplining of those subject to their power.

As this process unfolds, those in positions of power are confirmed in their original supposition that their lesser counterparts belong to another, different category of being, one that is not deserving, has no or few rights, and lacks the credentials or capabilities to participate as an equal—indeed, to participate at all. While ensuring that one's own needs are met, each higher-up affords him- or herself the final justification needed to disqualify those beneath from sharing in needs-defining, needs-satisfying processes. Should those excluded from participating in decisions that affect their lives begin to raise their voices in protest against their structurally thwarted and ignored needs, they are defined as threats to personal/organizational/national security and as requiring additional doses of harm—surveillance, discipline, and repressive power exercise.

POSTULATES ON CRIME AND SOCIAL HARM

For the most part, those who have taken on the task of studying "crime" accept the present distributions and place social justice and power exercise "beyond examination." As they measure it, the rate of "crime" might go up or down, but the level of social harm in our lives persists because institutionalized power exercise is not thought of in terms of harm or violence. Through its own structural configuration, criminal law cannot be utilized to indict the legal structural violence of power-based institutions or distributions, and certainly it cannot be utilized to indict the legal repressive violence (penal sanctions) of the state that serves to restore arrangements of structural violence when violations of the criminal law occur. The propagandizing and colluding efforts of state-certified professionals and the corporate or state mass media are quite effective, for the violence that is structured into the social arrangements that we experience on a daily basis rarely enters their, and subsequently our, thinking about what constitutes harm or crime. In our schools, children, in only the rarest of instances, are taught about the harms of a non-needs-based learning environment, even though they experience such an environment almost universally (Sullivan and Tifft 1998a; Kohn 1993, 1996). In our workplaces, as discussed earlier, the false self that many of us forges accedes to spending perhaps forty years in absence—following directives from above without opening its mouth to voice its ideas, feelings, and needs. In our families, children are disciplined for infractions of rules that apply only to them and in whose creation they were denied participation.

Dead before we die, many of us take such a way of life for granted. We see it as a necessary part of "the cost of living" (Sullivan 1986–87). When we look at criminal law from such a perspective, we see that for the most part, criminal law is solely responsive to interpersonal violence, what Gil (1998) calls counterviolence—the acts of those who are economically and socially marginalized in accord with the distributions. Eventually, then, we come to see crime and violence in terms of those acts committed "on the street" by the marginalized, which in our current society translates into the economic crimes and street violence of African American males (Miller 1996; Mauer 1999). But, once we begin to see the ways in which power is structured into our social arrangements and how those who exercise power manage to remain "beyond incrimination" (Kennedy 1970), we can develop some postulates to reformulate our thinking on the nature of crime and for responding to harm-based acts and arrangements.

The Postulates

First, our postulates suggest that every act of interpersonal violence that criminal law calls our attention to as a crime (e.g., theft, robbery, rape, battery, child abuse) has its mirror image harm in power relations on the social structural level—in the distributions (e.g., exclusion from voluntary participation, obedience to authority, subjugation to enforced scarcity, destruction of identity).

Second, our postulates suggest that, because social structural violence appears in masked or muted, slow-release, and ideologically justified forms and is often thoroughly interwoven with the ways we earn our daily bread, it is generally endured and eventually perceived by many as acceptable, as nonviolence, as nonharm (Sullivan and Tifft 1998a).

Third, our postulates suggest that the harms created by social structural violence are not acknowledged in criminal law because criminal law, as an administrative conduit of power-based political-economic institutions, is designed to direct our eyes toward the acts of those marginalized or disenfranchised by power. Law directs our attention to "reactive" and "reflective" counterviolence and away from the perpetrators and benefactors of structural violence, hierarchical relations, and an economy geared toward deficit creation for some in the interest of surplus enhancement for others (Gil 1996, 1998, 1999; Sklar 1994). Counter-violence and structural violence accompany one another wherever there are non-needs-based, power-based arrangements—in our political-economic and societal arrangements, in our families (Tifft 1993), in our schools (Sullivan 1999), and in our workplaces (Sullivan and Tifft 1998b; Sullivan et al. 1998). How these two modes of violence are differentially conceived and addressed can be found in any of these life spheres (Sullivan and Tifft 1998c).

As an illustration, Southerland, Collins, and Scarborough (1997) became interested in documenting the scope of violence in U.S. workplaces. They counted and examined acts of violence for their book *Workplace Violence*. The title suggests that structural violence might have been included in their study, but the researchers' focus was such that they counted only interpersonal acts of violence. Missing from the study is any hint of the numerous types of structural violence that workers are subjected to each day in the form of punishing and hazardous work conditions, inadequate and differential pay, and a lack of health insurance, all conditions that destroy presence and simultaneously foster resentment, if not rage.

In contrast, in his participatory observation of a number of poultry-processing plants in the United States, Horwitz (1994) could not avoid paying attention to structural violence. He saw in these plants a technology at work where large numbers of workers were increasingly consigned to "a Dickensian time warp, laboring not just for meager wages but also under dehumanized and often dangerous conditions" (Horwitz 1994: A3). Here, Horwitz says, automation had created for these workers, not freedom from backbreaking drudgery but "a new and insidious toil . . . work that is faster than ever before, subject to Orwellian control and electronic surveillance, and reduced to limited tasks that are numbingly repetitive, potentially crippling and stripped of any meaningful skills or the chance to develop them" (Horwitz 1994: A3). In some of these plants, workers who were new to the job were apprised of the hazardous chemicals present in only lip-service fashion, as if their health and earning capacity for their families did not matter. In one plant, a rule was enforced that said that walking off the line to relieve yourself was not allowed and was considered a voluntary quit. Indeed, at a Pilgrim's Pride plant, unexcused bathroom trips were punishable by a three-day suspension. One result of such conditions was that some workers had been forced to urinate on themselves because they were unable to locate a foreperson to ask permission to leave the processing line. And this is a processing line that has sped up over the past fifteen years from under sixty chickens a minute to the current allowable rate of ninety-one per minute. With the line moving at such a speed, workers in the cut-up department at B. C. Rogers must lift five-pound boxes at a rate of twelve boxes or more a minute into larger boxes that are then lifted onto a conveyor belt. These workers wind up lifting 3,600 pounds an hour during an eight-hour shift. Horwitz says (1994: A3) the work process "was so fast-paced that it took on a zany chaos, with arms and boxes and poultry flying in every direction. At break times I would find fat globulates and blood speckling my glasses, bits of chicken caught in my collar, water and slime soaking my feet and ankles, and nicks covering my wrists."

That so many of us seem unaware of such structural violence or are unwilling to define such conditions as violence or harm is not surprising. We live in an economy in which achievement of well-being is predicated on the accumulation and constant exercise of power, the creation and enforcement of hierarchical relationships, and threat-based work and living conditions that are geared toward one-way needs satisfaction (Sullivan and Tifft 1998c).

Finally, our postulates suggest that as those of us committed to living in and creating patterns of interaction designed to meet the needs of everyone begin to demystify the distinction between interpersonal and social structural violence, between worthy and unworthy victims, and culpable and nonculpable power wielders, many will object. They will assert again and again that the two forms of violence are neither comparable in nature nor equally harmful and, therefore, that the victims and perpetrators of structural violence do not deserve the same degree of attention as those who are the perpetrators of interpersonal and/or street violence. To the contrary, institutional or structural violence manifests itself in multitudinous life-denying situations and must be viewed as far more insidious because it is masked or obscured by procedures, processes, and ideological justifications that offer protection to power wielders by minimizing the impact and severity of the effects of their violence (Sullivan 1980; Gil 1989). Moreover, most of us tend to deny or minimize the existence of structural violence because we all, to varying degrees, share in its creation in our daily lives, and it is an exceedingly difficult cycle of violence to shake. The antidote requires that we rid ourselves of power-based interaction in all areas of our lives, which, in turn, requires that we detach ourselves from the benefits that power affords— privilege, feelings of superiority, and economic security. But, as we cannot comfortably live in a condition of resistance/detachment, we must move to create patterns of interaction/communities that promote relationships that are nonhierarchical, non–power based—in short, relationships that are organized to encourage and support each person to develop his or her talents while taking into account the needs of all.

A NEEDS-BASED, SOCIAL HARMS DEFINITION OF CRIME

A needs-based, social harms definition of crime allows us to recognize that violence and crime are historical, transcultural, and political variants. It also allows us to explore social harms/crimes in stateless societies and to make cross-cultural comparisons of social harms and legally defined crimes in differently organized

societies (Tifft 1994–95). A needs-based, social harms definition of crime extends our definition of crime to social conditions, social arrangements, or actions
of intent or indifference that interfere with the fulfillment of fundamental needs
and obstruct the spontaneous unfolding of human potential. The extent of social
structural harm or structural violence in a society thus reflects the degree to
which its members can neither meet their fundamental needs nor realize their
potentialities in the context of the normal workings of institutionalized social
arrangements (Gil 1999).

Interpersonal harms such as theft, rape, battery, and child abuse are significant
social harms. Nevertheless, these harms comprise only one set of the countless
actions that result in undeniable social harm and suffering (Elias 1986). Criminal law excludes from its definition of crime actions and patterns of interaction
that violate historically developed human rights (Schwendinger and Schwendinger 1970; Galliher 1989) and actions that assault human dignity. Moreover,
grave social injuries and harms (e.g., slavery, marital rape, crimes of state, and
crimes of economy) have been declared legal by those in positions to undertake
such maneuvers in support of social arrangements of power and privilege (Foucault 1977). Many of the most serious social harms and threats to human safety,
health, and life have been committed by those who have been successful in having their harms either embodied in the legal social arrangements of society or
excluded from the processes of penal law (Reiman 1998).

From a needs-based, social harms definition of crime, the twentieth century
poignantly demonstrated that we cannot accept the notion that a legal order is
either a moral or a just order. Numerous legal orders have justified the institutionalization of unimaginable harms (e.g., Hitler's Germany; Stalin's USSR;
South Africa's apartheid; United States' slavery, internment of Japanese Americans [Chang 1999; Brimner 1994], and policies of invasion, genocide, and pup-
pet dictatorships). Social harms for reasons of state are far too prevalent in our
present-day world. State terrorism, administrative torture, low-intensity warfare,
death squad killings, disappearances, covert and counterintelligence, political assassinations, ethnic cleansings, capital punishment, imprisonment, participatory
exclusion—there is no short list of crimes of state (Tifft 1994–95; Huggins 1998;
Clark 1999).

From a needs-based, social harms definition of crime, many twentieth-century
legal modes of production and distribution are criminal for they not only institu-
tionalize the systematic appropriation/theft of labor value but, as well, create
poverty, malnutrition, and death due to preventable starvation and disease (Elias
1986). Significant crimes of capital (Michalowski 1985) arise from the social
relations associated with the processes of capital accumulation, concentration,
and centralization. Crimes of capital are not limited to actions prohibited by
criminal, regulatory, or civil law, they include acts not presently under the control of either nation-state or international law (Michalowski and Kramer 1987).

Furthermore, law in the United States has historically guaranteed the right to deny access to one's person to only some members of society. Those bound into slavery had no guaranteed right to deny owners or masters access to their person until emancipation was legally enacted and rigorously enforced. Until the late 1980s, women bound into marriage in most states were not guaranteed the right to deny sexual access to their husbands. Physical slavery and marital rape were not acts that violated criminal laws. They were legally accepted appropriations of the human rights and potentialities of African Americans and married women, respectively. The legality of physical slavery and marital rape reflected the distributions, the institutionalized positions of these persons in the then-legal economic and power relations of society.

Unresponsiveness

Once again reflecting on power relations, social harms such as "crime," penal sanctions, and social arrangements of unilateral power exercise are variations of an underlying phenomenon—unresponsiveness. Unresponsiveness means forcing on others what they do not want (Pepinsky 1991). Unresponsiveness means suffering the pain of being denied one's humanity, difference, and capability to make a difference (Henry and Milovanovic 1993: 12). Unresponsiveness signifies loss, absence, and emptiness (Fromm 1941; Manning 1989; Scarry 1985). Responsiveness means that what one expects to achieve by one's intended actions is modified continually either to accommodate the experience and feelings of those affected or to allow the needs and desires of others to change the course of one's action (Pepinsky 1991). As we have argued, individual disregard for others in social interaction is often mirrored in unresponsiveness to others within the social arrangements of the society, as when the suffering of impoverished persons remains neglected in an economy of abundance and privilege. From the personal to the structural level, unresponsiveness leads to unresponsiveness— social harm leads to counter social harm; those subject to unresponsiveness in one context or relationship are likely to be unresponsive to others in a different context (Glaser 1986). Violence begins where responsiveness ends, as when a person intent on sexual intercourse overpowers another's resistance and torment, and rapes, or when the owners of a workplace knowingly and indifferently allow unsafe work conditions to persist, seriously injuring workers. Violence also begins when some members of a society or household deny participation in decision making to others in matters that directly affect them. In effect, they are charging them a price for their continued existence (Sullivan 1999: 6). When informed that this social arrangement assaults human dignity and thwarts developmental needs, those who forbid the desired participation act violently.

INTERPERSONAL AND SOCIAL STRUCTURAL VIOLENCE

Once again, it is most essential to reiterate that interpersonal and social structural violence cannot be understood apart from one another. They interact with and reinforce one another. They are different manifestations of the same under-lying social context: values, consciousness, social relations, and institutional dy-namics. The coercive processes by which social inequalities (the distributions) are established and conserved tend to induce resistance, resistance harms, and reactive or reflective counterharms from individuals and groups who are develop-mentally obstructed within these arrangements (Gil 1998, 1998; Tifft 1993). In turn, acts of resistance, resistance harms, and counterharms tend to lead to in-tensified repressive violence on the part of privileged and dominant groups, cre-ating vicious circles of ever-escalating violence and structural inequality (Gil 1989).

The counterharms set in motion by structural violence are not typically aimed at changing the social arrangements that embody inequality and thwart growth and expression. Rather, they are customarily displaced into interpersonal or self-destructive violence—battering, child abuse, rape, robbery, suicide, addiction, and psychopathology. Customarily, media and government spokespersons focus exclusively on the sensational interpersonal and intrapersonal counterviolence of individuals and groups. The structural violence that thwarts the develop-mental needs of these individuals is generally disregarded or discounted. As a consequence, the dynamics of violence in our society are obscured (Gil 1989), and the counterviolence and motives of those who choose these acts appear senseless or irrational (Albee 1986). The necessity of fundamental social struc-tural change toward responsive, egalitarian, needs-based institutions is dismissed, while structurally violated individuals and groups are scapegoated, assessed, and condemned (Gil 1989). When the motives and actions of these individuals and groups are recognized as violence in response to violent societal practices and conditions, they become understandable, though not acceptable.

Workplace Social Harms

To illustrate, once again consider the structural violence and counterviolence that occurs in the context of the inegalitarian and coercive social organization of work in the United States. Competition among enterprises to accumulate cap-ital and control resources and markets tends to shape the logic of everyday life. Economic decisions are primarily based on the criteria of profitability and the accumulation, concentration, and centralization of capital (Gil 1986). Far less important are the extent to which production and distribution arrangements meet the essential needs of the population; the nature of the social organization of these processes; and the consequences these processes have for communities, the environment, the conservation of resources, and people's consciousness and relationships. The social organization of production divides the population into a powerful minority of competing owners and controllers of the means of produc-tion and a majority of people who rent their energy, knowledge, and skills. These conditions of competition and social and economic inequality lead to attempts to retain or expand unequal distributions of resources, as in crimes of capital (e.g., hazardous workplace organization, hazardous consumer products, environmental destruction, restraint of trade) (Michalowski 1985) and to redistribute economic resources, as in crimes for personal gain (e.g., theft, burglary, embezzlement) (Gordon 1973). They also lead to frustration, anger, and stress-bred violence, as in expressive interpersonal violence (e.g., murder, rape, battering, child abuse).

The structural exclusion of many people from work, the fierce competition for scarce opportunities, and the insecurity of employment and advancement result not only in personal animosities but also in intergroup divisiveness, conflict, discrimination, and violence. This context also tends to prohibit caring, meaningful relationships both at work and in the community and gives rise to hopelessness and alienation, which, in turn, can result in depression, alcoholism, drug addiction, family violence, and both instrumental and expressive violence.

As illustrated in the chicken-processing plants, the social organization of work often allows workers little say in shaping and directing their work. Efforts to increase efficiency, productivity, and profits transform many work tasks into routines requiring little initiative, creativity, and intellectual effort. Perceived as "personnel" or "costs of production," many workers are treated as replaceable components of the production process, not whole and unique individuals (Goodman 1968). Work is regularly situated in an organizational context that arrests the development of talent; thwarts dignity, integrity, and autonomy (Goodman 1960; Gil 1986); excludes participation; and attacks a positive sense of self. These work arrangements constitute a form of violence akin to structural battering. Daily subjection to this context may inflict physical harm and spiritual emptiness that may result in a heightened need to reassert self-worth and importance.

Homeplace Social Harms

When working in such conditions, many men emerge from work without the tolerance required for either parenting or being an intimate companion or emotional restorer. Many attempt to control their partners or the nature of their intimate relationships to compensate for the dissatisfying, structurally violent conditions of work. Immersed in the cultural consciousness that some people have the legitimate right to control others, men who batter choose tactics that mirror those employed by others in positions of hierarchical power. They attempt to recover their lost sense of self through interpersonally reactive violence within the family (e.g., wife or partner battering, child abuse). Alternatively, many men who work in structurally violent work contexts imitatively organize and impose unilateral, unresponsive divisions of labor and decision-making processes within the family and thereby position themselves as inflictors rather than receivers of structural violence. Structural battering and interpersonal battering are intended to change how a partner acts, what she thinks and feels, and who she is. Battering deconstructs the partner's self and reality, and it obstructs the spontaneous unfolding of her human potential and thus constitutes a grievous social harm (Tifft 1993).

The presence of accepted male violence within intimate relationships and within the organizational relations of social life means that male hostility or anger, male criticism, and male disapproval serve as reminders of male physical violence and power. Men who rape, men who batter, men who execute and imprison, and men who declare war are the shock troopers of a violent, male-dominant society. Because some men rape, all women must become conscious of the power and presence of men; consider limiting their spatial, developmental, and psychic mobility; and restrict their interactions with others. Because some men batter, all women must become conscious and wary of male control and anger and fearful of confronting male "authority." Violence does not occur in a vacuum. Wittingly or unwittingly, male violence and control reinforce, and are reinforced by, patriarchal social arrangements and play an integral part in keeping women in a subordinate place.

Inspired by this very brief introduction to the essence of needs-based distributions—social justice, power, and a needs-based definition of crime—an illustrative criminological analysis follows.

A NEEDS-BASED, SOCIAL HARMS COMPREHENSIVE RESPONSE TO SOCIAL HARMS/CRIMES

Socially Injurious Economic Relationships

When corporate decision makers produce and distribute a known-to-be-harmful product in the interest of profit and market share (e.g., Dalkon Shield, Ford Pinto), we have a collective responsibility to respond, for these actions have led persons to lose their lives, their children's lives, their procreative potentialities, their positive self-identities, their full physical and spiritual capacities, and so forth. We respond to communicate that these actions are unacceptable and must not continue. Furthermore, we have a collective responsibility to change the social arrangements to prevent the production and distribution of harmful products. When and if we do not collectively respond, we indicate that it is acceptable for those who produce and distribute harmful products to thwart the needs and potentialities of others. When and if we do not take the responsibility to change the arrangements of production and distribution to prevent such social harms, we are stating that these arrangements are acceptable and that the lives, potentialities, talents, health, safety needs, and freedoms of others are not worth protecting or preserving (Tifft 2000).

Socially Injurious Intimate Relationships

When husbands decide to harm their wives knowingly, whether physically, psychologically, emotionally, sexually, or spiritually by battering them, we have a collective responsibility to respond. These acts, primarily motivated to create or maintain power, control, dominance, and superiority, lead to these women's loss of dignity, autonomy, self-confidence, physical health, and personhood. At the extreme, they lead to deconstruction and death (Tifft 1993). We collectively respond to these actions to communicate that they are unacceptable and must not continue. Furthermore, we have a collective responsibility to change these social arrangements to prevent the production and distribution of these violent and harmful patterns of interaction. When and if we do not collectively respond, we indicate that it is acceptable for some persons to thwart the needs and potentialities of others, to disrespect them, to disallow their voice and presence, to physically and spiritually injure them. When and if we do not take the responsibility to change these violent arrangements to prevent such social harms, we are stating that these arrangements are acceptable and that the lives, potentialities, needs, and freedoms of women are not worth protecting or preserving. We would thus be declaring that inequality, dominance, patriarchy, physical violence and control, marital rape, intimidation, social deprivation/isolation, and humiliation are the patterns of interaction we desire to preserve and pass on to the next generation (Tifft 2000).

Needs-Based Analysis

A comprehensive collective response to social harms, grounded in needs-based criminology, might suggestively be composed of the following features:

1. *Survivor needs.* Often collective responses have little connection with the reasons specific social harms are defined as unacceptable and designated crimes. A response that principally focuses on the "offender" or punishment may provide little support for the persons harmed and may not address their needs or ours. A needs-based response requires us to address the thwarted human needs, lost potentialities, lost senses of self-worth, lost freedoms, safety needs, health needs, and whatever other needs are specified by the victims/survivors. After all, these harms and losses are the reasons that these arrangements and acts (e.g., socially injurious production and distribution arrangements and socially injurious intimate relationships) were defined and designated as serious "crimes/social harms."

2. *Prevention.* Often collective responses do not propose and initiate a proactive, needs-based, primary prevention, public health, social structural/before-the-act prevention component. When this prevention component is missing, the prevalence of the undesired behavior or arrangements is un-

likely to be altered. Prevention strategies require that we address what alternative social arrangements and cultural idea changes might decrease the prevalence of these harms/crimes. What needs-based social arrangements are we going to create such that arrangements of production and distribution no longer produce harmful products, harmful conditions of work, and harmful distributions (poverty)? Similarly, how are we going to meet the needs of everyone such that battering is no longer a far too frequent pattern of interaction among intimates (Mika 1992; Zehr and Mika 1998; Morris 1994, 1995; Sullivan et al. 1998; Gil 1989, 1996, 1998, 1999)?

3. *Source/response correspondence.* Often collective responses are logically or substantively unrelated to the reasons a person made the decision to act in a socially harmful way and, as well, to the nature of the larger structural and cultural contexts within which this decision was made. The "why" or "cause" explanations are often out of sync with the substantive nature of the response. For example, incarceration may address neither the needs of the "offender" nor the direct health care or support needs of the "survivor" (Zehr and Mika 1998). Moreover, responses focused on the offender may address neither the immediate and long-run trust, safety and security needs of those specifically harmed nor those of community members (Zehr 1990). They may also address neither the collective responsibility issues presented earlier nor the social arrangements or cultural structures that "foster," "produce," or "encourage" harming choices. Garbage-can "community service" responses (e.g., leaf raking, working in a soup kitchen) may have nothing to do with either the nature of the harm (e.g., a bus stop robbery of an elderly man) or the specific motivations (e.g., unemployment, depression) to commit this crime.

   A needs-based response to this bus-stop robbery may entail meeting the survivor's needs for the restoration of trust and so forth, and the offender's needs with regard to his depression and his retraining and placement in a new workplace that is neither harmfully organized nor disrespectful of his human dignity. It may also address the manner in which employment/unemployment is organized so that there are only temporary unemployment and the provision of support groups, advisers, work finders, and notifications/warnings of an impending plant closing when unemployment is eminent. So, too, the social organization of production and distribution needs to be differently organized to provide far greater collective/public participation in decision making.

4. *Responses as crimes or social harms.* Often collective responses to the "offender" such as court-ordered treatment or physical confinement may themselves be social harms or "crimes" as defined by the criteria set out to explain why certain actions or arrangements should be considered "crimes." If we return to the illustrations given earlier (i.e., interaction patterns among intimates that yield battering and economic relationships that

yield socially harmful products), "crimes"/social harms were defined as actions or arrangements that physically and spiritually injure and/or thwart the needs, development, potentiality, health, and dignity of others. From a needs-based perspective, we need to develop nonharming responses to those who have harmed others. Offenders need to be provided with support and the opportunity to understand the harms they have "caused," to take responsibility to enter a dialogue concerning the survivors' feelings and needs and to help create an altered relationship. They need to be helped to accept personal responsibility for self-change and addressing their own needs (Zehr and Mika 1998). Critical of present-day criminal justice responses, we need to inquire whether, for example, capital punishment or stark or structurally violent prison living conditions fit the definition of "crime" and the reasons given for defining acts as "socially injurious"(Tifft 2000). If these responses meet these definitions or criteria, they are themselves violent harms and social injuries and therefore unacceptable. Furthermore, we need to assess what cultural values are embodied within a collective response. To use "murder" as an illustration, do our current-day responses embody and communicate that life is precious and sacred?

5. *Cultural and social arrangements advocated.* Often collective responses fail to directly identify the social arrangements-distributions and cultural values expected to be upheld through the response. We need to know exactly what social arrangements-distributions are being defined as legitimate or just and what values and ideas are fostered by the response. If collective responses legitimate an order, rather than order, what are the social arrangements and values defined as legitimate and institutionalized? We would argue that the responses (or omitted responses) that have upheld slavery, marital rape, and structural and physical battering and that currently uphold economic arrangements that consign people to death, despair, and poverty are themselves crimes and socially injurious. Collective responses are always designed to uphold an order and are organized to secure a specific set of relationships, beliefs, and desired ways of living.

CONCLUSION

We hope this brief excursion into the world of needs-based social organization, social justice, and criminology will inspire others to contribute to its full development and that as we join together we may increasingly live in a society, a global society, better organized to meet everyone's essential needs, making it easier for us all to be good and enjoy ourselves among each other. That is our prayer.

NOTE

This chapter is based on the following papers and publications: Sullivan and Tifft (1998a, 1998b, 1998c); Sullivan and Sullivan (1998); Tifft, Sullivan, and Sullivan (1997); Sullivan, Tifft, and Sullivan (1999); and Tifft (1999, 2000).

REFERENCES

Albee, George W. 1986. "Toward a Just Society: Lessons from Observations on the Primary Prevention of Psychotherapy." *American Psychologist* 41: 891–98.

Beirne, Piers, and James Messerschmidt. 1995. *Criminology*. 2d ed. Fort Worth, Tex.: Harcourt Brace College Publishers.

Bernard, Jesse. 1986. "The Good Provider Role: Its Rise and Fall." In *Family in Transition*, 5th ed., ed. Arlene S. Skolnick and Jerome H. Skolnick. Boston: Little, Brown, pp. 125–44.

Bose, Nirmal K. 1965. "Ghandhi: Humanist and Socialist." In *Socialist Humanism*, ed. Erich Fromm. Garden City, N.Y.: Doubleday, pp. 98–106.

Brazelton, T. Berry. 1982. *Becoming a Family*. New York: Dell.

———. 1992. *To Listen to a Child: Understanding the Normal Problems of Growing Up*. Redding, Mass.: Addison-Wesley.

Brimner, Larry D. 1994. *Voices from the Camps: Internment of Japanese Americans during World War II*. Danbury, Conn.: Franklin Watts.

Brock-Utne, Brigit. 1985. *Educating for Peace: A Feminist Perspective*. New York: Pergamon.

Chang, Gordon H., ed. 1999. *Morning Glory, Evening Shadow: Yamato Ichihashi and His Internment Writings, 1942–1945*. Stanford, Calif.: Stanford University Press.

Chomsky, Noam. 1994. *Keeping the Rabble in Line*. Monroe, Maine: Common Courage Press.

Clark, Ramsey. 1999. "The Celling of America, the Political Economy of Force, and the Violence of Economic Sanctions in International Relations: An Interview with Ramsey Clark." *Contemporary Justice Review* 2, no. 1: 5–21.

Coles, Robert A. 1997. *The Moral Intelligence of Children*. New York: Random House.

de Haan, Willem. 1990. "Universalism and Relativism in Critical Criminology." *Critical Criminologist* 4, no. 1: 1, 2, 7, 8.

Denzin, Norman K. 1984. "Toward a Phenomenology of Domestic Family Violence." *American Journal of Sociology* 90: 483–513.

Elias, Robert. 1986. *The Politics of Victimization: Victims, Victimology, and Human Rights*. New York: Oxford University Press.

Ferrell, Jeff. 1999. "Anarchist Criminology and Social Justice." In *Social Justice/Criminal Justice: The Maturation of Critical Theory in Law, Crime, and Deviance*, ed. Bruce A. Arrigo. Belmont, Calif.: West/Wadsworth, pp. 93–106.

Foucault, Michel. 1977. *Discipline and Punish: The Birth of the Prison*. New York: Pantheon.

Frankl, Victor E. 1973. *The Doctor and the Soul*. New York: Vintage.

Fromm, Erich. 1941. *Escape from Freedom*. New York: Holt, Rinehart & Winston.

Galliher, John F. 1989. *Criminology: Human Rights, Criminal Law, and Crime.* Englewood Cliffs, N.J.: Prentice Hall.

Gil, David. 1986. "Sociocultural Aspects of Domestic Violence." In *Violence in the Home*, ed. Mary Lystad. New York: Brunner/Mazel, pp. 124–49.

———. 1989. "Work, Violence, Injustice and War." *Journal of Sociology and Social Welfare* 16: 39–53.

———. 1996. "Preventing Violence in a Structurally Violent Society: Mission Impossible." *American Journal of Orthopsychiatry* 66: 77–84.

———. 1998. "Fostering Peace in Families by Ending Social Structural Violence." *Justice Professional* 11, nos. 1–2: 143–58.

———. 1999. "Understanding and Overcoming Social-Structural Violence." *Contemporary Justice Review* 2: 23–36.

Glaser, Daniel. 1986. "Violence in the Society." In *Violence in the Home*, ed. Mary Lystad. New York: Brunner/Mazel, pp. 5–31.

Goodman, Paul. 1960. *Growing Up Absurd: Problems of Youth in the Organized System.* New York: Random House.

———. 1968. *People or Personnel: Decentralizing and the Mixed Systems.* New York: Vintage.

Gordon, David M. 1973. "Capitalism, Class, and Crime in America." *Crime and Delinquency* 19: 163–186.

Hagan, John. 1977. *The Disreputable Pleasures.* Toronto: McGraw-Hill Ryerson.

———. 1985. *Modern Criminology: Crime, Criminal Behavior and Its Control.* New York: McGraw-Hill.

Heller, Agnes. 1987. *Beyond Justice.* Oxford: Basil Blackwell.

Henry, Stuart, and Dragan Milovanovic. 1993. "Back to Basics: A Postmodern Redefinition of Crime." *Critical Criminologist* 5, nos. 2/3: 1, 2, 6, 12.

———. 1996. *Constitutive Criminology: Beyond Postmodernism.* London: Sage.

Horwitz, Tony. 1994. "Jobs to Nowhere." *Times Union* (Albany, N.Y.). 4 December, A3.

Huggins, Martha K. 1998. *Political Policing: The United States and Latin America.* Durham, N.C.: Duke University Press.

Kennedy, Mark. 1970. "Beyond Incrimination: Some Neglected Facts of the History of Punishment." *Catalyst* 5: 1–16.

Kierkegaard, Søren. 1941. *The Sickness unto Death.* Princeton, N.J.: Princeton University Press.

Kohn, Alfie. 1993. *Punished by Rewards: The Trouble with Gold Stars, Incentive Plans, A's, Praise, and Other Bribes.* Boston: Houghton Mifflin.

———. 1996. *Beyond Discipline: From Compliance to Community.* Alexandria, Va.: Association for Supervision and Curriculum Development.

Kozol, Jonathan. 1996. *Amazing Grace: The Lives of Children and the Conscience of a Nation.* New York: Crown.

Kropotkin, Peter K. 1924. *Ethics.* New York: Mother Earth.

Lanier, Mark M., and Stuart Henry. 1998. *Essential Criminology.* Boulder, Colo.: Westview.

Le Guin, Ursula K. 1975. *The Dispossessed.* New York: Avon.

Manning, Peter K. 1989. "On the Phenomenology of Violence." *The Criminologist* 14: 1, 4, 5, 6, 22.

Mauer, Marc. 1999. "The Sentencing Project." In *Race to Incarcerate*. New York: New Press.

Michalowski, Raymond J. 1985. *Order, Law, and Crime: An Introduction to Criminology*. New York: Random House.

Michalowski, Raymond J., and Ronald C. Kramer. 1987. "The Space between Laws: The Problem of Corporate Crime in the Transnational Context." *Social Problems* 34, no. 1: 34–53.

Mika, Harry. 1992. "Mediation Interventions and Restorative Justice: Responding to the Astructural Bias." In *Restorative Justice on Trial: Pitfalls and Potentials of Victim–Offender Mediation: International Research Perspectives*, ed. Heinz Messmer and Hans-Uwe Otto. Dordrecht, The Netherlands: Kluwer, pp. 559–67.

Miller, David. 1976. *Social Justice*. Oxford: Oxford University Press.

Miller, Jerome. 1996. *Search and Destroy: African-American Males in the Criminal Justice System*. New York: Cambridge University Press.

Morris, Ruth. 1994. *A Practical Path to Transformative Justice*. Toronto: Rittenhouse.

———. 1995. "Not Enough!" *Mediation Quarterly* 12: 285–91.

Mumford, Lewis. 1967. *The Myth of the Machine: Technics and Human Development*. New York: Harcourt, Brace Jovanovich.

Pepinsky, Harold E. 1991. *The Geometry of Violence and Democracy*. Bloomington: Indiana University Press.

Pepinsky Harold E., and Richard Quinney, eds. 1991. *Criminology as Peacemaking*. Bloomington: Indiana University Press.

Pfohl, Stephen. 1994. *Images of Deviance and Social Control: A Sociological History*. New York: McGraw-Hill.

Pieper, Josef. 1996. *The Four Cardinal Virtues*. South Bend, Ind.: University of Notre Dame Press.

Piercy, Marge. 1976. *Woman on the Edge of Time*. New York: Fawcett Crest.

Prejean, Helen. 1993. *Dead Man Walking: An Eyewitness Account of the Death Penalty in the United States*. New York: Vintage.

Quinney, Richard. 1995. "Socialist Humanism and the Problem of Crime." *Crime, Law & Social Change* 23: 147–56.

———. 1998. "Criminology as Moral Philosophy, Criminologist as Witness." *Contemporary Justice Review* 1, nos. 2/3: 347–64.

Reiman, Jeffery. 1998. *The Rich Get Richer and the Poor Get Prison: Ideology, Class, and Criminal Justice*. 5th ed. Boston: Allyn & Bacon.

Rogers, Carl R. 1961. *On Becoming a Person*. Boston: Houghton Mifflin.

———. 1980. *A Way of Being*. Boston: Houghton Mifflin.

Scarry, Elaine. 1985. *The Body in Pain: The Making and Unmaking of the World*. New York: Oxford University Press.

Schwartz, Pepper. 1994. "Modernizing Marriage." *Psychology Today* (September/October): 54, 56, 58, 59, 86.

Schwendinger, Herman, and Julia Schwendinger. 1970. "Defenders of Order or Guardians of Human Rights?" *Issues in Criminology* 5: 123–57.

Simpson, Christopher. 1994. *Science of Coercion*. New York: Oxford.

Sklar, Holly. 1994. *Scapegoating the Poor*. Boulder, Colo.: Barsamain.

Southerland, Mittie D., Pamala A. Collins, and Kathryn. E. Scarborough. 1997. *Workplace Violence: A Continuum from Threat to Death*. Cincinnati, Ohio: Anderson.

Sullivan, Dennis C. 1980. *The Mask of Love: Corrections in America—Toward a Mutual Aid Alternative*. Port Washington, N.Y.: Kennikat.

————. 1986–87. "The True Cost of Things, the Loss of the Commons and Radical Change." *Social Anarchism* 6: 20–26.

————. 1999. "Peacemaking and the Way to End All War." Paper presented at the Annual Meeting of the American Society of Criminology, Toronto, November.

Sullivan, Dennis C., and Kathryn Sullivan. 1998. "The Political Economy of Just Community: A Radical Interpretation." Paper presented at the Annual Meeting of the American Society of Criminology Washington, D.C., November.

Sullivan, Dennis C., and Larry L. Tifft. 1998a. "Criminology as Peacemaking: A Peace-Oriented Perspective on Crime, Punishment, and Justice That Takes into Account the Needs of All." *Justice Professional* 11: 5–34.

————. 1998b. "Restorative Justice: Exploring Its Economic and Transformative Dimensions." *Humanity and Society* 22: 38–54.

————. 1998c. "A Social Structural Alternative to the Punishment Response: Toward A Regrounding of the Imagination in a Needs-Based Economy." Paper presented at the annual Meeting of the Academy of Criminal Justice Sciences, Albuquerque, N.M., March.

Sullivan, Dennis C., Larry L. Tifft, and Peter Cordella. 1998. "The Phenomenon of Restorative Justice: Some Introductory Remarks." *Contemporary Justice Review* 1: 7–20.

Sullivan, Dennis C., Larry L. Tifft, and Kathryn Sullivan. 1999. "Justice without Violence: Exploring the Transformative and Economic Dimensions of the Restorative Justice Movement." Paper presented for roundtable discussions at Emmaus House, the Catholic Worker Community, Albany, N.Y., February, and at Saint Joseph House, the Catholic Worker Community, New York, March.

Sullivan, John. 1998. "Meeting the Individual Needs of all Learners in the Inclusion Classroom." *Justice Professional* 11, nos. 1–2: 175–87.

Tifft, Larry L. 1979. "The Coming Definitions of Crime: An Anarchist Perspective." *Social Problems* 26: 392–402.

————. 1993. *The Battering of Women: The Failure of Intervention and the Case for Prevention*. Boulder, Colo.: Westview.

————. 1994–95. "A Social Harms Definition of Crime." *Critical Criminologist* 7, no. 1: 9–13.

————. 1998. "Justice, Kinship, and Childcare: The Coming Definition of Family." Paper presented at the Annual Meeting of the American Society of Criminology, Washington, D.C., November.

————. 1999. "Peacemaking Evolved: An Introduction to Needs-based Criminology." Paper presented at the Annual Meeting of the American Society of Criminology, Toronto, November.

————. 2000. "Social Justice and Criminologies: A Commentary." *Contemporary Justice Review* 3, no. 1: 43–52.

Tifft, Larry L., and Dennis C. Sullivan. 1980. *The Struggle to Be Human: Crime, Criminology, & Anarchism*. Over the Water, U.K.: Cienfuegos.

Tifft, Larry L., John Sullivan, and Dennis C. Sullivan. 1997. "Discipline as Enthusiasm: An Entry into the Recent Discussion on the Moral Development of Children." Paper presented at the Annual Meeting of the Association for Humanist Sociology, Pittsburgh, November.

Wieck, David. 1975. "The Negativity of Anarchism." *Interrogations: Revue internationale de recherche anarchiste* 5: 25–35.

Young, Iris M.1990. *Justice and the Politics of Difference*. Princeton, N.J.: Princeton University Press.

Zehr, Howard. 1990. *Changing Lenses*. Scottdale, Pa.: Open University Press.

Zehr, Howard, and Mika Harry. 1998. "Fundamental Concepts of Restorative Justice." *Contemporary Justice Review* 1: 47–56.

Part III

Integrating Approaches

12

Crime as Disrepute

Scott Greer and John Hagan

Crime is criminal because somebody could and did legitimately ban it. Attempts to define crime all face the problems inherent in basic definition: what is criminal is what somebody tried to ban, what they had the authority to ban, and that there was at least some public acceptance of their authority to ban. Some things arguably should be crimes, even though they are not, and vice versa. Often, a gap exists between what is criminal and what should be criminal according to widely held principles: a widely held norm forbidding murder turns out to lack legal application when it is in a poorly maintained, leaky chemical plant that causes deaths; indignant victims of an apparent fraud can find that there is no criminal remedy despite the clear norm against fraud; or nobody even considers the possibility of a criminal prosecution for heinous crimes against whole peoples. Political and legal systems in their different ways distort norms, giving some far more force than they have in society, and others far less; marijuana smoking is probably more accepted than knowingly dumping toxins, but the former is more personally dangerous to those who are caught doing it. Despite all this, norms and law cannot be disentangled. Even the most authoritarian state cannot maintain a legal regime by coercion alone.

Defining disreputable acts and the criminal acts among them is difficult precisely because society is complex and the political and coercive institutions of the state have their own internal complexity and relationship to different aspects of society. This chapter's definition of deviance builds on efforts of various scholars to establish frameworks for the study of crime and deviance. These efforts are inevitably linked to concepts of how norms evolve in societies, how the political system interacts with the society, and how individuals respond to and apply normative pressure. Building on these prior efforts, this chapter formulates a "pyramid of deviance" as a conceptual metaphor to be used in guiding and focusing the empirical understanding of crime. The last sections of this chapter examine some implications of the pyramid and suggest weaknesses and new dimensions of crime and disrepute highlighted by the pyramid.

SEVEN APPROACHES TO DEVIANCE

Sociologists defining deviance have faced problems of cultural variation, logical inconsistency of crimes, and measurement and normative judgment. Seven approaches delimit much of sociology's response to crime and deviance. They are (1) a legal-consensus definition, (2) a sociolegal definition, (3) a cross-cultural definition, (4), a statistical definition, (5) a labeling definition, (6) a human rights definition, and (7) a critical, somewhat utopian definition. Particular authors, discussed here, enunciate the definitions, but many others echo some or all of their arguments.

THE LEGAL-CONSENSUS APPROACH

The most articulate advocate of a legalistic definition of deviance was the lawyer-sociologist Paul Tappan (1947). Tappan insisted that we limit our study of criminality as it is legally constructed: "Crime is an intentional act in violation of the common law . . . committed without further defense or excuse, and penalized by the state" (100). He further insisted that persons studied as criminals must be adjudicated (i.e., convicted) as such. Acknowledging that cultures vary in what they call criminal, Tappan argued that governing statutes provide the only clear and definitive indication of what any specific cultural group holds deviant: "Here we find *norms* of conduct, comparable to mores, but considerably more distinct, precise, and defined" (100). In short, Tappan suggested that the criminal law provides a reliable guide to what is consensually defined as deviant in any given society.

The salient difficulty with Tappan's approach is that it systematically ignores much of what analysts of deviance wish to study: the noncriminal but nonetheless disreputable pleasures of various deviant lifestyles. At the same time, the legal-consensus approach neglects the basic issue of why some acts are legislated as criminal while others remain only informally the subject of disrepute. Furthermore, this approach misleads us in suggesting that legal definitions clearly reflect societal consensus about what is deviant. Finally, being legally called a criminal depends on being caught and convicted. This sampling process results in not only a narrowly defined but also a nonrepresentative collection of subjects for study.

The Sociolegal Approach

Edwin Sutherland (1945) suggested a relaxation of legal criteria that allowed an expansion of attention to various "antisocial behaviors." Retained, however, was an emphasis on criminality as designated by two explicit criteria: "legal description of acts as socially injurious and legal provision of a penalty for the act" (132). Sutherland demonstrated with the use of these criteria that it is possible to consider "criminal" many unethical business practices handled in the civil courts. The demonstration consisted of a comparative analysis of the procedures and punishments used in the prosecution of corporate interests in the civil and criminal courts. The conclusion was that "the criteria which have been used in defining white-collar crimes are not categorically different from the criteria used in defining other crimes" (135).

Sutherland's redefinition of the field of study facilitated a new and important emphasis in criminological research on the economic crimes of "upperworld" offenders. However, Sutherland's reluctance to widen the scope of attention beyond statutory matters leaves his definition open to two earlier criticisms of the legalistic approach: first, noncriminal forms of deviance continue unnoticed; second, like the criminal courts, the civil court dockets probably represent a biased sample of illegal enterprises. Finally, it should be noted that Sutherland's emphasis on white-collar crime neglects undetected occupational indiscretions among workers of lesser social status (Horning 1970).

A Cross-Cultural Approach

Sellin (1938) proposed a definition of deviance that goes beyond the realm of law. His argument is that every group has its own standards of behavior called "conduct norms" and that these standards are not necessarily embodied in law. "For every person, then, there are from the point of view of a given group of which he is a member a normal (right) and an abnormal (wrong) way of reacting, the norm depending on the social values of the group which formulated it" (1938: 30). Beyond this, however, Sellin argued that some conduct norms are *invariant* across *all* cultural groups. Furthermore, he insisted that these norms were the appropriate focus for research: "Such study would involve the isolation and classification of norms into *universal categories* transcending political and other boundaries, a necessity imposed by the logic of science" (1938: 3).

Unfortunately, Sellin did not specify what the universal conduct norms might be. The weakness of his strategy is the dubious proposition that such norms can be found either inside or outside the law. The lesson of a large body of anthropological research is that norms of conduct are remarkably varied, with the universals of human behavior, if any, limited primarily to the trivial necessities of everyday life. Universal *and* nontrivial conduct norms might be very rare or nonexistent.

A Statistical Approach

Wilkins (1964) suggested a more plausible approach to our subject matter, while remaining attentive to the problem of cultural variation. He begins with the assumption that "[a]t some time or another some form of society . . . has defined almost all forms of behavior that we now call 'criminal' as desirable for the functioning of that form of society" (46). Wilkins then took as his criterion of deviance the frequency with which various forms of behavior occur in any particular society. Said simply, high-frequency behaviors are considered normal and low-frequency behaviors deviant. The resulting definition of deviance is thus pictured in the form of a normal bell-shaped curve: "it may be supposed that the model given by the normal frequency distribution shown in this chart represents the distribution of ethical content of human action" (47). Serious crimes and saintly acts form the two extremes in this definition. The range of additional acts to be considered deviant remains at the discretion of the researchers.

One weakness of this approach lies in its simplicity. While infrequency of behavior is one measure of deviance, the statistical approach neglects the role of societal groups in selecting from infrequent acts those considered undesirable and those considered saintly. Obviously, all infrequent occurrences are not designated as deviant or criminal. Beyond this, "saintly acts" are seldom of interest to analysts of deviance unless the acts become problematic for those who observe them. What is required, then, is an addition of analytical content to the quantitative framework provided.

The Labeling Approach

If the statistical approach minimizes the importance of the societal response, the labeling approach clearly does not. Becker (1963) provided a concise statement of this viewpoint: "The deviant is one to whom that label has successfully been applied; deviant behavior is behavior that people so label" (9). Becker's point is that behaviors are not recognized as deviant unless others, as members of cultural groups, react to them as such. This approach is important in making us aware of the significance of the ways in which we respond to deviance (Hagan and Palloni 1990). However, as a definition of deviance, the labeling approach also creates problems.

Bordua (1969) observed that the labeling definition tends to make deviance "all societal response, and no deviant stimulus." His point is that the labeling approach characteristically assumes a passive subject who plays little or no part in eliciting a response (Hagan 1973). In some cases, this will be true, but often it will not. Thus, a more useful definition of deviance will incorporate both possibilities.

The Human Rights Approach

The next approach we consider proposes a dramatic reconception in what we define as *criminal deviance*. This reconception is urged by Herman Schwendinger and Julia Schwendinger (1970). They begin with the assumption that "[a]ll persons must be guaranteed the fundamental prerequisites for well-being, inducing food, shelter, clothing, medical services, challenging work, and recreational experiences, as well as security from predatory individuals or repressive and imperialistic social elites" (145). The Schwendingers regard these as rights (rather than rewards or privileges) that the criminal law should guarantee and protect. They argue that it is the *conditions* that result in the denial of these rights that should be called criminal. The importance of this shift in focus is that it allows the Schwendingers to recommend a radical change in what should be called criminally deviant, for "[i]f the terms imperialism, racism, sexism and poverty are abbreviated signs for theories of social relationships or social system which cause the systematic abrogation of basic rights, then imperialism, racism, sexism and poverty can be called crimes according to the logic of our argument" (148).

While many, if not most, analysts of deviance might agree with the moral position taken in asking this question, it may nonetheless be the case that this approach to the definition of crime confuses more than it clarifies. A basic problem is that in its concern to condemn imperialism, racism, sexism, and poverty, this approach confuses presumed causes of criminal behavior with the behavior we wish to study.

A Utopian-Conflict Approach

Another provocative approach to the definition of deviance with echoes in today's Foucauldian analyses is presented by "new criminologists" of the 1970s, Taylor, Walton, and Young (1973). They suggest that we redefine deviance as "human diversity" and argue that deviance represents a normal and purposeful attempt to correct or protest human injustice. In response, society seeks to repress this challenge by criminalizing (i.e., arresting, prosecuting, and incarcerating) the actors involved. In short, deviance is born of the conflict between the oppressed and the oppressors. The solution proposed demands a reversal of this situation: "For us . . . deviance is normal . . . The task is to create a society in which the facts of human diversity . . . are not subject to the power to criminalize" (282).

This approach is both useful and utopian. On the one hand, it alerts us to the possibility that some behaviors (e.g., disorderly conduct offenses, political crimes, and some property offenses) may be called deviant or criminal mostly because they are offensive or threatening to the privileged. On the other hand, to assume that all acts of deviance, particularly the most serious (e.g., murder, rape, and child abuse) are justifiable components of a politically meaningful lifestyle is utopian.

What, then, is the appropriate definition of deviance? Taking these positions into account, the next section suggests a framework for the analysis of crime that integrates insights from these different writers.

THE PYRAMID OF CRIME

A basic assumption in considering what is important in defining crime is that we have a definition that takes into account not only what is formally considered criminal by law, but also a range of behaviors that, for all practical purposes, are treated as crimes (e.g., Sutherland's white-collar crimes). Such a definition should also include those behaviors that across time and place vary in their location in and outside the boundaries of criminal law. We need a definition that considers behaviors that are both actually and potentially liable to criminal law. In this sense we will follow Sellin's (1937) dictum that as social scientists, criminologists cannot afford to permit nonscientists—in this case legislators and other agents of the law who make and enforce the criminal law—to fix the terms and boundaries of the systematic scientific study of crime. Rather, the criminological approach must recognize that separating crime from other kinds of deviance is a social and political phenomenon.

The basic definition is simple: crime is a kind of deviance, which in turn consists of variation from a social norm that is proscribed by criminal law. More generally, there are many varieties of crime and deviance, which can be divided and subdivided into several categories, and these categories can be conceived theoretically as ranging from those considered least to most serious in any given society. This can be said more concretely. For example, there is an obvious difference in our society between multiple murder and adolescent marijuana use. The most deviant acts can be located empirically on a continuum of seriousness between these two extremes.

Not all persons or groups, in any given societal context, will agree or have strong feelings about the wrongfulness of each act. For example, most persons will have no strong feelings about whether it is "decent" or "indecent" to dress in "erotic clothing" or about what "public indecency" or "erotic clothing" is. However, this in itself is our first measure of seriousness: *the degree of agreement about the wrongfulness of an act*. This assessment can vary from confusion and apathy, through levels of disagreement, to conditions of general agreement. We will regard this as an index of agreement about the norm.

Our second measure of seriousness is the *severity of the social response* elicited by the act. Social penalties vary from public execution to polite avoidance, with a range of responses in between. The more severe the penalty prescribed, and the more extensive the support for this sanction, the more serious is the societal evaluation of the act.

Our third measure of seriousness involves a *societal evaluation of the harm* inflicted by the act. As we noted earlier, some possibly harmful acts, for example drug abuse, seem largely personal in their consequences, and therefore are increasingly regarded as "victimless." Other acts, such as gambling, are "victimless" in the sense that the persons involved are frequently willing and anxious participants. Finally, some acts (e.g., most crimes of violence) are more clearly interpersonal, or social, in their consequences. Here there is also a more definite sense of victimization, although the issue is sometimes resolved by nothing more than who first had access to the most effective weapon. Thus, much of the debate that goes into an evaluation of harmfulness is concerned with the degree of victimization and the personal or social harm that a set of acts may involve.

In most modern societies, including our own, the three measures of seriousness are closely associated. In other words, the more serious acts of deviance, which are most likely to be called "criminal," are likely to involve (1) broad agreement about the wrongfulness of such acts, (2) a severe social response, and (3) an evaluation as being very harmful. However, the correlation among these three dimensions certainly is not perfect, and for many acts, there is disagreement as to their wrongfulness, an equivocal social response, and uncertainty in perceptions of their harmfulness. It is precisely this kind of ambivalence that our approach attempts to capture. Thus, the form of our approach can be visualized as a pyramid (see figure 12.1), with the less serious forms of deviance rarely called "criminal" at the base, the more serious forms of deviance usually called "criminal" at the peak, and a range of uncertain behaviors in between. Each vertical axis of this pyramid represents one of our measures of seriousness. The form of the pyramid purposefully suggests that the most serious acts of crime and deviance in a society tend also to be less frequent, while less serious acts may be considerably more common. Acts included in the pyramid include two general categories (criminal and noncriminal forms of deviance) and four subdivisions (consensual crimes and conflict crimes; social deviations and social diversions). The divisions between these categories are represented with broken lines in figure 12.1. Our purpose is to indicate that across time and place, the particular location of behaviors on the pyramid will vary. In other words, the divisions between the categories are intentionally imprecise. Nonetheless, each of the categories can be discussed individually.

Our discussion proceeds generally from the most to the least serious forms of crime and deviance. It needs to be emphasized, however, that the designation of seriousness is empirically, rather than ethically, determined. Some students of crime and deviance point out that unethical but noncriminal business practices are often morally more serious than rapes, robberies, or even murders. They argue, for example, that unethical multinational business arrangements can create conditions of poverty, inhumanity, degradation, and famine. From an ethical viewpoint, these arguments are extremely important. However, our purpose here is not to create a universal scale of immorality. Our goal is to describe and explain the institutionalization and the violations of the norms of an existing social order. The results of this approach will likely be relevant to, although not sufficient for, the formation of moral judgments.

CRIMINAL FORMS OF DEVIANCE

The forms of deviance regarded as most serious are defined by law as criminal. However, this should not be taken to mean that there is permanence to such

Figure 12.1 The Pyramid of Crime

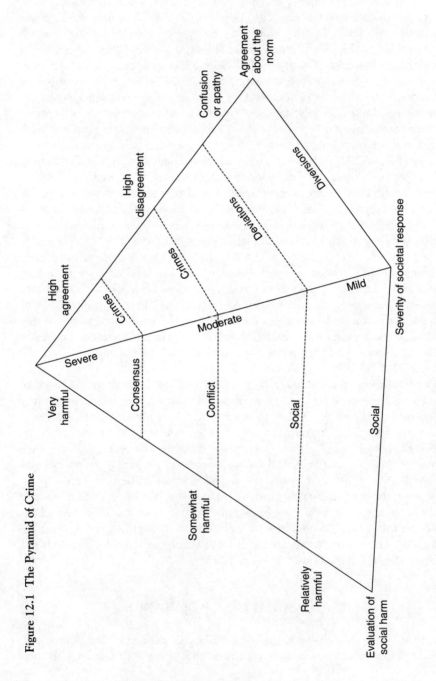

Source: John Hagan, 1977. *The Disreputable Pleasures.* Toronto: McGraw-Hill Ryerson, p. 14.

designations. The point has been made in this book that conceptions of crime change. Berk, Brackman, and Lesser (1977) first made this point by actually classifying and counting changes made in the California penal code between 1955 and 1971. In doing this, all laws affecting the kinds of behavior labeled "illegal" were taken into account, with particular attention given to whether the net effect was to bring more or less behavior under control. Among the results is a graphing of the cumulative changes for all behaviors included or excluded from the California code over this period. Perhaps the most important finding apparent from this exercise is that for no part of this period was the overall net effect of the state legislature's actions to decriminalize behavior. That is, while specific kinds of behavior were taken out of the code during this period, the overall effect was to increase the range of behavior included (referred to as *net widening*). Indeed, a variety of different kinds of behaviors are liable to this fate.

The Consensus Crimes

Our attention is directed first to the crimes that concern most of us, the more visible, predatory crimes. Legal philosophers at one time characterized such acts of deviance as *mala en se*, or "wrong in themselves." However, modern sociologists emphasize that few, if any, human behaviors are universal or timeless in their criminal character. Nonetheless, for several centuries most Western societies have shown considerable consensus in designating as criminal a select group of behaviors. Among the most easily listed of these offenses are premeditated murder, forcible rape, and kidnapping for ransom. A number of researchers have attempted to extend this list and to see just how widespread agreement is currently in our society and others about the seriousness of a number of different acts that are usually designated as crimes.

The pioneering work of this kind was done by Sellin and Wolfgang (1969). Using samples of judges, police, and college students in Philadelphia, they obtained ratings of the seriousness of 141 offenses. A subgroup of fifteen offenses was then selected from the larger list and supplemented with descriptions of the consequences to victims of the criminal acts (e.g., amounts of property stolen or personal injury). A set of fifteen descriptions of these criminal acts and scale scores for each resulted, along with two major conclusions. The first conclusion was that respondents were able to complete the rating tasks rather easily, suggesting that people make judgments of this kind in their everyday lives. The second conclusion was that there was considerable agreement among subgroups about both the relative ordering of criminal acts and the scale scores given. Several replications of this work suggest that American, English Canadian, and French Canadian samples ranked the relative seriousness of these offenses similarly (Akman, Normandeau, and Turner 1967). Another major piece of research of this kind was reported by Rossi et al. (1974) from a survey of an adult population drawn from Baltimore, Maryland. This survey found that in a sample of two hundred adults there was very substantial agreement on the relative seriousness of 140 offenses, including various kinds of white-collar as well as more conventional crimes (see also Blumstein and Cohen 1980).

The terms *"consensus"* and *"conflict"* refer first to sentiments of the general population on a particular issue, as measured, for example, by a frequency distribution of attitudinal expressions indicating what proportion of a group as a whole approves or disapproves of a particular behavior. They refer, second, to the attitudes of specific status groups, as related to a particular issue and indicated by some measure of association—for example, the difference in the percentage of black as contrasted with white Americans who approve of assault. Using both of these criteria, consensus can be said to exist where a population generally is agreed in its attitudes and where these attitudes are related weakly, if at all, to few, if any, status group memberships. In contrast, conflict can be said to exist where attitudes are related more widely and more strongly to status group memberships (regardless of whether members of the society at large are generally agreed or disagreed). Using these criteria, criminal behaviors can be located relative to one another and with reference to an overall continuum of attitudes toward criminal behaviors. Our position is that "consensus crimes" are located toward one end of this continuum, while "conflict crimes" are located toward the other (see Hagan, Silva, and Simpson 1977). It is essential to note that the group of behaviors we have called "consensus crimes" is neither immutably nor permanently criminal. Nonetheless, the fact that some behaviors have been consensually defined as crimes for successive generations makes them of primary interest to some criminologists.

The Conflict Crimes

Continuing controversy surrounds the presence of many offenses in our criminal codes. These crimes are sometimes referred to as *mala prohibita,* or "wrong by prohibition"—for example, as proscribed and punished by statute. As one moves away from the statutes, however, it becomes clear that public opinion is divided about the appropriate status of such offenses. Most important, social class and interest groups are the frequently cited roots of such conflict. The sociological concern is that the criminal law may be used by one class or interest group to the disadvantage of another.

A nonexhaustive list of the conflict crimes would include the public disorder offenses (malicious mischief, vagrancy, and creating a public disturbance), chemical offenses (alcohol and narcotics offenses), political crimes (treason, sedition, sabotage, espionage, subversion, and conspiracy), minor property offenses (petty theft, shoplifting, and vandalism), and the "right-to-life" offenses (abortion and euthanasia). The feature that unites these offenses is the public debate that surrounds them. This is a different way of saying that we lack societal consensus on the dimensions of public disorder, the use of comforting chemicals, permissible politics, the protection of private property, and the limits of life. Lacking a consensus, many of us, given the opportunity or need, may feel free to deviate. It is not surprising, then, that criminologists usually are less interested in asking why individuals are involved in conflict crimes, and are more concerned with the reasons why such persons are considered criminals by law.

NONCRIMINAL FORMS OF DEVIANCE

Not all forms of deviance are designated as criminal, yet many noncriminal forms of deviance are treated in ways analogous to those required by criminal law, while other forms of noncriminal deviance are not. In general, the more serious a noncriminal form of deviance is considered, the more likely it is to be treated in a criminal fashion. Because our scientific interest is as much in behavior and its treatment as in its stated definition, and because these forms of noncriminal deviance constitute a pool, behaviors that in the past may have been, or in the future may become criminal, the noncriminal forms of deviance also are an important source of concern for criminologists. Two types of noncriminal deviance concern us: what we call the "social deviations" and the "social diversions."

The Social Deviations

Although social deviations are sometimes treated as if they were criminal, there are clearly some very important differences. The most frequent of these deviations are of three types: adolescent (juvenile delinquency), vocational (noncriminal violations of public and financial trust), and interpersonal (psychosocial disturbances). The feature that unites these experiences is that although they are not considered criminal, they are nonetheless considered disreputable. Of particular interest is the stigma that may follow contact with noncriminal agencies of social control and how this stigma may compare to that consequent to processing by agencies of crime control. Noncriminal agencies typically attempt to minimize their stigmatizing effects. Juvenile courts "treat" rather than convict "delinquents," professional bodies "suspend" and "expel" occupational "violators," civil courts "process technical violators," and psychiatric agencies protect the identities of their "patients." These efforts vary in their effectiveness, and sociologists and criminologists have been particularly interested in determining how access to personal resources and professional protection affect the outcomes. For example, in an innovative piece of research, Schwartz and Skolnick (1964) demonstrated that while doctors can be found in malpractice without experiencing a loss of income, "common criminals" encounter a stigma that makes earning their future livelihoods difficult. This study illustrates how significant the distinction between criminal and noncriminal forms of deviance can be and the relevance to criminology of their comparative study.

The Social Diversions

The social diversions are regarded as less serious forms of deviance and consequently are less likely to be criminalized. Included among the social diversions are varied expressions of preferences with regard to sex, clothing, language, and leisure. We include them in our discussion partly for the sake of completeness but also because they, too, are occasionally liable to criminalization, and because they display some significant parallels to things called "criminal." The latter point has been made in a number of interesting ways. Sykes and Matza (1961), for example, note that U.S. society contains a set of "subterranean values," including the search for adventure, excitement, and thrills, that exists alongside such conformity-producing values as security, routinization, and stability (see also Davis 1944; Veblen [1899] 1967). A result is that the lines drawn between crime, deviance, and diversion in our society are uncertain and subject to change.

CRIME AND DISREPUTE?

The pyramid approach begins not with crime but with deviance. It examines the seemingly most appalling crimes in the same terms as minor and amusing deviations, and in this sense, it is primarily an empirical analysis of proscribing norms. Almost any norm might be plotted on it (e.g., the norm that discourages house guests from tracking mud into the hosts' home could be evaluated for its agreed-on status, agreed-on evaluation of its impact on the visit, and the likelihood that you will be invited back if you soil the carpets with dirt and slush). In this, it differs from the more self-consciously critical theories of crime, which more unilaterally view criminalization as an exercise of social power.

This framework began with perspectives that from a social scientist's position sought to give meaning to the descriptive category of deviance through the use of observable concepts. The framework of the pyramid regards state sanctions—criminalization—as a strong form of social disapprobation. The strength of this categorization is empirical. Evaluation of social harm, severity of response, and agreement about the norm *are* generally correlated. The gap between generally accepted norms and law, and the gap between individual ethics and generally accepted norms, should not obscure the extent of this agreement on norms. Neither should it obscure the interplay of law and norms: a deviant labeled is often a deviant created (Becker 1963). This interplay might be highly objectionable, but it produces an empirical correlation between response, evaluation of harm, and relationship to norms.

In addition to its presumed empirical usefulness, the advantage of seeing crime as a subset of disrepute is that the social underpinnings of criminalization lie in the societal refusal to accept deviance. If state action lacked any grounding in social evaluation of harms and norms, it would itself be seen as a gross deviation from the state's proper role. In aggregate, *the justification of criminalization is like the justification of any social sanction*. Both criminalization and milder forms of sanction gain much of their social power and legitimacy from their relationship to a commonly accepted norm and understanding. The law might be based in state power, but it also derives much of its ethical force and legitimacy from the degree to which it agrees with popular norms. If popular norms laud an act that could plausibly be considered criminal, then, for better or for worse, the act is not deviant and goes unpunished.

Finally, the pyramid incorporates a conceptual framework to reveal the shifting positions of crimes by schematizing the internal structure of disrepute. Criminalization or social sanctions work best when they are most legitimate, which in turn means they work best when the locations of the acts on the three axes are correlated. Any deviant act that is toward one side of the pyramid is vulnerable to a campaign to bring it back toward the center. It is possible to discuss the changing status of acts within the pyramid because the three axes of the pyramid reflect the major ways people and institutions evaluate and sanction deviance. A sanction that is far out of line on one axis is vulnerable to the charge of illegitimacy.

Viewing crime as a subset of deviance makes an explicit choice to limit the theory's critical powers to increase its empirical powers. Critical and philosophical theories, broadly, derive lists of crimes from norms that a society empirically does hold, or logically should hold. A social contractarian theory such as that of Rawls (1971) attempts to derive rules and ethics from the preconditions of a just society by asking whether people would agree to the rule if they did not know what their standing would be in the society. Less ambitious efforts seek fundamental norms in constitutional law, or society, and might argue that the United States is a classically liberal country and therefore should consistently tolerate victimless crimes.

Compiling a list of crimes as an exercise in logic and social thought will produce a list that differs from the list of ones that are actually criminal or even disreputable: it is difficult to envision a coherent philosophic theory that would leave tobacco and alcohol legal while criminalizing marijuana or that holds different penalties for corporate and solo poisoners. Theory—whether ambitious social contract arguments or appeals to widely held but abstract norms—might be used to criticize either the specific norms or the system that created the gap. If the United States is a classically liberal polity, then antidrug laws can be criticized as un-American and an anomaly. A theory of justice might suggest that they are illegitimate. The gap between general and specific norms, or even between different instances of specific norms, is a better opening for critique than a framework for analysis. Critics can point to the gap between a general norm or principle (e.g., individualism) and a specific one (e.g., a ban on recreational drugs), while investigators can only turn their attention to the reasons the gap emerged.

If critical writing requires identification of a gap between what is and what should be, then a study of what is can be a prerequisite to a theory of what should be. Critiques of common understandings of crime can be coherent because they seek to recategorize a behavior, changing it from the category of business to the category of criminal, or from criminal to pleasurable. Such critiques presume a gap between crime as society, sees it and crime as it should be seen, and they thereby validate the empirical usefulness of frameworks that identify crime as society sees it. Redefining crime with coherent ethical or merely logical arguments would drastically limit the empirical usefulness of a framework while making it more difficult to substantively critique current ideas of crime and punishment.

This strategy of linking disrepute and crime within the broader category of deviance does, of course, run the risk of legitimating philosophically indefensible legal outcomes. Poorly handled, an argument that invokes norms can seem to put the weight of a whole society behind a law that most people don't even know about. This risk is serious when the state is the enforcer, because an unfair policy outcome can masquerade as the general will. Regardless of that, defining crime at a given time "freezes" it and can delegitimate other proposed crimes (a 1950 definition of disrepute would almost wholly exclude environmental destruction that is illegal and unacceptable today). Such problems are best remedied with careful empirical research. Any tool can be misused.

The framework does not, however, lack all normative implications. First, following the strategy of students of white-collar crime, it is possible to make a serious argument from simple principles of identity: theft is theft regardless of whether it is done through sophisticated accounting or by breaking and entering. Second, the pyramid has very broad foundations. It takes very little to question a practice or suggest that it has harms. The dimension of agreement is why it is not vulnerable to the classic critique of norm-based arguments that they overstate consensus and understate strain and diversity. Third, it is a pyramid and not a post. The fact that evaluation, severity, and agreement are often correlated does not mean that they are always correlated. Tension between the three dimensions creates a clear opening for activists: they can argue that an unenforced law with high agreement and evaluation requires more enforcement or that a law with little agreement and less harm should be repealed *simply because of the gap*. In other words, critics and activists can use the fact that law benefits from the legitimation of norms.

"Who Are We?" I: Subgroups and Deviancy

The most troubling objections to the applicability of the pyramid in understanding ordinary crime are the objections that question the existence of the society. By implying that there is a society that might be more or less agreed about a norm, the pyramid appears vulnerable to the classic critique of norm-based arguments since Durkheim: what is the society that holds these norms? It is always possible to critique an argument that posits a social norm (or a social anything) by pointing out groups that are not consulted, or visibly disagree, or perhaps should for some reason have a different attitude than they do. Any society, and especially the enormous and diverse societies of developing and developed countries, contains many groups that are not classic deviant subgroups yet are largely excluded from politics and law and occupy ambiguous stances regarding commonly held norms (e.g., consider attitudes toward illegal immigration among "average" French people compared to French citizens of Algerian descent whose kinship networks include Algerians in Algeria as well as legally or illegally in France). This critique would seem to suggest that it is meaningless or badly insufficient to create an axis of agreement, for it overstates the extent of commonality among groups in society. Agreement suggests willingness and ability to agree.

The simplest response is empirical: there is a great deal of agreement in most societies, and political mechanisms in democracies generally eliminate the most glaring distortions. The strongest response, however, looks beyond the agreement to the social forces that create it. Crime is always in some sense a social construct, produced by the interaction of social groups and institutions, including the state. Disrepute entwines norms and institutions. The lack of unanimity among subgroups in a society does not lessen the power of institutions and widely held norms to create a category of crime and disrepute that may be analyzed and related to other aspects of society.

If there is a strong and stable cleavage between major groups in issues of criminal law or in any other serious issues, it suggests empirically that the law, lacking an agreed-on norm, will lack legitimacy, while politics will be ridden with conflict. In fact, prosecuting everyday deviancy might not be a major issue in such driven societies. In cases where a small and powerless group exists in a larger and coherent society (e.g., illegal immigrants in the developed countries), then the pyramid reflects their powerlessness: regardless of their agreement on norms, evaluation of harms, and the response they would select, their deviance will be treated according to the larger normative structure of society. Worse, they might be classed into a category that has different demands for behavior placed on it: a misdemeanor for a citizen can mean relatively little, whereas it can mean deportation for an alien. The structure of the pyramid holds, but the three axes are set by others who are not accountable to them. This reflects fundamental inequalities of legal and social status: some people are held to norms and sanctions that are not their own, and their disagreement counts for little. The pyramid highlights inequalities but still requires a basic delineation of membership to be a useful model of crime.

"Who Are We?" II: Can Deviancy Be Global?

Like many other concepts in social science, the pyramid of crime suffers from potential scaling problems. Specifically, it works best when there is a fairly coherent society, with integuments of media links, shared institutions, similar economic positions, and other social similarities and when there is a state ruling and responsive to that society. Innovations from cheap airfare and international telephony to the construction of supranational legal systems and transnational capital markets—the stuff of "globalization" debates—challenge these assumptions in three ways, reflecting differences in political structure, ambiguity about units, and the difficulty of defining the society.

In the analysis, "severity of social response" ranges from polite disapprobation to, in some countries, execution. This category includes both social sanctions and the actions of the state. The state (in general) takes responsibility for more serious violations of norms while the lesser infractions are policed largely by raised eyebrows and snickers. The defining characteristic of international society—the lack of a sovereign rule—has to date meant that there was no state to enforce even the most serious infractions. Hitler's Germany was not defeated by a police force on account of its normative violations but by dozens of countries, most of them fighting for their existence and unconcerned with matters like the Holocaust. This is the first problem: The construction of international criminal law is an effort to establish the rule of law at the upper reaches of the pyramid, but without the state and with a far broader range of societies. Who must agree on the norm for it to be a norm, and through whose framework shall events be interpreted? Insofar as norms in a complex society depend on institutions for their transmission, the fact that many institutions stop at state borders creates normative disagreement and enforcement problems.

Ambiguity about units is the second part of this problem. The pyramid reflects society at its best when citizens are like and equal. It throws political inequalities into sharp light when they are not, as in the case of illegal immigrants. But it also faces a problem with larger units than individual people. Agreement about a norm means one thing when debating whether to try individuals for a given act. It is very different when there is no agreement on who or what is being sanctioned or tried.[1] For example, the juridical personality of corporations remains a counterintuitive concept, yet individuals are only very rarely tried for the acts they commit in the interests of their firm. The problem becomes worse, however, when the individuals are part not of a corporation but of sovereign states. Their liability is blurred by the rhetoric of sovereignty, the complex command lines of a state, and the suspicion that foreigners belong to a different moral community.

This has only recently become a problem (as against a fact of life). For centuries, states have gained more and more control over law, slowly eliminating older nonstate legal traditions such as manor law, canon law, merchant law, and city law as well as many and various legal traditions and structures in non-European countries. Coupled with the doctrine of absolute state sovereignty and the exigencies of power politics, this effectively reduced the remit of law to domestic trials of individuals. However, the situation is arguably reversed today, as international legal regimes in areas ranging from human rights and war crimes (Ratner and Abrams 1997) to commercial arbitration and trading regimes (Dezalay and Garth 1996) seem to demonstrate that there are both global norms of conduct and opportunities for the construction of global legal systems that can enforce global norms. Confusion about norms stems from the probable fact that norms have outrun law in this case, and law has outrun policing.

Finally, the third challenge to the extension of the pyramid model lies in the difficulty of defining a global society. It might be that some widely held norms—such as the norm forbidding genocide—are actually norms without societies, specific requirements for conduct adopted by many different societies rather than (thankfully) derived from experience. Given the range of behaviors found worldwide and the difficulties of prosecuting criminals when states stand between the law and the criminal, many actions would be plastered against one edge of the pyramid, the edge that marks considerable harm, little agreement, and no response.

Rwanda as an Example

The 1994 Rwanda genocide and the subsequent establishment of an international tribunal to try crimes against humanity[2] show how the pyramid of crime can illuminate serious social and moral questions and what limits it might face in understanding crime. Internally, the genocide questions the existence of a society with a responsive state and citizens who are fairly similar and equal. Were the Hutu *genocidaires* who perpetrated the massacres an enormous deviant subgroup, or was Rwanda becoming two societies laid atop one another with two different normative structures, or was the level of agreement about norms (including the acceptability of *being* Tutsi) so low in Rwandan society that there is no agreement on even the most sickening crimes? Here *"disagreement"* is a weak term.

Rwanda, on the international plane, might be seen as a case in which high worldwide agreement existed about the norm: genocide is unacceptable. Yet there was a conflicting norm: that of sovereignty. Also, the evaluation of social harm could vary radically depending on the observer: its social harm is enormous, viewed in terms of Rwandan lives, but harm to Rwandan lives might not seem an enormous social harm in Dallas. Moreover, the levels of possible societal response are radically reduced: most measures of disrepute simply do not work if the people who disapprove are in Milwaukee and the disapproved-of are in Kigali.[3] The most important people who disapproved were the Tutsi-led guerrilla force that overthrew the genocidal Hutu regime and the French politicians who sent in a French expeditionary force (although it is unclear just who the French troops were supposed to help). In other words, the forces that mattered were the ones, however admirable, that were beyond the law of Rwanda and subject to the rule of others. Since the collapse of the genocidal regime in Rwanda, a war crimes tribunal has been investigating and prosecuting *genocidaires* in the name of humanity (hence the term *"crimes against humanity"*). While few will speak up for genocide, both the criminal (Rwanda or Rwandans) and the plaintiff (humanity) remain ambiguous in public debates, even as the international tribunal begins to try individual Rwandans.

To try the international criminals of the Rwandan genocide might be to construct an international norm and an international epistemology that accepts the idea that individuals can violate global norms. The empirical argument for having one scale of agreement in a complex society is that widely held views and institutions combined can create and maintain a norm. The trials for Rwanda and the former Yugoslavia, thus, might help create, as an empirical matter, a norm that holds for all the societies of the globe. It might create a coherent narrative with comprehensible actors that people understand worldwide and a sanction that is universally legitimate. It is thus partly a set of normative sanctions that are willing a society into self-consciousness.[4] The pyramid of crime is an empirical analysis of extant norms and sanctions, and the very act of trying the crimes against humanity in Rwanda and the former Yugoslavia might create as an empirical fact a norm and a sanction that overcome the massively institutionalized differences between different groups worldwide.

CONCLUSION

The pyramid of crime, like the empirical criminological theories of Sutherland, Sellin, and others, faces two major challenges. One challenge is that it is inadequately critical. The other is that it depends on, if not a nation-state, at least a stable society yoked to a fairly predictable and democratic state. The first challenge is accepted: to use ethical interrogation, or even to derive coherent ethical theories from existing norms, would be to change the meaning of crime in a way that would distance the definition of crime from everyday institutional and individual usage and practice. The world might thereby be improved, but understanding crime requires examining it in its current definitions.

The second challenge is more difficult to face. For a subgroup within a state, its disagreement with norms and evaluations of harms is in part reduced to simple contestation by the fact that it shares a political and institutional framework with others. The common institutions of the state and civil society reduce group cleavage to the level of disagreement within the society or demarcate certain groups subjected to alternative and nondemocratic normative structures. Membership delimits the applicability of the pyramid; intergroup conflict can only with difficulty be modeled in this norm-based framework. Two truly conflictual normative structures probably cannot harmoniously coexist when one controls a modern state.

The international level, however, introduces problems of accountability, comprehension, and agency as well as far more difficult requirements for both norms and response. Within a normal polity, deviants are still individuals considered like other members of the society. On a global level, however, the deviants are harder to identify, as they can seem to be states, whole societies, or just renegade leaders. Norms, such as those banning genocide, enjoy wide legitimacy and serious enforcement problems. The creation of international criminal tribunals might create the very society, with normative agreement, that would solidify existing global norms, while also creating a mechanism for policing that uncouples sovereignty and societal response.

NOTES

1. The American prosecutors at Nuremburg created serious legal problems with their efforts to try Nazi leaders for conspiracy to wage aggressive war. In part, this was because conspiracy presupposes individuals voluntarily joining a conspiracy, and Nazi Germany was a state rather than a burglary ring or a plot. The result was that the conspiracy charge disappeared amidst arguments about who and what was actually being tried: the men in the dock, Nazi organizations such as the SS, the German state, or the German people. See Smith (1977: chap. 5).

2. Masterfully analyzed in Prunier (1995) and Klinghoffer (1998).

3. In addition, there is nothing like an international police force or other meaningful international agency with full-time responsibility to watch for deviations from international norms. Until midway through the genocide, for example, France regarded Rwanda as a French ally and ignored internal events (Greer 2000).

4. The problem with Sellin's concept of universal conduct norms was that such norms are almost impossible to find. If institutions can help create and sustain norms, the existence of institutionalized international criminal law might strengthen or even create universal conduct norms.

REFERENCES

Akman, D. D., A. Normandeau, and S. Turner. 1967. "The Measurement of Delinquency in Canada." *Journal of Criminal Law, Criminology, and Police Science* 58 (September): 330–37.

Becker, Howard. 1963. *Outsiders: Studies in the Sociology of Deviance.* New York: Free Press.

Berk, Richard, Harold Brackman, and Selma Lesser. 1977. *A Measure of Justice.* New York: Academic Press.

Blumstein, Alfred, and Jacqueline Cohen. 1980. "Sentencing of Convicted Offenders: An Analysis of the Public's View." *Law and Society Review* 14: 223–62.

Bordua, David. J. 1969. "Recent Trends: Deviant Behavior and Social Control." *Annals of the American Academy of Political and Social Science* 369 (January): 149–63.

Davis, Arthur K. 1944. "Veblen's Study of Modern Germany." *American Sociological Review* 9: 603–09.

Dezalay, Yves, and Bryant G. Garth. 1996. *Dealing in Virtue: International Commercial Arbitration and the Construction of a Transnational Legal Order*. Chicago: University of Chicago Press.

Greer, Scott L. 2000. "Mutual Benefit? France in Africa, from Stabilizer to Saboteur." In *Questioning Geopolitics*, ed. Georgi Derluguian and Scott L. Greer. Westport, Conn.: Greenwood.

Hagan, John. 1973. "Labeling and Deviance: A Case Study in the 'Sociology of the Interesting.' " *Social Problems* 20, no. 4: 448–58.

Hagan, John, and Alberto Palloni. 1990. "The Social Reproduction of a Criminal Class in Working Class London, Circa 1950 through 1989." *American Journal of Sociology* 96, no. 2 (September 1990): 265–99.

Hagan, John, Edward Silva, and John Simpson. 1977. "Conflict and Consensus in the Designation of Deviance." *Social Forces* 56, no. 2: 320–40.

Horning, Donald N. 1970. "Blue-Collar Theft: Conceptions of Property, Attitudes toward Pilfering, and Work Group Norms in a Modern Industrial Plant." In *Crimes against Bureaucracy*, ed. Erwin O. Smigel and H. Laurence Ross. New York: Van Nostrand Reinhold.

Klinghoffer, Arthur J. 1998. *The International Dimensions of Genocide in Rwanda*. New York: New York University Press.

Prunier, Gérard. 1995. *The Rwanda Crisis: History of a Genocide*. New York: Columbia University Press.

Ratner, S. R., and J. S. Abrams. 1997. *Accountability for Human Rights Atrocities in International Law: Beyond the Nuremberg Legacy*. Oxford: Clarendon.

Rawls, John. 1971. *A Theory of Justice*. Cambridge, Mass.: Belknap.

Rossi, Peter H., Emily White, Christine E. Bose, and Richard E. Berk. 1974. "The Seriousness of Crimes: Normative Structure and Individual Differences." *American Sociological Review* 39 (April): 224–37.

Schwartz, Richard, and Jerome Skolnick. 1964. "Two Studies of Legal Stigma." In *The Other Side: Perspectives on Deviance*, ed. Howard Becker. New York: Free Press.

Sellin, Thorsten. 1937. *Research Memorandum on Crime in the Depression*. New York: Social Science Research Council, Bulletin 27.

———. 1938. *Culture Conflict and Crime*. Bulletin 41. New York: Social Science Research Council.

Sellin, Thorsten, and Marvin E. Wolfgang. 1969. *Delinquency: Selected Studies*. New York: Wiley.

Smith, B. F. 1977. *Reaching Judgment at Nuremberg*. New York: Basic Books.

Sutherland, Edwin. 1945. "Is 'White Collar Crime' Crime?" *American Sociological Review* 10: 132–39.

Sykes, Gresham, and David Matza. 1957. "Techniques of Neutralization: A Theory of Delinquency." *American Sociological Review* 22: 664–70.

Tappan, Paul. 1947. "Who Is the Criminal?" *American Sociological Review* 12 (February): 96–102.

Taylor, Ian, Paul Walton, and Jock Young. 1973. *The New Criminology: For a Social Theory of Deviance*. London: Routledge & Kegan Paul.

Veblen, Thorsten. [1899] 1967. *The Theory of the Leisure Class*. New York: Viking.

Wilkins, Leslie. T. 1964. *Social Deviance*. London: Tavistock.

13

The Prism of Crime: Toward an Integrated Definition of Crime

Stuart Henry and Mark M. Lanier

Our purpose in this concluding chapter is to further integrate into a comprehensive definition the seemingly contradictory views of crime identified in the previous chapters of this book. However, we aim not for an ultimate or finalized definition but for one that accommodates the range of constitutive dimensions of crime. This is in the spirit of Arrigo's (1995: 465) argument that integration is "not a systematic, reconstitutive closure to possibilities; rather, it is an opening-up to multiple, discordant, and different expressions by which meaning and being are articulated." We shall do this by drawing on the integrational insights of John Hagan (1977, 1985; and this volume, chap. 12), who is one of the few theorists to have addressed the problem.

LIMITS TO THE PYRAMID OF CRIME ANALYSIS

As we have argued elsewhere (Lanier and Henry 1998; Henry and Lanier 1998), Hagan's pyramid is one of the few attempts to integrate the multiple dimensions of crime, yet it does not go far enough. The pyramid is incomplete for several reasons.

Crime's Visibility

First, it neglects public awareness of crime—that is, the realization that one has been a victim. Crime takes many forms, all of which involve harm, but not all of those harmed necessarily realize they have been victimized. Participants in victimless crime may claim that the criminal label is wrong. In the case of victims of government and corporate crime, it is often a long time before the victims become aware that they have been harmed, and many never realize it. For example, the effects of environmental crime may be so slow and diffused that no one notices any harm or change in the environment. Yet, over a period of years a particular area may become uninhabitable due to environmental crime. Such crimes can result in insidious injuries when the links between the causes and the effects are obscure, take a long time to appear, affect only a segment of the population, result in increased risk of injury or disease, and are widely dispersed through the population (Calhoun and Hiller 1986). Thus, we argue that crime can range from being "obvious" or "readily apparent" to "relatively hidden" and, finally, so "obscure" that it is accepted by many as normal, even though it harms its victims (e.g., environmental crimes, racism, and patriarchy). Hagan acknowledges this but does not include the measure of obscurity as one of his dimensions.

Extent of Victimization

A second missing, though implied, dimension of the "pyramid of crime" is the number of victims. If only one person is affected by crime, this is certainly tragic and serious. Nevertheless, this crime is qualitatively different from acts of violence affecting many people as in terrorist attacks. These two additional dimensions, visibility and numbers harmed, are implied in surveys that depict the perceived seriousness of various acts. Absolute numbers of victims influences a society's perception as to the seriousness of crime, as is dramatically illustrated in the Oklahoma City terrorist bombing of a federal building.

Severity of Response

A third limitation of Hagan's pyramid relates to the dimension of seriousness of response. This dimension fails to capture the probability or likelihood that a convicted offender will receive a serious response, even though the law may set such a penalty. Crimes of the powerless (e.g., robbery, theft, larceny) are far more likely to receive the full weight of the law than are crimes of the powerful (e.g., insider trading, corporate fraud, price fixing) (Calavita and Pontell 1993).

Visual Constraint

A final limitation of Hagan's analysis is in its visual structure: the way that it is displayed does not allow the other elements that we have noted to be included. The pyramid suggests that where conflict exists about the criminality of some crimes, these are only somewhat harmful. However, some crimes may be extremely harmful yet still not be perceived as harms by society, not least because the media presents them in a way that favors the perpetrators. Until recently, this was the case with crimes of gender, such as sexual harassment and date rape, in which the (generally) male offender was shown as having poor judgment, but not intending harm. It is clear to us that consensus is not always present on the seriousness of harms such as corporate crimes or crimes by institutions and organizations on their members or clients. Corporate crimes can be extremely harmful. This lack of consensus is in spite of the moderate societal response and conflict among interest groups in society over the need for regulations and whether their violation constitutes crimes. For example, corporations historically oppose health and safety regulations if they slow production or add to cost, depicting consumer or environmental protections as needless government interference in the workings of industry.

THE PRISM OF CRIME

To solve these problems, we suggest a redesigned visual presentation, making it a double pyramid or what we call the "crime prism" (see figure 13.1). In our schema, we place an inverted pyramid beneath the first pyramid. The top pyramid represents the highly visible crimes, typically of the structurally powerless, that are committed in public. These include crimes such as robbery, theft, auto theft, burglary, assault, murder, stranger rape, and arson. These crimes are similar to many of what for years have been called "index crimes" by the FBI. The bottom-inverted pyramid represents relatively invisible crimes. These include a variety of crimes committed by the powerful. These would be offenses by government officials, corporations, and organizations, as well as crimes by people committed through their occupations, such as fraud and embezzlement, and even some crimes such as date rape, sexual harassment, domestic violence, sexism, racism, ageism, and hate crimes. These crimes are typically conducted in private contexts, such as organizations and workplaces, and involve violations of trusted relationships. Together crimes of the powerless and crimes of the powerful constitute the visible and invisible halves of our prism of crime.

We use the term *prism* not only because of its visual appearance but also because, just as a prism is used to analyze a continuous spectrum, so in our case it is used to analyze the spectrum of dimensions that constitute "crime." Furthermore, light is refracted in a prism to reveal various colors; likewise, through our crime prism, people may view the same criminal act in different contextual terms depending on their prior experiences, socialization, and worldview. The revised dimensions of the crime prism need some further elaboration before we can explain how they constitute an integrated definition.

Social Agreement

This feature spans from the top of the crime prism (graphically located on the right side) representing the greatest agreement, through moderate agreement, down to the widest section of the pyramid where there is apathy or disinterest.

Figure 13.1 The Prism of Crime

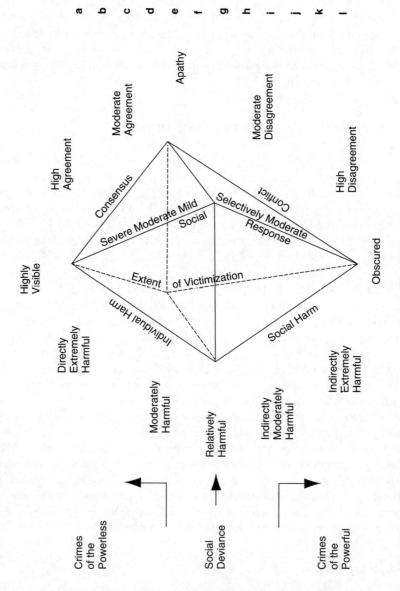

Source: Mark M. Lanier and Stuart Henry, 1998. *Essential Criminology*. Boulder, Colo.: Westview, p. 28.

It then ranges through the lower half of the prism to crimes where there is moderate disagreement to those in which there is high disagreement, or extreme conflict at the opposite extreme. Beginning in the visible area (top half) of the prism, a planned random mass murder would be placed at the top of the pyramid, since there is likely to be most agreement about the seriousness of such an act. A planned murder (at times this type may generate controversy as in the O. J. Simpson case, but for most of these crimes little controversy is expressed) might be placed at position B, depending on the circumstances of the case, whereas the crime of robbery at gunpoint would rank on the agreement scale at position C. Acts of social deviance, such as punk hairstyles or wearing rings piercing various parts of the skin, would rank at position F, since these are acts about which many people are generally apathetic.

Moving down to the invisible area, a doctor cheating on claims made to a federal health insurance plan for patients would be placed at position H, whereas a factory discharging polluted waste in a way that results in pollution of the city water supply would rank at K. This placement is because people disagree about the need for government regulation, the intended or accidental nature of the action, and so on. Considerable conflict exists over these "invisible crimes" located in the lower half of the pyramid, such as whether workplace deaths and injuries result from accident or criminal negligence of safety standards are crimes.

Probable Social Response

The upper segment of this dimension (graphically located on the prism angles closest to the reader) runs from a high probability of severe sanctions for convicted offenders (e.g., death penalty or life prison), through moderate sanctions (e.g., shorter prison sentences, fines, probation), to a high probability of mild sanctions (e.g., community service, counseling, public condemnation). In other words, it represents the legal perspective outlined at the outset of this book. In our revision of Hagan's pyramid into the lower inverted half of the prism, this dimension now also extends from mild through selectively severe sanctions (e.g., fines, probation, and restitution) and continues to symbolically severe sanctions at the lowest point. "Symbolically severe" refers to the low probability that severe sentences will be widespread and the recognition that these will often be reduced on appeal. As DeKeseredy and Schwartz (1996: 47) forcibly argue:

> [P]oor people who accidentally kill bank tellers while attempting to rob them are labeled as murderers and are subject to harsh punishment. . . . Corporate executives who create unsafe working conditions are often exempt from both formal censure and prosecution, despite the fact that their decisions result in injuries and even death for thousands of people each year.

The probable social response dimension in the crime prism thus reflects the ability of powerful interests to mediate the effects and working of the law, reflecting

some aspects of the interactionist, social constructionist, and power/conflict perspectives discussed in this book.

Individual and Social Harm

This dimension is also the same as in Hagan's analysis for the upper section,
except that in our crime prism it refers to direct individual harm, where the offender has specifically targeted the victim (this is presented on the left edge of
the prism). The most harmful crimes here include those in which the victims
are killed and those in which they become permanently injured and maimed;
through crimes that are harmful through some temporary loss of capability,
money, property, or position; to those that might offend moral sensibilities but
do not directly result in personal loss.

However, this dimension also spans into the lower half of the prism which
includes offenses creating moderate social harm (e.g., price fixing that increases
the costs of products to consumers) to those social harms in which people have
been physically injured and killed in the course of the general need to meet an
organizational goal. This dimension of the pyramid incorporates the aspect of
defining crime begun with Sutherland and extended by the Schwendingers and
Tifft and Sullivan in earlier chapters of this book.

Extent of Victimization

This final dimension, omitted but implied in Hagan's measure of harm, represents the number of victims affected by a crime. Put simply, this feature spans
from those in which numerous random victims result from highly visible individual crimes located at the top of the prism (A), through those where several are
affected by random crime (C), to those where a few are affected at the center of
the prism (F). As this dimension extends into the lower prism of invisible crime,
more people are affected, but now by being members of a particular "targeted"
social category—for example, employees who work with hazardous materials;
people who are employed in high-risk occupations, such as mining, construction,
or chemicals; or individuals who are buying a particular kind of faulty product
(e.g., Firestone tires sold on Ford sport utility vehicles) or are living in an area
where pollutants have contaminated the drinking water.

INTEGRATING THE DIMENSIONS

Now that we have briefly illustrated the dimensions of the crime prism, it is possible to discuss the spatial location of a few specific examples. Take the earlier
example of terrorism. Here crime is obvious, highly visible, extremely harmful,
and noncontroversial with regard to the measure of consensus-conflict. Smith

and Orvis (1993) indicate that this kind of crime can be horrifying to the sensibilities of virtually all people, while directly harming relatively few (obviously family members and friends and acquaintances may also be hurt, but still in lesser numbers). Societal response and outrage to this type of crime are immediate and pointed. Law enforcement agencies devote all available resources and form special task forces to deal with these crimes. Punishment is severe and can include the death penalty. Consequently, it would be placed on the top or very near the apex of the prism, near position A. However, this only holds true if several people were harmed. If few were harmed, its ranking on the extent of victimization scale moves it down nearer B.

Further down the prism, but still at its upper end, are violent acts of individual crime. These are also readily apparent as being criminal. They are *mala in se* crimes. Relatively few people are hurt by each act, yet societal reaction is severe and involves little controversy. Law enforcement considers these crimes a top priority. Sanctions are very severe, ranging from lengthy penal confinement to death (located around C). Beneath these come acts of robbery, burglary, larceny, and vandalism located toward the upper quarter of the prism (D). At the lowest levels of the upper segment is where Hagan (1985: 59) placed social deviations and social diversions. Deviance, the higher placed of the two, includes acts such as public drunkenness, juvenile status offenses (acts that if committed by an adult would be legal), and trespass (position E). It should be noted, however, that these are small-scale or low-value violations. Beneath the social deviations are what Hagan terms social diversions of unconventional lifestyles or sexual practices, and so forth. In either case, these offenses are relatively harmless and result in confusion or apathy with no consensus about their criminal status and little formal law enforcement. These offenses would be located at the center of the prism at position F.

From this point on for the inverted pyramid of our modified visual, the perception of criminality is relatively hidden. Offenses here are mildly responded to by law enforcement and often are merely subject to a variety of informal social sanctions or by systems of internal social control.

As we move into the lower section of the prism and toward the lower point, the obscurity of the crime increases. Its harm becomes less direct. Conflict over its criminal definition increases and the seriousness of society's response becomes more selective. *Mala prohibita* acts are positioned here. Mala prohibita definitions of crime necessarily involve a social, ecological, and temporal context. As we have seen, these acts may be criminal in one society but noncriminal in another. Likewise, an act that is criminal in one county or state may be legal in another (e.g., prostitution). Such crimes also change over time. Crimes that do not reflect a consensus in society move toward the lower inverted part of the prism. Many more people are harmed by similar acts, yet societal responses are moderate. The police exercise considerable discretion when dealing with these types of offenses. Often, fines and "second chances" are given to violators of these laws. These crimes would be placed at G and H.

At a lower level, crime is not apparent (hidden) and indirect, yet it hurts many people over an extended time (e.g., the savings and loan scandal and the Ford–Firestone tire case at J and I). Yet, the impact of this type of crime is diffused, and societal reactions are diluted. Law enforcement is rarely equipped to handle it. Prison sentences are rarely given; the more common sanctions are fines, restitution settlements, censure, and signs of disapproval. Regulatory agencies (e.g., the Occupational Safety and Health Association, the Federal Trade Commission), rather than law enforcement, are responsible for law enforcement. Unless the offense is made public, corporations and their trade associations will likely handle these problems through their own disciplinary mechanisms. They will be located at the lower quarter of the prism.

At the final level (positions K and L), crimes are so hidden that many may deny their existence, while others may argue as to whether they are crimes. For example, an institutionalized type of crime may be sexism, which is patriarchal, subdued, and so ingrained into the fabric of a society as to be unnoticed, yet its impact is very influential. The law enforcement community generally scoffs at consideration of these crimes being criminal. These crimes are rarely, if ever, punished. Those sanctions that occur generally involve social disapproval (though some groups will voice approval) and verbal admonishment.

APPLICATION OF THE INTEGRATED PRISM ANALYSIS TO THE CRIMES OF SCHOOL VIOLENCE

In this final section we provide a contemporary example to illustrate the utility of the crime prism. In the analysis of school violence, commentators tend to define the scope of the problem narrowly. Typically they focus on interpersonal violence: among students toward each other or by students toward their teachers. In terms of our prism, they focus on the visible harms between school students, which would be located in the top half of the prism, but fail to see the broader dimension of the crimes that extend into the lower levels of the prism. We argue that the complexity of crimes such as school violence defies such a simplistic framing. It fails to address the wider context of school violence, the wider forms of violence in schools, and the important interactive and causal effects arising from the confluence of these forces. What is demanded is an integrated, multilevel definition of the problem that will lead to a multilevel causal analysis and a comprehensive policy response that takes account of the full range of constitutive elements. It is our view that the prism provides us with a conceptual framework to define the full dimensional scope of the problem.

The Scope of the Problem: The Paucity of the School Violence Concept?

Public analysis of social problems tends to be framed very narrowly. Violence is visible and manifest among school students, so it is assumed that they constitute the scope of the problem. Yet, any analysis of school violence that simply looks at one factor, such as human fallibility, gun availability, or cultural toxicity, is in grave danger of missing the wider constitutive elements.

Violence is generally defined as the use of force toward another that results in harm. Simplistic versions limit the concept to "extreme physical force" (Champion 1997: 128; Rush 1994: 54), which may include intimidation by the threat of force (Bureau of Justice Statistics 1998). Omitted here are several critical elements of harm: (1) emotional and psychological pain that result from domination of some over others; (2) harms by institutions or agencies *on* individuals; (3) the violence of social processes that produces a systemic social injury, such as that perpetuated through institutionalized racism and sexism; and (4) the "symbolic violence" of domination (Bourdieu 1977) that brings coercion through the power exercised in hierarchical relationships.

In the school context, studies of violence typically refer to student-on-student and student-on-teacher acts of physical harm or interpersonal violence: "Violence refers to the threat or use of physical force with the intention of causing physical injury, damage, or intimidation of another person" (Elliott, Hamburg, and Williams 1998: 13–14).[1] This definition clearly refers to acts located in the upper half of our prism. However, considering the lower half of the prism is suggestive since it draws our attention to other hidden dimensions of the problem that we have described as the hidden crimes of the structurally powerful in society (Henry and Lanier 1998). It also sensitizes us to the symbolic social harms that deny humanity through violating human rights (see the chapters in this volume by Milovanovic and Henry, Schwendinger and Schwendinger, and Tifft and Sullivan). In the school context, these harms, located in the lower half of the prism, include harms committed by teachers on students and by school administrators on both students and teachers. They also include the organization of schooling where this creates harm to both student creativity and the educational process. Conventional definitions of school violence, located in the upper half of the prism, neglect harmful institutionalized social and educational practices. These include acts and processes of institutionalized racism/sexism, discrimination, labeling, and tracking (Yogan 2000), authoritarian discipline (Adams 2000), militaristic approaches to school security (Thompkins 2000; Pepinsky 2000), sexual harassment, and predation, all of which would be located in the lower half of the prism.

For example, gender discrimination has been shown to create harmful effects on female students' learning experience. When teachers favor male students over females because of their seemingly extroverted classroom participation, they disadvantage females and oppress their potential development, which can lead to feelings of inadequacy, anger, and long-term depression. Such practices are not defined as violence, but they are symbolically violent with long-term harmful consequences.[2]

Consider, as further examples, a school administration that exercises arbitrary, authoritarian discipline or teachers who "get by" without their best effort and who lack commitment to their students' education. Consider also the message conveyed to students about "trust" and "freedom" of educational thought when we deploy metal detectors, video cameras, identity tags, drug-sniffing dogs, and guards to "secure" that freedom (Adams 2000; Thompkins 2000). This "hidden curriculum" can have a significant negative impact on students' moral and social development (Yogan and Henry 2000).

At a broader level, consider the harm of inequitable school funding, such that one school will receive better funding due to its location in a wealthy area, compared to a school located in a poverty-stricken urban setting. Finally, consider the harm created by celebrating competitive success while condemning academic failure; is it any wonder that "children who do poorly in school, lack educational motivation, and feel alienated are the most likely to engage in criminal acts"? (Siegel 1998: 197–98). This analysis does not even begin to address how competitive success corrupts the morality of the successful, driving them to win at all costs, regardless of the harm they cause to others in the process (Nicholson 2000; Staples 2000).

Toward an Expansive Integrated Concept of School Violence

Because of the omission of these broader dimensions of school violence, we are missing much of the content and causes of violence in schools. We are blind to the part played by this wider context of violence in shaping the more visible forms of interpersonal physical violence manifest by some students. A more inclusive integrated concept of school violence is necessary.

With regard to the perpetrators of harm, the concept for those who exercise the power to deny others, conventionally described as "offenders," is limiting since it assumes that only individuals offend. Yet the manifestation of power that denies people their humanity can operate at many levels, from individual to organization or corporation, community and society to nation-state. Furthermore, the exercise of the power to harm, as mentioned earlier, can also be accomplished by social processes, such as sexism, ageism, and racism, which goes beyond the individual acts of people. The exercise of power to deny others their humanity by some agency or process also takes place in a spatial social context. Even though the term *school violence* implies that the spatial location is the "school building, on the school grounds or on a school bus" (Bureau of Justice Statistics 1998), such a limited definition denies the interconnections between the school context and the wider society of which it is a part. It ignores the ways in which these acts of violence permeate social and geographic space. As a result, it fails to recognize that what may appear as an outburst in the school is merely one manifestation of more systemic societal problems. These may begin in, or be modified by, activities in other spatial locations such as households, public streets, local neighborhoods, communities, private corporations, public organizations, national political arenas, global marketplace, or the wider political economy. As such, the social and institutional space of the school is merely one forum for the appearance of a more general systemic problem of societal violence.

The Pyramidal Analysis of Dimensions of School Violence

In this section, we will relate school violence to the dimensions of the prism. How does the acknowledgment of multiple dimensions of defining school violence affect our analysis? First is the dimension of relative seriousness of crime based on the harm it has caused. Some acts, like alcohol use and truancy, are victimless crimes in that they only harm the participants; others, such as the recent high-profile shootings in schools, harm more than one person at a time, and that pain can extend to the victims' relatives, friends, and community (see Nicholson 2000).

Second is the degree of moral consensus or agreement as to whether an act is right or wrong, which "can range from confusion and apathy, through levels of disagreement, to conditions of general agreement" (Hagan 1985: 49). Thus, although there is consensus that drugs should not be in schools, the consensus is much greater against heroin and cocaine than marijuana, and against all three compared to alcohol and cigarettes (see Venturelli 2000).

The third dimension is the severity of society's formal response. Severity may range from social ostracism by school peers toward their fellow students, through informal reprimands by teachers, official warnings, expulsion and exclusion from school, prosecution, imprisonment; ultimately to the death penalty.[3]

As we have seen, school violence takes many forms, all of which involve harm, but not all of those harmed necessarily realize they have been victimized. This point relates, then, to the visibility dimension of the crime prism. For example, it is difficult to see the negative effects of tracking, yet the "track system" has been shown to reinforce class and racial segregation, and over time this practice operates as a crime of repression, limiting the intellectual, social, and moral development of those subject to it (Yogan 2000). The harmful effects of this practice are obscure and may take a long time to appear (in lowered expectations for self, poor self-esteem, etc.). Visibility of some aspects of school violence is an important dimension because it is partly a reflection of the force of existing legal definitions, themselves shaped by powerful economic, political, and class interests. These interests, in turn, partly reflect the commercial interests of the mass media, which limit their framing of the crime question (see the chapters in this volume by Surette and Otto and by Russell). In part, they reflect the popular culture's trivialization and sensationalization of direct interpersonal "true

crimes" in preference to complex, diffuse social harms and injuries that have become institutionalized, compartmentalized, privatized, and justified via the organization's legitimate goals.

In light of the pyramid discussion and analysis, an expansive integrated definition and reconception of school violence allow us to reframe our analysis of
types of school violence. Types of school violence can be distinguished by the
level of their perpetrators within the social structure, and these in turn reflect
their positioning at different levels within the prism. Five levels of violence are
identified, though the accuracy of the distinction between levels is less important
than that the range of levels be addresses:

Level 1: student on student; student on teacher; student on school
Level 2: teacher on student; administrator on student; administrator on
    teacher; teacher/administrator on parents; parent on teacher/administrator.
Level 3: school board on school/parent; school district on school/parents; com-
    munity on school/parent; local political decisions on school and on parent
Level 4: state and national educational policy on school; state and national
    juvenile justice policy on student; media and popular culture on student and
    on administrator; corporate exploitation on students; national and state
    policies on guns and drugs
Level 5: harmful social processes and practices that pervade each of the prior
    four levels. Here social processes are the patterns of interaction that over
    time take on the appearance of a natural order or social reality existing
    above the individuals whose actions constitute that structure.

Discussion on school violence tends to be restricted to level 1 and some aspects of level 4. Even within level 1, some important distinctions can be made.
In contrast to the excessive discussion of level 1 and some of 4, there has been
virtually no discussion of levels 2, 3, and 5, which, given the interrelations between these types, represents a glaring deficiency.

Causal Implications of the Prismatic Analysis of School Violence

This expansive integrated approach to defining school violence allows us to
better identify different types of school violence. But it also raises the question
of whether the different levels of violence manifest in the school setting are interrelated. In other words, are the different levels of violence in school causally
interrelated, such that invisible institutional violence at the level of, say, administrators and teachers, is generative of visible violence among school students?
Clearly this is an empirical question, and some evidence supports that this may
be the case (Welsh 2000). Although individuals may contribute to these social
processes, it is the collective and cumulative repetition of actions by different
people that creates harm to others. In the context of school violence, these proc-

esses comprise the practices and policies of the school, or what Welsh (2000) calls "school climate." It can include the policies and practices of school boards and their detrimental effects on school districts and the local politics of communities. At a broader level, the collective actors can operate on the state and national levels to include educational policy. An example would be the decision to expand prison-building programs at the expense of school building, to hire corrections officers rather than schoolteachers, and even to submit to the apparent "economy of scale" that leads to building large schools over small ones, when all the evidence suggests that these are more alienating and more criminogenic. While these collective and policy decisions may seem distant from the school's day-to-day activities, their effects reach long into the classroom and constitute part of the formative context for violence that is played out there.

For example, Kramer (2000) distinguishes between three types of student violence: (1) predatory economic crimes, which involves the pursuit of material goals by any means, including violence; (2) drug industry crimes, which involve violent gang turf wars; and (3) social relationship violence from powerless angry youths who use acts of violence to resolve issues of humiliation from their alienation (see also Staples 2000; Cintron 2000). This third type may be a manifestation of the deeper social processes of harm in the lower level of our prism. In addition, we have argued that not all school students respond in the same way to the conditions that generate violence, even within level 1, and this has much to do with the influence of class, race, and gender (Yogan and Henry 2000; see also Russell, in this volume).

Thus, the prismatic definitional framework outlined here suggests that we need to take a much broader approach to examining the causes of school violence. Rather than operating simply on the individual analytical level that looks to psychological and situational explanations for why students act violently, we need to address the context of students lives—their families, race, ethnicity, gender, and social class. We need to explore how these dimensions interconnect through social processes to shape and structure human thinking, moral development, and individual choices. We need to examine how these social forces shape school curriculum, teaching practices, and educational policy. Thus, at a deeper level we should be concerned to identify the way parents and schools themselves harm the lives of students and the way they shape the content of young people's lives. Finally, at the wider level we need to examine the ways the culture and the economic, social, and political structure of U.S. society is reproduced and how it reproduces harmful processes. Although it may seem that this level has been addressed through the discussions, analysis, and attempt to legislate against "toxic culture," this is an inadequate approach to macrolevel analysis. Discussion of cultural causes of school violence has focused on the role of violence in the media—in movies, in rap music lyrics, in videos, in video games, and on the Internet—and on gun culture. The argument is that cultural violence amplifies young male aggressive tendencies. It devalues humans into symbolic object images of hate or derision, trains youth to use violent skills, celebrates death and destruction as positive values, and provides exciting and colorful role models who use violence as the solution to problems, glorifying the most powerful and destructive performances via news media infotainment. While this may be true, it is not enough to simply blame toxic culture for poisoning kids' minds without also looking at the ways in which corporate America invests in the exploitation of violence for profit that feeds this cultural industry. A macroanalysis of "culture," therefore, has to connect that culture to the political economy of the society in which it is generated.

Policy Implications of the Prismatic Analysis of School Violence

The use of the prismatic analytical framework to defining crime may allow us to identify the multiple interrelated causes of such violence, but this also has implications for policy and practice. Indeed, it affects the societal response dimension of the prism. Such an analysis is likely to provide for a more comprehensive approach to policy that reaches deeper into the roots of systemic violence than superficial quick-fix responses. It allows us to see the interconnections between different types of school violence and develop integrated policies designed to respond to them. An adequate policy response must be comprehensive, dealing *simultaneously* with each of the causes identified at each of the levels of definition. It must penetrate the built-in protections of systems that conceal their own practice from analysis and change. It must be reflexive enough to recognize that policy itself can be part of the problem rather than the solution; policy should be self-critical and self-correcting. While this chapter does not allow us to expand on the immensity of the policy question called for by such an analysis, the question of "dispute resolution" can be indicative in illustrating how a restrictive verses an expansive definition of school violence would operate (see Adams 2000; Pepinsky 2000; Caulfield 2000; Nicholson 2000).

Dispute Resolution

A narrow approach to school violence prevention policy would begin by assuming a level 1 definition of the problem. For example, kids are violent in schools because they are taught to use violence to solve their problems or, at best, because they are not taught nonviolent ways of dealing with conflict. The simplistic restrictive policy response would suggest that dispute resolution training in techniques of nonviolent problem solving would be appropriate.

In contrast, an expansive definition and an integrated causal analysis would tie the use of violence by students to the use of symbolic and other forms of violence by adults, whether these are parents, teachers, administrators, or politicians. Instead of just implementing such training for students, it would argue for all school personnel, at every level, to undergo and practice nonviolent problem solving. Furthermore, the school organization, curriculum, and educational processes would be subject to the same "violence cleansing" scrutiny to be replaced by what Pepinsky (2000) calls "educating *for* peace" rather than "educating *about* peace."

In short, viewed through the prism of crime the issue of school violence is not just about kids in schools; it is about the total coproduction of our society by each of its constituent elements. To approach school violence another way is not merely shortsighted; it is to do more violence to those who have already suffered so much pain.

CONCLUDING COMMENTS

The increasingly complex visual representations of crime, from the "pyramid of crime" to our "crime prism," graphically illustrate the increasingly recognized complexity associated with defining crime. No longer is a simplistic reliance on written law and claims of moral indignation on behalf of a majority, sufficient to answer the question "What is crime?" The analytical tools we employ in defining the problem of crime, whether school violence or corporate fraud, needs a framework to disaggregate the constitutive elements of the problem. That is why we believe the prismatic analysis offers a glimpse at how to proceed. A prism reflects light differently depending on the angle from which ones views it, and it disperses light into its constitutive elements. In our crime prism, this approach allows varied views of the same act to give different perceptions of the same reality, while also exposing the various elements that together mask the underlying components of the problem. Use of the prismatic framework to define crime has other implications, also.

First, the positioning of crimes in the prism varies over time, as society becomes more or less aware of them and recognizes them as more or less serious. For example, consider the changing position of domestic violence or sexual harassment, both of which have recently begun to move from the lower half to the upper half. In contrast, other acts that were once in the upper half have become so common as to be hidden; they are relatively harmless and invoke neither public sentiment nor societal response. In short, the prism of crime is not a static depiction but affords us a dynamic model of how what counts as crime changes over time.

Second, as we have seen, the upper half of the prism contains predominantly conventional crimes, or "street crimes," whereas the lower half of the prism contains the greater preponderance of white-collar crimes, or "suite crimes." This analysis raises the important question of whether these invisible crimes of the powerful are causally related to the more visible crimes of the powerless. If so, what does that say for crime policy? Ultimately, it may well be that our myopic conception of crime, focusing as it presently does on crimes in the visible realm, misses the very harms that are their driving force beneath the surface. We hope that future empirical research will be able to resolve this issue and in doing so substantiate the value of the integrated prism perspective on defining crime.

NOTES

1. Even at the level of individual violence, this restrictive approach ignores student acts of damage and destruction toward a school or the educational and learning process, as in the examples of vandalism or drug taking.

2. Similar exclusionary practices have recently been argued to be contributing to male violence in schools (see Pollack 1998; Yogan and Henry 2000).

3. Increasingly, children are being tried as adults, juvenile court cases are being waived to criminal court, and in some states, such as Illinois, they are now eligible for the death penalty for committing mass murder in schools. In 1996, 10,000 juvenile court cases were waived to criminal court compared, with 6,800 in 1987; 15 percent of those involved youth under sixteen years old, compared with 7 percent in 1987 (Office of Justice Programs 1999: 1).

REFERENCES

Adams, A., Troy. 2000. "The Status of School Discipline and Violence." In *School Violence*, vol. 567: *Annals of the American Academy of Political and Social Science*, ed. W. Hinkle and S. Henry. Thousand Oaks, Calif.: Sage.

Arrigo, Bruce. 1995. "The Peripheral Core of Law and Criminology: On Postmodern Social Theory and Conceptual Integration." *Justice Quarterly* 12, no. 3: 447–72.

Bourdieu, Pierre. 1977. *Outline of a Theory of Practice.* Cambridge: Cambridge University Press.

Bureau of Justice Statistics. 1998. *School Crime Supplement to the National Crime Victimization Survey, 1989 and 1995.* Washington, D.C.: U.S. Department of Justice, Office of Justice Programs.

Calavita, Kitty, and Henry Pontell. 1993. "Savings and Loan Fraud as Organized Crime: Toward A Conceptual Typology of Corporate Illegality." *Criminology* 31: 519–48.

Calhoun, Craig, and Henry K. Hiller. 1986. "Coping with Insidious Injuries: The Case of Johns-Manville Corporation and Asbestos Exposure." *Social Problems* 35: 162–81.

Caulfield, Susan L. 2000. "Creating Peaceable Schools." In *School Violence*, vol. 567: *Annals of the American Academy of Political and Social Science*, ed. W. Hinkle and S. Henry. Thousand Oaks, Calif.: Sage.

Champion, Dean, J. 1997. *The Roxbury Dictionary of Criminal Justice.* Los Angeles: Roxbury.

Cintron, Ralph. 2000. "Listening to What the Streets Say: Vengeance as Ideology?" In *School Violence*, vol. 567: *Annals of the American Academy of Political and Social Science*, ed. W. Hinkle and S. Henry. Thousand Oaks, Calif.: Sage.

DeKeseredy, Walter S., and Martin Schwartz. 1996. *Contemporary Criminology.* Belmont, Calif.: Wadsworth.

Elliott, Delbert S., Beatrice A. Hamburg, and K. R. Williams. 1998. *Violence in American Schools*. Cambridge: Cambridge University Press.

Hagan, John. 1977. *The Disreputable Pleasures*. Toronto: McGraw-Hill Ryerson.

———. 1985. *Modern Criminology*. New York: McGraw-Hill.

Henry, Stuart, and Mark M. Lanier. 1998. "The Prism of Crime: Arguments for an Integrated Definition of Crime." *Justice Quarterly* 15: 609–27.

Kramer, Ronald C. 2000. "The Role of Poverty, Inequality and Social Exclusion in Shaping the Problem of Youth Violence." In *School Violence*, vol. 567: *Annals of the American Academy of Political and Social Science*, ed. W. Hinkle and S. Henry. Thousand Oaks, Calif.: Sage.

Lanier, Mark M., and Stuart Henry. 1998. *Essential Criminology*. Boulder, Colo.: Westview.

Nicholson, Jane. 2000. "Reconciliations: Prevention and Recovery for School Violence." In *School Violence*, vol. 567: *Annals of the American Academy of Political and Social Science*, ed. W. Hinkle and S. Henry. Thousand Oaks, Calif.: Sage.

Office of Justice Programs. 1999. "Delinquency Cases Waived to Criminal Court, 1987–1996." In *OJJDP Fact Sheet 99*. Washington D.C.: U.S. Department of Justice, Office of Justice Programs.

Pepinsky, Hal. 2000. "Educating for Peace." In *School Violence*, vol. 567: *Annals of the American Academy of Political and Social Science*, ed. W. Hinkle and S. Henry. Thousand Oaks, Calif.: Sage.

Pollack, William. 1998. *Real Boys: Rescuing Our Sons from the Myths of Boyhood*. New York: Random House.

Rush, George E. 1994. *The Dictionary of Criminal Justice*. 4th ed. Guilford, Conn.: Dushkin.

Siegel, Larry J. 1998. *Criminology: Theories, Patterns and Typologies*. 6th ed. Belmont, Calif.: West/Wadsworth.

Smith, Brent, and Gregory Orvis. 1993. "America's Response to Terrorism: An Empirical Analysis of Federal Intervention Strategies during the 1980s." *Justice Quarterly* 10: 661–81.

Staples, J. Scott. 2000. "The Meaning of Violence in Our Schools: Rage against a Broken World." In *School Violence*, vol. 567: *Annals of the American Academy of Political and Social Science*, ed. W. Hinkle and S. Henry. Thousand Oaks, Calif.: Sage.

Thompkins, Douglas E. 2000. "School Violence: Gangs and a Culture of Fear." In *School Violence*, vol. 567: *Annals of the American Academy of Political and Social Science*, ed. W. Hinkle and S. Henry. Thousand Oaks, Calif.: Sage.

Venturelli, Peter J. 2000. "Drugs in Schools: Myths and Realities." In *School Violence*, vol. 567: *Annals of the American Academy of Political and Social Science*, ed. W. Hinkle and S. Henry. Thousand Oaks, Calif.: Sage.

Welsh, Wayne N. 2000. "The Effects of School Climate on School Disorder." In *School Violence*, vol. 567: *Annals of the American Academy of Political and Social Science*, ed. W. Hinkle and S. Henry. Thousand Oaks, Calif.: Sage.

Yogan, Lissa J. 2000. "School Tracking and Student Violence." In *School Violence*, vol. 567: *Annals of the American Academy of Political and Social Science*, ed. W. Hinkle and S. Henry. Thousand Oaks, Calif.: Sage.

Yogan, Lissa, and Stuart Henry. 2000. "Masculine Thinking and School Violence: Issues of Gender and Race." In *School Violence: A Practical Guide for Counselors*, ed. D. Sandhu and C. B. Aspey. Alexandria, Va.: American Association of Counselors.

Index

About the Contributors

Mortimer J. Adler is one of the most enduring of American scholars. He has published extensively since 1927; just since his seventieth birthday he has written more than twenty of his sixty books. Professor Adler has a colorful and informative past. He attended Columbia University to study philosophy. However, since he did not complete the required physical education courses, he never graduated. Columbia awarded him a doctorate of philosophy after a few years teaching there in the 1920s. In 1929–1930 he joined the faculty at the University of Chicago, where he remained until 1952. He was chairman and cofounder of the Center for the Study of Great Ideas, founder and director of the Institute for Philosophical Research, cofounder and honoree trustee of the Aspen Institute, and is professor emeritus from the University of Chicago. Now living near San Francisco and nearing a century in age, he is still active and promoting social progress. His current book is *The New Technology: Servant or Master* (with Phillip Goertze).

Kathryn Farr is professor of sociology at Portland State University. Dr. Farr's research interests are in women, crime, and mental illness, and the social constructions of gender and deviance. She is currently involved in a multicity study on surviving an attempted homicide by an intimate partner. Publications from a recently completed project on women and death row are "Defeminizing and Dehumanizing Female Murderers: Portrayals of Lesbians on Death Row," *Women & Criminal Justice* (2000); "Representations of Female Evil: Cases and Characterizations of Women on Death Row" (coauthored with S. J. Farr), *Quarterly Journal of Ideology* (1998); and "Aggravating and Differentiating Factors in the Cases of White and Minority Women on Death Row," *Crime and Delinquency* (1997).

Marc Gertz, Ph.D., is professor of criminology and criminal justice in the School of Criminology and Criminal Justice at Florida State University. His recent publications deal with the media and fear of crime, public perceptions in establishing community attitudes, and the use of guns. His articles have appeared in *Crim-*

inology, *Social Problems*, *Journal of Research in Crime and Delinquency*, *Journal of Criminal Law and Criminology*, and many other books and journals. The eighth edition of *The Criminal Justice System: Politics and Policies* with George Cole is in press.

Don Gibbons is professor emeritus of urban studies and sociology, Portland State University. He is author of eight books dealing with criminology and deviance, including *Society, Crime, and Criminal Behavior* (1991), *Delinquent Behavior* (with Marvin D. Krohn, 1992), *The Criminological Enterprise* (1979), and *Talking about Crime and Criminals* (1994). He has also written more than sixty articles dealing with crime, criminality, and deviance. His major areas of interest center on criminological theories and theory building, including the investigation of crime types and criminal patterns, the study of citizens' perceptions about crime and corrections, and criminal justice policy formulation.

Leroy C. Gould has been professor of criminology and criminal justice at the Florida State University since 1981. Before joining the faculty at Florida State University, Professor Gould served as assistant professor of sociology and psychiatry and as research associate at Yale University. Besides teaching sociology, Dr. Gould served as director of research for the Drug Dependence Unit of the Connecticut Mental Health Center and did "energy-related" research at the Yale Institution for Social and Policy Studies. Dr. Gould's Ph.D. is in sociology from the University of Washington; his B.A. is in social relations from Harvard. Dr. Gould has coauthored three books and written many articles about crime, drugs, and social perceptions of energy technology. He is married and has three daughters.

Scott Greer is a doctoral candidate in political science at Northwestern University and a former law and social science fellow at the American Bar Foundation. He is coeditor with Georgi Derluguian of *Questioning Geopolitics* (2000) and has done research and published on French and Scottish politics, international criminal law, and the politics of health care in the United States. He is currently writing a dissertation on the politics of regionalism in Spain and Britain.

John Hagan is the John D. MacArthur Visiting Professor of Sociology and Law at Northwestern University, a senior research fellow at the American Bar Foundation and professor of law and sociology at the University of Toronto. Dr. Hagan is author or coauthor of numerous books on crime and deviance, including *Quantitative Criminology* (1982), *Modern Criminology* (1984), *Crime and Inequality* (1995), *Structural Criminology* (1989), *Crime and Disrepute* (1994), and *Mean Streets: Youth Crime and Homelessness* (1998). He also coedits the *Annual Review of Sociology*. He is currently working on a study of the lives of Vietnam War resisters in Canada with the support of a John Guggenheim Fellowship.

Stuart Henry is professor and director of interdisciplinary studies at Wayne State University in Detroit, where he also serves as associate dean of the College of Lifelong Learning. He has researched varieties of marginalized knowledge and informal institutions, including mutual aid groups, informal economies, nonstate systems of discipline and social control, and cooperatives. Most recently, he examined the relationship among social norms, private discipline, and public law. Dr. Henry has nineteen books published, and over seventy of his articles have appeared in professional journals or as book chapters. His books include the classic works *The Hidden Economy* (1978), *Informal Institutions* (1981), and *Informal Economy* (1987). His most recent works include *Criminological Theory: An Analysis of Its Underlying Assumptions* (with Werner Einstadter, 1995) and *Constitutive Criminology: Beyond Postmodernism* (1996) and *Constitutive Criminology at Work* (1999) (both with Dragan Milovanovic), *Essential Criminology* (with Mark Lanier, 1998), and *School Violence* (with Bill Hinkle, 2000). Dr. Henry serves on the editorial board of *Theoretical Criminology* and the *Law and Society Review*.

Gary Kleck is professor of criminology and criminal justice in the School of Criminology and Criminal Justice at Florida State University. His recent research has concerned the defensive use of guns by crime victims, the impact of drug use and drug enforcement levels on violence rates, and the links among unemployment, criminal opportunities, and crime. His articles have been published in the *American Sociological Review*, *American Journal of Sociology*, *Social Forces*, *Social Problems*, *Journal of Criminal Law and Criminology*, *Law & Society Review*, *Journal of Quantitative Criminology*, and many other journals. He is the author of *Point Blank: Guns and Violence in America* (1991) and *Targeting Guns: Firearms and Their Control* (1997), and he is coauthor (with Don B. Kates, Jr.) of *The Great American Gun Debate: Essays on Firearms and Violence* (1997).

Mark M. Lanier is associate professor of criminal justice and legal studies at the University of Central Florida. He holds an interdisciplinary doctoral degree in social science from Michigan State University with concentrations in criminology, sociology, and psychology. He has published research in a variety of disciplinary journals, including public health, criminal justice, criminology, law, and psychology. His funded research has involved studies of youth and HIV/AIDS and community policing. Dr. Lanier was nominated for the American Society of Criminology Young Scholar of the Year Award in 1996–1997; was awarded Distinguished Researcher of the Year from the College of Health and Public Affairs at the University of Central Florida in 1997; and in 2000 was identified among the top 4 percent of academic "stars" from criminology and criminal justice doctoral programs, according to a study reported in the *Journal of Criminal Justice Education*. He coauthored *Essential Criminology* (1998) with Stuart Henry.

Jerome Michael was (from 1927 to 1953) Nash Professor of Law at Columbia University and has a Jury Trials Moot Court Award at Columbia University named after him. He is coauthor with Mortimer J. Adler of the seminal work *Crime, Law and Social Science* (1933).

Dragan Milovanovic is professor of criminal justice at Northeastern Illinois University. He has written (authored, coauthored, edited) sixteen books and has numerous publications in the area of sociology of law and criminology. These include *Weberian and Marxian Analysis of Law* (1989); *Postmodern Law and Disorder* (1992); *The Sociology of Law* (1994); *Constitutive Criminology* (with Stuart Henry, 1996); *Race, Gender and Class in Criminology* (with Martin Schwartz, 1996); *Chaos, Criminology and Social Justice* (1997); *Thinking Critically about Crime* (with Brian MacLean, 1997); *Postmodern Criminology* (1997); and *Constitutive Criminology at Work* (with Stuart Henry, 1999). His current research interests are in postmodern criminology and law, constitutive criminology, chaos theory, Lacanian semiotics, catastrophe theory, topology theory, and edgework. In 1993 he received the Distinguished Achievement Award from the Division on Critical Criminology of the American Society of Criminology. He is editor of the *International Journal for the Semiotics of Law*.

Charles Otto is a graduate teaching assistant in the department of criminal justice and legal studies at the University of Central Florida. He is currently completing his Ph.D. in public affairs. His dissertation topic is an evaluation of a computer vision-assisted camera surveillance system for an urban downtown area.

Katheryn K. Russell is an associate professor of criminology and criminal justice at the University of Maryland, College Park. Professor Russell received her undergraduate degree from the University of California, Berkeley (1983), and her law degree from Hastings Law School (1986). She received her Ph.D. from the criminology department at the University of Maryland, College Park (1992). Dr. Russell's teaching, research, and writing have been in the areas of criminal law, sociology of law, and race and crime. Her 1994 article "The Constitutionality of Jury Override in Alabama Death Penalty Cases," published in the *Alabama Law Review*, was cited by the U.S. Supreme Court in *Harris v. Alabama* (1995). Professor Russell has also taught at the American University School of Law, the City University of New York (CUNY) Law School, Howard University, and Alabama State University. She also worked at the Southern Poverty Law Center as a legal intern. She is a member of the American Society of Criminology and the Academy of Criminal Justice Sciences. Professor Russell's first book, *The Color of Crime: Racial Hoaxes, White Fear, Black Protectionism, Police Harassment and Other Macroaggressions*, was published in 1998. She is currently working on her second book.

Paul Schnorr is director of the Urban Studies Program of the Associated Colleges of the Midwest. Dr. Schnorr grew up in small-town Wisconsin and moved to Chicago in 1986 to do graduate studies in sociology at Northwestern University. During graduate school, he worked on community crime control in West Chicago, tutored at Cook County Jail, and spent several years with a program resettling families from Chicago to a small town in Indiana. Dr. Schnorr's primary interests are to understand the different forms of community in Chicago and linking that understanding with programs of appropriate community action. He has participated in a national forum discussing the issues and challenges facing nonprofit organizations and continues to learn about where and how community members can best participate in the management of those organizations. Schnorr also serves on the board of directors of Chicago Community Midwives, an organization dedicated to making natural childbirth accessible to women of all incomes.

Julia and Herman Schwendinger are currently professors in the department of criminology at the University of South Florida. Julia Schwendinger was a cofounder of the first antirape crisis group in the United States. She has counseled the antirape group in New York state, has served as a private consultant for defense attorneys and judges, and has been a parole commissioner and director of the Women's Resource Center for San Francisco Jails. Herman Schwendinger is a member of the New York Academy of Sciences. He retired as a professor emeritus from the department of sociology, State University of New York, New Paltz, where he was bestowed the title of State University of New York Faculty Exchange Scholar and received the State University of New York Excellence Award. Both have worked in the University of California's Berkeley's Institute for the Study of Social Change and have been exchange scholars at universities in Berlin, St. Petersburg, Moscow, and central Asia. The Schwendingers have published numerous articles and books on crimes against women, human rights, adolescent subcultures, and delinquency, including *The Sociologists of the Chair* (1974), *Rape and Inequality* (1983), and *Adolescent Subcultures and Delinquency* (1985). Since 1993, they have been working on methods for graphing large informal networks. The first of a series of articles proposing research strategies based on group dynamics, ethnographic observations, and network analysis has been published in the *British Journal of Sociology*. They are writing a book centering on the actual or potential effects of adolescent subcultures on teenage rapists, scholastic achievement, school vouchers, and so forth. Their seminal writings have received the Distinguished Scholar Award from the Crime, Law, and Deviance Section of the American Sociology Association; the Outstanding Scholar Award from the Society for the Study of Social Problems; the Tappan Award from the Western Society of Criminology; the Major Achievement Award from the Critical Criminology Division of the American Society of Criminology; and an award for special recognition of their scholarship and research on women and crime from the Women's Division of the American Society of Criminology.

Ray Surette is a professor of criminal justice and legal studies at the University of Central Florida. His research interests involve the interactions of the mass media, media technology, and media culture with public perceptions of crime and justice, copycat crime, and criminal justice policy. He has published numerous articles on media, crime, and criminal justice topics and is the author of three books in the area: *Media, Crime, and Criminal Justice: Images and Realities*; *Justice and the Media* (1998); and *The Media and Criminal Justice Policy* (1990).

Paul Tappan was professor of criminology and law at the University of California, Berkeley, until his death in 1964.

Larry Tifft and Dennis Sullivan have been collaborating on writing and activist projects about justice since they first taught together at the University of Illinois, Chicago, in 1972. In 1980, their book *The Struggle to Be Human: Crime, Criminology, and Anarchism* was published in the Orkney Islands, Scotland. It was the first pacifist-anarchist treatise to appear on crime, punishment, and justice. This was followed by Sullivan's *The Mask of Love: Corrections in America: Toward a Mutual Aid Alternative* the same year. In 1993, Tifft's *Battering of Women: The Failure of Intervention and the Case for Prevention* was published; and, in 1997, Sullivan's *The Punishment of Crime in Colonial New York: The Dutch Experience in Albany During the Seventeenth Century* appeared. Tifft and Sullivan have also written many articles together and are currently near completion of a book, *Restorative Justice as a Transformative Process: A Personalist Vision*. In the past several years, they founded and currently serve as editors of the international journal *Contemporary Justice Review*, and both were instrumental in establishing the Justice Studies Association, an international association of scholars, practitioners, and activists committed to restorative and social justice.